Fodor's

PHILADELPHIA

WELCOME TO PHILADELPHIA

The first World Heritage City in the United States celebrates its past at sites such as Independence Hall and revels in its present as a funky, modern metropolis on a cultural upswing. Founded by William Penn and nurtured by Benjamin Franklin, Philadelphia today buzzes with lively neighborhoods, excellent restaurants, and fun nightlife. Die-hard sports fans, avid art lovers, and history buffs all have plenty to explore. Whether you enjoy fine dining or a bike ride through Fairmount Park, one thing is certain: there is much to love in the City of Brotherly Love.

TOP REASONS TO GO

★ **Local Cuisine:** Cozy BYOBs, cheesesteaks, Reading Terminal Market.

★ **Iconic Landmarks:** The Rocky Steps, the LOVE Statue, Boathouse Row.

★ **Eclectic Neighborhoods:** Historic Society Hill, funky Fishtown, chic Rittenhouse Square.

★ **Revolutionary History:** The Liberty Bell, Independence Hall, Valley Forge Park.

★ **Art:** World-class museums, street murals, high-end galleries and everything in between.

★ **Bar Scene:** From lively beer gardens to chic cocktail lounges, nightlife flourishes.

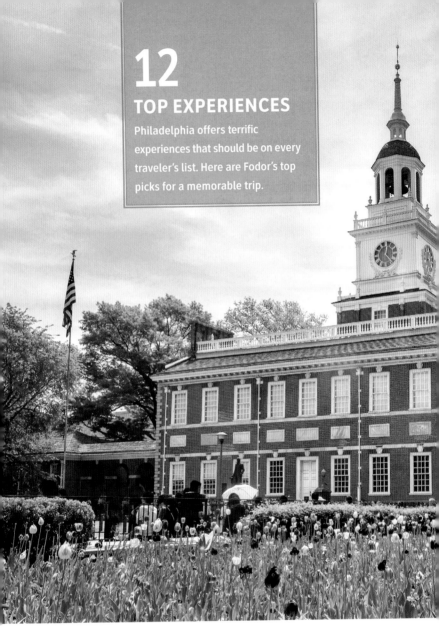

12
TOP EXPERIENCES

Philadelphia offers terrific experiences that should be on every traveler's list. Here are Fodor's top picks for a memorable trip.

1 Independence National Historical Park

The early history of the United States is recalled at the famous sites in this park, including the Liberty Bell, Congress Hall, and iconic Independence Hall, where the Declaration of Independence was signed in 1776. (Ch. 2)

2 Fairmount Park

One of the world's largest city parks, Fairmount boasts trails, bike paths, and historic mansions—as well as stunning views of Boathouse Row on the Schuylkill River. *(Ch. 2)*

3 Sports

Philadelphia is famous for its sports teams—and for its die-hard fans. Experience the local culture and enjoy a baseball game at the Phillies' Citizen's Bank Park. *(Ch. 1)*

4 Reading Terminal Market

This historic public market is a must-visit for any food lover. Head to longtime favorite DiNic's for a famous pork sandwich, and then try Bassets delicious ice cream. *(Ch. 3, 6)*

5 Bike Rides

For a fresh look at the city, rent wheels through the Indego bike share program. One place to explore is the Schuylkill Banks Boardwalk with its striking city views. *(Ch. 1)*

6 Rittenhouse Square

One of city founder William Penn's five original squares, Rittenhouse is known for its elegance and charm. Restaurants, shops, and apartments line this green refuge. *(Ch. 2)*

7 Cheesesteaks

Pat's or Geno's? You can be the judge in this famous food face-off. A trip to Philly isn't complete without trying the city's most legendary sandwich. *(Ch. 1, 3)*

8 Parkway Museums

Splendid, tree-lined Ben Franklin Parkway is home to some of the city's most famous museums including the Barnes Foundation, Rodin Museum, and Philadelphia Museum of Art. *(Ch. 2)*

9 Old City

Known for its cobblestone streets and historic sites, the city's oldest neighborhood is a mix of 18th-century charm and lively nightlife spots, galleries, and restaurants. *(Ch. 1, 2)*

10 Murals and Street Art

The city's wonderful Mural Arts Program, begun in 1984, views every blank wall as a canvas. You can see the work of local artists showcased all around town. *(Ch. 2)*

11 Brewery Scene

Beer lovers can sip great suds at many craft breweries or brew pubs; new spots continue to pop up in funky neighborhoods like Fishtown and Northern Liberties. *(Ch. 3, 5)*

12 South Street

With an unapologetically edgy vibe, this famous street combines ethnically diverse restaurants, shops, and bars into one lively area that always buzzes with activity. *(Ch. 1, 2)*

CONTENTS

ABOUT THIS GUIDE

Fodor's Ratings

Everything in this guide is worth doing—we don't cover what isn't—but exceptional sights, hotels, and restaurants are recognized with additional accolades. Fodor'sChoice★ indicates our top recommendations. Care to nominate a new place? Visit Fodors.com/contact-us.

Trip Costs

We list prices wherever possible to help you budget well. Hotel and restaurant price categories from **$** to **$$$$** are noted alongside each recommendation. For hotels, we include the lowest cost of a standard double room in high season. For restaurants, we cite the average price of a main course at dinner or, if dinner isn't served, at lunch. For attractions, we always list adult admission fees; discounts are usually available for children, students, and senior citizens.

Hotels

Our local writers vet every hotel to recommend the best overnights in each price category, from budget to expensive. Unless otherwise specified, you can expect private bath, phone, and TV in your room. For expanded hotel reviews, facilities, and deals visit Fodors.com.

Top Picks

★ Fodor'sChoice

Listings

✉ Address
📨 Branch address
☎ Telephone
📠 Fax
🌐 Website
📧 E-mail
🎫 Admission fee
🕒 Open/closed times
[M] Subway
✥ Directions or Map coordinates

Hotels & Restaurants

🏨 Hotel
🛏 Number of rooms
🍽 Meal plans
✕ Restaurant
✍ Reservations
👔 Dress code
💳 No credit cards
[$] Price

Other

⇨ See also
☞ Take note
⛳ Golf facilities

Restaurants

Unless we state otherwise, restaurants are open for lunch and dinner daily. We mention dress code only when there's a specific requirement and reservations only when they're essential or not accepted. To make restaurant reservations, visit Fodors.com.

Credit Cards

The hotels and restaurants in this guide typically accept credit cards. If not, we'll say so.

EUGENE FODOR

Hungarian-born Eugene Fodor (1905–91) began his travel career as an interpreter on a French cruise ship. The experience inspired him to write *On the Continent* (1936), the first guidebook to receive annual updates and discuss a country's way of life as well as its sights. Fodor later joined the U.S. Army and worked for the OSS in World War II. After the war, he kept up his intelligence work while expanding his guidebook series. During the Cold War, many guides were written by fellow agents who understood the value of insider information. Today's guides continue Fodor's legacy by providing travelers with timely coverage, insider tips, and cultural context.

EXPERIENCE PHILADELPHIA

WHAT'S WHERE

1 **The Historic Downtown.** Given its historical importance, *everything* in Old City is a highlight. Well-preserved Society Hill is filled with cobblestone streets and hidden courtyards. Penn's Landing has become a 37-acre riverside park.

2 **Center City.** City Center is anchored by City Hall and has many of the city's best restaurants and bars. The vibrant and diverse Chinatown is also here, as are landmarks like the Reading Terminal Market. You'll also find Rittenhouse Square, the heart of upper-crust Philadelphia.

3 **Benjamin Franklin Parkway and Fairmount.** From City Hall the Benjamin Franklin Parkway stretches northwest to the Philadelphia Museum of Art. Fairmount is home to solid dining, drinking, and shopping, while 8,500-acre Fairmount Park is the largest landscaped city park in the world.

4 **South Philadelphia.** South Philadelphia gave the world Rocky Balboa and 9th Street's Italian Market. Bella Vista, the residential area around the market, is home to a number of bars and restaurants. Farther south are East Passyunk and Queen Village.

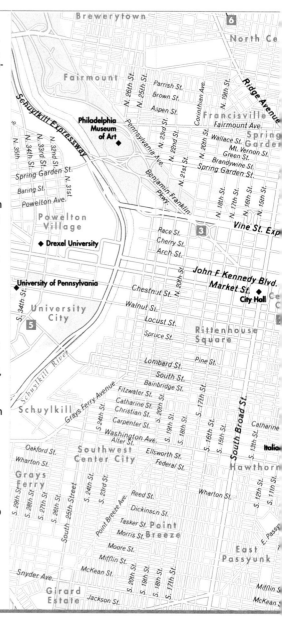

1

5 **University City.** The University of Pennsylvania and Drexel University are the anchors of University City, the easternmost portion of West Philadelphia. Beyond is a high concentration of bars, restaurants, and cafés.

6 **Northwestern Philadelphia.** The old mill town of Manayunk, wedged between the Schuylkill River and some very steep hills 7 miles northwest of Center City, was once crucial to Philadelphia's industrial fortune. Today it's bringing in dollars with its restaurants and boutiques. Charming residential areas Chestnut Hill and Mount Airy are sometimes referred to as suburbs. Germantown, 6 miles north of Center City, features beautifully preserved historic homes.

7 **Northeastern Philadelphia.** The area encompassing North Philadelphia, Northeastern Philadelphia, and Northern Liberties are all slowly gentrifying areas a short cab ride north from Center City.

PHILADELPHIA PLANNER

Street Finder

If you ever feel lost, you can orient yourself by gauging where you stand in relation to the two main thoroughfares that intersect at the city's center: Broad (or 14th, Street, which runs north–south; and Market Street, which runs east–west. Where Broad and Market meet, neatly dividing the city center into four quadrants, you'll find massive City Hall, Philadelphia's center of gravity.

Within Center City, the numbered streets start on the eastern side, from the Delaware River beginning with Front Street (consider it "1st Street") all the way west to 25th Street on the banks of the Schuylkill (pronounced "SKOO-kull") River. In between Market to the north and Lombard to the south, most of the east–west streets have tree names (from north to south: Chestnut, Walnut, Locust, Spruce, Pine).

Center City has four roughly equal-size city squares, one in each quadrangle. In the northwest quadrangle there's Logan Square; in the southwest is Rittenhouse; in the northeast there's Franklin Square; and in the southeast is Washington Square. Running along the banks of the Delaware River is Columbus Boulevard/Delaware Avenue.

Getting Around

Driving

Laid out in a grid pattern by its founder William Penn, Center City is relatively easy to navigate by car. Just remember that many streets are one-way, and the main thoroughfares are often congested with traffic. A spot at a downtown parking meter—if you're lucky enough to find one—costs $2.50 per hour. Philadelphia Parking Authority officers are seriously vigilant about ticketing. If you plan on spending a good amount of time in the city, supplementing your visit with walking and public transportation, your best bet might be a parking garage; there are a number throughout Center City.

Public Transportation

Philadelphia's **SEPTA** buses provide good coverage of Old City and the Historic Downtown, Center City, and farther west to University City. A bus ride costs $2.25 in cash (exact change only). A transfer costs an additional $1. Find fares, maps, and schedules at the Independence Visitor Center and online at ⊕ *septa.org*. Purple **PHLASH trolleys** follow a Center City route to 22 downtown sights; you can buy a hop-on, hop-off all-day pass for $5 at the Independence Visitor Center or when you board the trolley.

SEPTA, Philadelphia's subway system, runs regular trains throughout the day, but their geographic reach is somewhat limited, so trips may need to be supplemented with bus, taxi, or car service rides. The Market-Frankford Line, or Blue Line, runs east–west along Market Street; the Broad Street Line, or Orange Line runs north–south along Philly's main thoroughfare.

Taxi Travel

Taxis are plentiful in Center City, especially along Broad, Market, Walnut, and Chestnut streets and near major hotels and train stations. They're hailed streetside; smartphone users can also download 215GetACab, a free Android/iOS app that allows you to schedule pickups instantly. Fares rise according to distance: $2.70, plus 23¢ for each one-tenth of a mile. The standard tip for cabdrivers is about 20% of the fare.

iladelphia Online Resources

ts and Entertainment

lling itself as a guide to experiencing illy like a local, **Uwishunu** is an in-the-iow blog extension of the city's more mprehensive visitor site. Written by a verse staff with different interests, it lives to its local point of view. **Visit Philly** is comprehensive guide to events through-it the year; it also includes new entries Philly dining, attractions, and shopping.

or events listings and more local blog-ng, visit *Philadelphia* magazine's website, here staffers hold forth on everything om street style to restaurants to shop-ng. **Philly.com**, the online home of the *hiladelphia Inquirer* and *Philadelphia aily News*, covers many of these same pics, as well.

od

illy has more than its fair share of food ogs, which just shows you how impor-nt the dining scene is to Philadelphians. **obooz** (🌐 *foobooz.com*), which is part of *hiladelphia* magazine, mixes news of res-urant openings and closings with food-dustry gossip and restaurant reviews. also acts as a clearinghouse for other lline reviews. **Eater** (🌐 *philly.eater.com*) is a very active Philly branch, as does **igat** (🌐 *zagat.com/philadelphia*). Those ho pride themselves on being in the iow about the restaurant scene check it "Table Talk" by Michael Klein in the *hiladelphia Inquirer*, as well as Klein's og, **The Insider** (🌐 *philly.com/theinsider*).

afety

iiladelphia once got a bad rap for a high ime rate, but since Mayor Michael Nutter ok office in 2008, overall violent crime is dropped significantly. As in any major ty, visitors should always exercise caution id be aware of their surroundings.

When to Go

Any time is right to enjoy the area's attractions, and a variety of popular annual events take place throughout the year. To avoid the largest crowds and be assured that all seasonal attractions are open, visit in May–June or September–October. If you don't mind waiting in longer lines to see popular attractions, visit around July 4, when the city comes alive with fireworks, parades, and festivals. The top draw is the Wawa Welcome America! festival, which often includes a performance by a blockbuster musician or two. There are special activities in the Historic Downtown area all summer long. Concert and theater seasons run from October through the beginning of June. You may find some better lodging deals—and a beautiful snowfall—in winter, if you don't mind bundling up. In spring, the city's cherry blossoms bloom, rivaling those of the Tidal Basin in Washington, D.C. Like other northeastern American cities, Philadelphia can be hot and humid in summer and cold in winter.

GREAT ITINERARIES

In a city with as many museums, historical sites, parks, gardens, and more that you'll find in Philly, you risk seeing half of everything or all of nothing. With a day, you'll be hard-pressed to move beyond the city's primary historical sights, but if you have a week, you can delve deeper as you explore both the top attractions and what's off the beaten path.

The Best of Philadelphia in 1 Day

Sign up at the **Independence National Historical Park Visitor Center** for a walking tour hosted by a National Park Service guide, or try a go-at-your-own-pace tour offered by **The Constitutional Audio Walking Tour** (⊕ *www.theconstitutional.com*). At the very least you'll want to see the Liberty Bell, Independence Hall, the Carpenter's Hall, and Franklin Court. If you get started early, you can finish all that in about three or four hours. For lunch, visit **Reading Terminal Market**, where you can sample the cuisine Philadelphia is known for—like cheesesteaks, soft pretzels, and Bassett's ice cream. If you're interested in art (and make a reservation in advance), you can visit **The Barnes Foundation** on the Benjamin Franklin Parkway. Then walk nine blocks east on Arch Street to Old City; **Christ Church**, the **Betsy Ross House**, and **Elfreth's Alley** are all in close proximity. In the late afternoon, head back toward Independence Hall for a horse-drawn carriage ride. Have dinner in Old City; then catch the **Lights of Liberty** 3-D show.

Philadelphia in 5 Days

Five days is enough time to take in Philadelphia's cultural and historic highlights as well as spend some time exploring the appealing neighborhoods, and take a day trip Valley Forge, the Winterthur Museum, or Longwood Gardens.

Day 1: History

It's possible to get a good taste of what the city has to offer even if you only have a couple of days. You'll want to get the tour of the historic sights accomplished on Day 1.

There's no getting around the fact that colonial history is the primary reason most people visit Philadelphia, and most visitors will want to devote their first morning to exploring **Independence National Historical Park**. The two most popular sights are **Independence Hall** and the **Liberty Bell Center**. But don't neglect the **Independence Visitor Center**, where you must make a reservation (March through December) to tour Independence Hall; be sure to set aside 28 minutes from your schedule to see the film *Independence,* directed by John Huston, or the 20-minute *Choosing Sides.* There are usually lines to see the Liberty Bell, so do that while you wait for your tour time. If you have extra time, visit the Benjamin Franklin Museum on Franklin Court. Have lunch at nearby **Reading Market.** In the afternoon, you have a choice. You can keep up your historical pursuits, staying in Old Town to see more historic sights, including the **Carpenter's Hall**, **Christ Church**, the **Betsy Ross House,** and **Elfreth's Alley,** or you can delve deeper into the Constitution at the **National Constitution Center**, which has fascinating programs and interactive exhibits. At night, dinner and nightlife beckon in nearby Center City.

Day 2: Art and Museums

Philadelphia has more than enough museums to occupy a visitor for a full week, but it's worth spending one day to visit a couple that are particularly interesting. The **Philadelphia Museum of Art** on Benjamin Franklin Parkway, followed by lunch in the museum's lovely dining room, will be njoyable to almost anyone; it's the city's widest ranging art museum. But if your interest is impressionist, post-impressionist, and early modern American art, **The Barnes Foundation** may be a better destination (reservations required). In the afternoon you could visit **Eastern State Penitentiary Historic Site** for a tour of a former prison or to the **Franklin Institute**. Another option is to explore one of Philadelphia's distinct neighborhoods. Stroll around **Rittenhouse Square** and stop in at the **Rosenbach Museum and Library,** which has a diverse collection ranging from the original manuscript of James Joyce's *Ulysses* to the works of beloved children's author Maurice Sendak. There's also Society Hill, Queen Village, and South Philadelphia for the **Mummer Museum** on 9th Street and the outdoor **Italian Market**. Set aside time to dine in one of the city's best restaurants or take in a concert.

Day 3: Neighborhood Exploration

With more time, you can go deeper into your personal interests, whether they include art, shopping, history, the outdoors, or keeping your kids happy and occupied.

The best way to do that is to delve into more Philly neighborhoods. Check out Chinatown or Northern Liberties, or take a drive through Germantown and Chestnut Hill (stopping at **Cliveden**). If the weather's nice, you can drive or bike to the northwestern tip of **Fairmount Park** and check out the **Wissahickon**—a local favorite for all sorts of activities, from strolling to cycling. Afterward, head back into the city to check out the **University Museum of Archaeology and Anthropology** in University City and stroll down Locust Walk, the heart of University of Pennsylvania's leafy urban campus. In the evening, drive or catch the SEPTA R6 train to

Manayunk, where you can have dinner in one of the restaurants lining Main Street; many stores here are open late, too.

Day 4: Further Adventures

On Day 4, families will enjoy spending the morning visiting Penn's Landing, where they can check out the **Independence Seaport Museum** and take the ferry across the river to the **Adventure Aquarium** and **Camden Children's Garden**. In the afternoon hit the **Philadelphia Zoo**. If you didn't already visit, it, consider the **Eastern State Penitentiary** or the **Franklin Institute**—whichever attractions you didn't get to visit on Days 2 and 3—or another neighborhood, where you can dine at a local **BYOB** (Locate the nearest wine store at ⊕ *www.lcb.state. pa.us*). Check the local papers for an evening activity—perhaps a sporting event at the South Philadelphia stadiums, a show in Center City, or live music at a jazz club. If it's the first Friday of the month, go to Old City for First Friday, when stores and galleries stay open late.

Day 5: Time for an Excursion

Head out of the city by car to **Valley Forge National Historical Park,** where you can hike or picnic after you've taken the self-guided auto tour of General Washington's winter encampment, or take a day trip to the **Brandywine Valley**. Your first stop will be the **Brandywine River Museum** in Chadds Ford, which features the art of Andrew Wyeth and his family. Next, head south to **Winterthur**, Henry Francis du Pont's extraordinary mansion. Last, stroll through **Longwood Gardens** in Kennett Square, which is in bloom even in winter. If it's a Tuesday, Thursday, or Saturday in summer, stay for dinner and the fountain light show.

PHILADELPHIA'S REVOLUTIONARY HISTORY

More than just the home of Independence Hall or the Liberty Bell, Philadelphia was instrumental in the rise of the American Revolution, and an essential staging ground in the fight for the country's permanent independence from the British Empire.

The Founding of a City

The earliest European settlers to the area came from Sweden in the 1600s. The Commonwealth of Pennsylvania wasn't officially established until 1681, when King Charles II of England ceded a large portion of his New World holdings to William Penn, satisfying a debt to Penn's father. One year later, Penn established Philadelphia, which grew into a formidable center of colonial activity over the course of the next century.

Rising Resentment

By the 1760s, heavy tariffs instituted by the Crown—the Stamp Act of 1765, the Townshend Acts of 1767, and the Tea Act of 1773 among the most prominent—began strangling commerce in the colonies. Anger over the ever-increasing financial burden, especially since the colonies enjoyed no representation in Parliament, became palpable, especially in Philadelphia.

"Philadelphia's response to these and to various other irritants showed an intensity of feeling, expressed by people of all classes," wrote Russell F. Weigley in *Philadelphia: A 300 Year History*. Indeed, the city had a reputation for political awareness and activism not dictated by wealth or social stature, bolstered by its large and cultured population, a powerful merchant class, and an influential press.

Philadelphia Joins the Cause

In May 1774, Paul Revere, the patriot known best for his "Midnight Ride" warning colonists of the British incursion at Lexington and Concord that kicked off the Revolutionary War, rode into Philly, imploring Pennsylvania leadership to support the rising resistance. This led to the First Continental Congress, held in an under-construction Carpenters' Hall in the autumn of that same year.

Philadelphia was also the site of the Second Continental Congress in the summer of 1775, the meeting that led to the drafting and signing of the Declaration of Independence. But the city's importance to the revolution was as logistical as it was symbolic. This second convening of delegates from throughout the colonies also resulted in the formation of the Continental Army, not to mention the appointment of George Washington to lead that fighting force. In addition to its political importance, the city became an invaluable hub for training and equipping Revolutionary troops, including naval forces; sites of wartime significance, including Fort Mifflin, Washington Crossing, and Valley Forge, are close by the city's present-day borders.

Given its value to the conflict, Philadelphia was eventually taken by British forces in 1777, but they would evacuate after a year. The city continued to be a gem of the fledgling nation after the war ended in 1783, serving as a haven for the period's greatest political thinkers as well as the temporary capital from 1790 to 1800. Its importance to the American Revolution, and to America itself, cannot be overstated.

REE IN PHILLY

Many of Philadelphia's most historic and best-known attractions are free—or suggest a small donation for admission—every day. This lengthy list includes **Independence Hall,** the **Liberty Bell, Carpenter's Hall, Frank-Court,** and the other buildings and sites **Independence National Historic Park.**

Music and Theater

Check the calendar of the **Curtis Institute of Music** (⊕ *www.curtis.edu*) to catch one of the frequent free concerts. **The Philadelphia Orchestra** (⊕ *www.philorch.org*) also gives free neighborhood concerts. Visit **Macy's** across from City Hall; the former Wanamaker's boasts the largest pipe organ in the world, and there are daily free concerts. The Christmas show around the holidays is a definite favorite with shoppers. Check out a dress rehearsal or pay-what-you-can performance at the **Arden Theater**—they're open to the public and accept donations for admission. Local independent radio station **WXPN** offers free concerts Fridays at noon at its home base, **World Café Live** (⊕ *www.xpn.org*).

Outdoor Fun and Festivals

Take your pick of activities in **Fairmount Park:** hike the trails of the **Wissahickon** (⊕ *www.fow.org*), bring a picnic to **Belmont Plateau** and enjoy the view; or meander around the **Horticultural Center,** and look for the scattered pieces of public art. All summer long, multicultural festivals at **Penn's Landing** feature live music and dance instruction.

Architecture, Art, and Literature

Take a tour of **City Hall.** See Maurice Sendak's original illustrations and James Joyce's *Ulysses* manuscript, among other treasures, at the **Rosenbach Museum and Library.** Visit the lobby of the **Curtis Center** to gawk at the giant *Dream Garden* by Maxfield Parrish. Tour the **Masonic Temple,** a masterpiece inside and out, that's also historically significant as the birthplace of freemasonry in America. Visit the **Galleries at the Moore College of Art & Design,** the first and only women's visual arts college in the United States.

It's always fun to stroll the galleries in Old City, but it's especially fun on **"First Fridays"**—the first Friday of every month is celebrated with wine receptions, and galleries keeping later hours. Visit the **African American Museum** (free from 5 to 7). The first Sunday of each month is "pay what you wish" all day at the **Philadelphia Museum of Art.** The **Institute of Contemporary Art** at the University of Pennsylvania is free all the time. You can check out contemporary art at any time by taking a free tour of the city's many vibrant **murals** (⊕ *www.muralarts.org*).

History Tours

Take yourself on a walk by downloading and printing the self-guided **Constitutional Walking Tour** of more than 30 sites around historic Philadelphia from ⊕ *www.theconstitutional.com.* Take a guided house-by-house tour of **Elfreth's Alley,** one of America's oldest residential streets, or go solo with a call-in cell-phone tour of **Valley Forge National Historical Park** (☎ *484/396–1018*). In the summer, look for the elaborately costumed storytellers with **Once Upon a Nation,** who set up at 10 benches throughout Philadelphia's historic area. Hop from bench to bench for a free, interactive tour, during which actors in character relay stories of Philadelphia in Colonial times.

A HISTORIC WALK THROUGH THE OLD CITY

Touring through Old City, the neighborhood that encompasses the majority of Philly's Historic Downtown, doesn't have to begin and end with the Liberty Bell. Rely on this walk to make sure you hit all the highlights — and some under-the-radar locations as well.

A Jumping-off Point

Start off with a stop at the **Independence Visitor Center**, where you can get your bearings, talk to park rangers and concierges, and take in two short films chronicling Philadelphia's Revolutionary War history. The Center also has a café, public restrooms, and free Wi-Fi.

Independence National Historic Park and Vicinity

From here, it's off to the **Liberty Bell Center**, which is close by. Admission to lay eyes upon this gargantuan beacon of American freedom is free, but it's also very popular, so expect lines. You should also anticipate consistent crowds at **Independence Hall**, though there's quite a bit more to this portion of the Independence National Historical Park than the one-and-done Bell. Timed tours of the birthplace of both the Constitution and the Declaration of Independence are available free of charge; the most popular times are available on a first-come, first-served basis, though you can also reserve tickets over the phone for a small fee. Don't miss the other features of the park complex, including **Carpenter's Hall** (site of the First Continental Congress); and **Franklin Court**, Benjamin Franklin's former residence, featuring a mix of original architecture and restored features, including a fully operational post office.

Walk just a few blocks east down Market Street and you'll find the **Christ Church**, the beautifully maintained circa-1695

house of worship that also happens to be Franklin's final resting place. One block from here: the **National Constitution Center**, a gorgeous modern structure dedicated to celebration and analysis of America's most important political document. Three blocks northeast of the church sits **Elfreth's Alley**, considered one of the oldest residential blocks in America. Two adjoined houses in the alley, which featured mostly hybrid businesses/residences in its heyday, serve as a museum and gift shop. Around the holidays, current residents host "Deck The Alley," an open-house fund-raiser with food, drink, and costumed revelry.

Beyond the Biggies

There are plenty of other draws worthy of your attention besides the "big five." The **National Museum of American Jewish History**, the **National Liberty Museum**, the **Chemical Heritage Foundation**, **Betsy Ross House**, the **Independence Seaport Museum**, and the **Fireman's Hall Museum** are but a few of the historic/academic draws in the neighborhood. Attractions like **Race Street Pier, Morgan's Pier**, and **Spruce Street Harbor Park** allow visitors to enjoy a view of the Delaware River.

Refreshment Stops

Old City also has a number of well-regarded, award-winning bars, restaurants, and cafés enjoyed by locals; look for High Street on Market, Zahav, Amada, or Olde Bar.

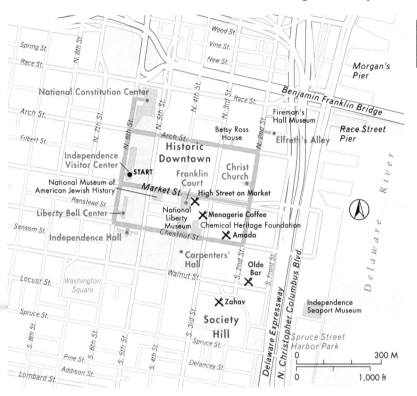

Where to Start	Independence Visitor Center, 6th and Market streets
Getting Here	It's only a few minutes' walk from 30th Street Station to the visitor center, or you can park directly underneath. Enter the underground parking (41 N. 6th St.); it costs only $13.50 to park for the day if you arrive before 9 and leave by 6.
Length	Less than 2 miles (but seeing all the sights takes at least one full day).
Where to Stop	If you continue beyond Elfreth's Alley, consider stopping at the Betsy Ross House (239 Arch St.), which is near the Constitution Center.
Best Time to Go	When the weather is conducive to strolling outdoors.
Worst Time to Go	Sunday morning, when the National Constitution Center is closed, or on particularly cold or wet days, when walking isn't fun.
Writer's Choice	If you visit on a weekend, Olde Bar, which is also a good lunch stop, has happy hour starting at 4 pm.

PHILADELPHIA WITH KIDS

Philadelphia has fantastic activities and sights for tots. Best of all, these stops appeal to adults as well.

Historic Area

The **National Constitution Center**'s interactive exhibits are way better than learning from a textbook. Nearby **Franklin Square**, however, is the perfect place to take a break from all the history. There's a carousel, miniature-golf course, and an excellent burger stand that also serves up Cake Shakes (milk shakes made with Butterscotch Krimpet Tastykakes). Kids love the 3-D **Lights of Liberty** show; for something spookier, check out one of the **Ghost Tours** offered around the Historic Area.

Fairmount Park

The **Please Touch Museum** is essentially a giant playground for kids. In its location in Fairmount Park's majestic Memorial Hall—one of the few remnants from the 1876 Centennial Exhibition—the museum is bigger (38,000 square feet of exhibits) and better than ever before. The nearby **Philadelphia Zoo** is another great spot, with a petting zoo, tree house, and "Big Cat Crossing," a series of overhead passageways that allows lions, tigers, pumas, and other large cats to roam. The sprawling indoor–outdoor **Smith Memorial Playground and Playhouse** nearby has a giant wooden slide and a mansion-like playhouse.

Benjamin Franklin Parkway

At the **Franklin Institute**, kids can't resist walking through the giant heart and seeing their hair stand up in the static-electricity exhibit. The nearby **Academy of Natural Sciences** has great, kid-friendly exhibits about dinosaurs and architectural digs. If you want to top off all the science adventures with a treat, stop in at the **Four Seasons** for a once-in-a-lifetime tea party.

Penn's Landing

At **Penn's Landing** kids can climb in the bunks used in steerage or hop in a scull and row along the Schuylkill at the **Independence Seaport Museum**. Next take the **RiverLink Ferry** across the river to the Camden Waterfront to explore the **Adventure Aquarium.** The **Shark Realm,** an enormous tank filled with sharks, stingrays, and sawfish, is the central attraction here. The **Camden Children's Garden** is an interactive horticultural garden with exhibits that allow you to taste, smell, and touch different elements.

Around Town

There are plenty of great snacks to pick up for days on-the-go at the **Reading Terminal Market**. Kids will like watching the workers at **Miller's Twist** wind the dough into pretzel shapes. They can also feed pennies to Philbert, the bronze pig at the market's center (the money goes to local charities). For a sit-down meal option, the **City Tavern** is a great way into history, and it has a good kids' menu. If you're in the mood for a ball game, **Citizens Bank Park**, home to Major League Baseball's Phillies, is one of the most kid-friendly major-league ball parks, with features like the Phanatic Phun Zone play area.

HILLY BOOKS AND MOVIES

OOKS

ction

urnalist Steve Lopez set his hard-edged vel *Third and Indiana* in gritty Kens-gton. *Philadelphia Fire* by John Edgar ideman is about the police firebomb-g of a black cult in West Philadelphia. uane Swierczynski, a Northeast Philly tive, is a prolific author of crime novels d comics. *Philly Fiction* and *Philly Fiction 2*, two collections of short stories set Philadelphia by local writers, are good troductions to the city's neighborhoods d people.

est-selling novelist Jennifer Weiner has t most of her books here, including *In er Shoes* and *Good in Bed*. Mystery riter Lisa Scottoline grew up in South hiladelphia and writes a column for the *hiladelphia Inquirer*.

istory

rank Rizzo: The Last Big Man in Big City merica by journalist Sal Paolantonio, out the city's revered and despised for-er mayor, and Buzz Bissinger's *A Prayer r the City*, about then-Mayor Ed Rendell the 1990s, are two great introductions local politics. *Philadelphia: A 300-Year istory*, an essay collection, was edited y Russell F. Weigley. Catherine Drinker owen's *Miracle at Philadelphia* tells the ory of the Constitution. *Up South: Civil ights and Black Power in Philadelphia*, y Matthew J. Countryman, examines the ostwar civil rights movement.

rchitecture

he stunning architectural photographs f Tom Crane, in *Historic Sacred Places f Philadelphia* and *Historic Houses of hiladelphia*, peek into some highlights. he Foundation for Architecture's *Phila-elphia Architecture: A Guide to the City* overs almost 400 historical sites.

MOVIES AND TELEVISION

The classic Philadelphia film is *Rocky* (1976), and fans still run up the Art Museum steps like the titular boxer every day. *Rocky Balboa* (2006) serves as a love letter to the city. *The Philadelphia Story* (1940) was inspired by the romantic hijinks of Helen Hope Montgomery Scott, a real-life Main Line socialite.

In the past 40 years most Philadelphia films have emphasized the city's majestic gritti-ness (much of which no longer exists). See the cityscape in *Blow Out* (1981) or *Trad-ing Places* (1983) as opposed to what it looks like today. Oscar hits like *Philadel-phia* (1993) and *Silver Linings Playbook* (2012) explore the beautiful and challeng-ing aspects of the city at once.

M. Night Shyamalan's *The Sixth Sense* (1999) has terrific shots of Philly. Terry Gilliam's *12 Monkeys* (1995) places ele-phants in front of City Hall and uses the Eastern State Penitentiary as an insane asylum (visit and you'll know why). *National Treasure* (2004) has Nicolas Cage stepping all over Independence Hall. *Shame of a City* (2006), a documentary by local filmmaker Tigre Hill, is an eye-opening look into city politics through the lens of the 2003 mayoral race between Sam Katz and John Street. The cast and crew of popular television shows like *It's Always Sunny in Philadelphia* are fre-quently spotted around the city.

BIKING IN PHILADELPHIA

While it still lacks the bipedal caché of cities like San Francisco, Portland, and Denver, Philadelphia has made great bounds in becoming a progressive bicycle-friendly town.

Where to Bike

The city has made a decent effort to install a wider network of bike lanes on major thoroughfares, traveling both north to south and east to west. Major streets, like Pine and Spruce streets through Center City, feature spacious bike-only lanes adjacent to traffic lanes, and other highly trafficked drags, like Broad Street and Spring Garden Street, are equipped with bike lanes, as well. Cyclists looking for a more isolated riding experience can visit paths along the Schuylkill River, in Fairmount Park, and in Wissahickon Valley Park. Many of Philly's older, narrower single-lane streets are still frequented by cyclists, though they might prove trickier to navigate for inexperienced riders and/or visitors.

Rules of the Road

It is completely legal for a rider to use a lane in the same manner as a motor vehicle, though some cyclists opt to one side of the street to let auto traffic pass. Like many cities, there is intermittent friction between cyclists and motorists when it comes to issues of road-sharing, traffic laws, and safety. It's wise to obey all signs and directives as if one was in a car when riding a bike in Philly.

Where to Park

The most difficult part of biking in the city may be finding a safe place to stash your bike while you run into a restaurant for lunch or a historic sight for a visit. The installation of street racks designed for bicycle lock-ups hasn't increased to meet the amount of active riders just yet, though more permanent racks and corrals seem to be popping up regularly. Invest in a quality, heavy-duty lock, whether you're locking up your bike at a rack or on a fence or street sign.

Bike Sharing

Visitors who haven't brought along their own bicycles can rent them in the short term via **Indego** (⊕ *www.rideindego.com*), Philadelphia's bike-sharing program. Dozens of bike-stocked Indego kiosks are scattered throughout the city, offering instant rentals via a high-tech kiosk system. Conveniently, you're able to pick up a bike in one area and drop it off at the kiosk closest to your destination.

Want to Know More?

For information on biking in Philadelphia, visit the website of the **Bicycle Coalition of Greater Philadelphia** (⊕ *bicyclecoalition.org*)

PORTS IN PHILADELPHIA

e reputation of Philadelphia sports ns precedes them—and not always in e most flattering manner, either. Among e most high-profile sporting cities in the untry, with a professional franchise in ch of the major sports, Philly has a long d storied athletic heritage, which natu- lly translates to a deep passion for the cal teams among the populace. That ssion, for better or worse, manifests elf in some blunt and at times inelegant ys, resulting in the large-scale vilifica- n of Philly supporters.

seball

e Phillies won a World Series title in 08. Philadelphia fans are most incensed nen their arch-rivals, the New York ets, are in town.

iladelphia Phillies. Since 2004 the Phila- lphia Phillies have played in **Citizens nk Park**, a beautiful stadium that akes for a great day or night outing in ring, summer, or fall. The season runs m April to October. Tickets start at 0. ⊠ *Citizens Bank Park, 1 Citizens nk Way* ☎ *215/463–1000* ⊕ *philadel- ia.phillies.mlb.com.*

sketball

iladelphia consistently produces first- te basketball prospects, and vigorous, mpetitive pickup games can be found hundreds of courts around the city. The ers, the city's National Basketball Asso- tion franchise, last won a title in 1983, d are in the midst of a loss-heavy, multi- ason "rebuilding" phase that is testing e patience of some diehards.

iladelphia 76ers. The Philadelphia 76ers ay at the Wells Fargo Center from ovember to April. Tickets start at $15. *Wells Fargo Center, 3601 S. Broad St.* *215/339–7676* ⊕ *www.nba.com/sixers.*

Collegiate Big Five basketball. Collegiate Big Five basketball features teams from LaSalle, St. Joseph's, Temple, the Univer- sity of Pennsylvania, and Villanova. The season runs from December to March. ⊠ *Big Five Office, the Palestra, 235 S. 33rd St., University City* ☎ *215/898– 4747* ⊕ *www.philadelphiabig5.org.*

Football

The Eagles, who have never won a Super Bowl but do have a 1960 NFL champi- onship on their mantles (predating the Super Bowl era), are the most beloved team in town.

Philadelphia Eagles. The Philadelphia Eagles can be seen in action at their state-of-the- art facility, from September through Janu- ary. The stadium has a grass playing field and holds up to 68,000 fans. Many of the best seats go to season-ticket holders; individual tickets begin at $55. ⊠ *Lin- coln Financial Field, 11th St. and Pattison Ave., South Philadelphia* ☎ *267/570–4000* ⊕ *www.philadelphiaeagles.com.*

Hockey

The Flyers, Philly's National Hockey League team, last won the Stanley Cup, the NHL's ultimate prize, in 1975.

Philadelphia Flyers. The Philadelphia Fly- ers hit the ice at the Wells Fargo Center from October to April. Tickets start at $46. ⊠ *Wells Fargo Center, 3601 S. Broad St., South Philadelphia* ☎ *215/952–7300* ⊕ *flyers.nhl.com.*

ON THE
CALENDAR

WINTER	
January 1	**Mummers Parade.** One of Philadelphia's most unique traditions, the annual New Year's Day celebration is a bacchanal of music, dance, and ridiculous costumes with roots in 17th-century European folk celebrations. The parade begins at City Hall and proceeds south down Broad Street. "String bands" feature instruments; "comics" put on humorous themed skits; "fancies" place the focus on attire. Mummer "brigades" earn prizes; onlookers are traditionally high-spirited, and possibly still drunk from the night before. There's even an official Mummers Museum in South Philly. ⊕ *www.phillymummers.com*

SPRING	
Early March	**Philadelphia Flower Show.** One of the city's most high-profile happenings, Philly's Flower Show is the oldest continuously running indoor floral exhibition in the world. Attracting more than a quarter-million viewers, the show features rare and ornate displays, a judged competition, hands-on instruction, and live entertainment. It's hosted every March at the Pennsylvania Convention Center. ⊕ *theflowershow.com*
April	**Cherry Blossom Festival.** The Japan Society of Greater Philadelphia organizes the city's take on the elaborate welcome-to-spring celebrations held in Japan and beyond, with events throughout the city and its suburbs. The occasion culminates with "Sakura Sunday," a vibrant celebration at the Horticulture Center of Fairmount Park. ⊕ *subarucherryblossom.org*
Late April	**Penn Relays.** Established in 1895 by the University of Pennsylvania, the Penn Relays are among America's oldest athletic traditions, now an international affair that attracts teams from around the globe to race over a three-day period. Held at Penn's historic Franklin Field, it regularly draws six-figure crowds. ⊕ *www.thepennrelays.com*
Early May	**Rittenhouse Row Spring Festival.** This annual festival, which takes place along the main vein of Walnut Street, highlights all the neighborhood's offerings and is a bit more democratic in its invite policy than some of the more exclusive goings-on in the area. Food, drink, live music and entertainment, and even fashion segments make up the programming at the fest, traditionally held in early May. ⊕ *rittenhouserow.org*

SUMMER	
Late May	**Roots Picnic.** Even though they're now the big-time house band for *The Tonight Show Starring Jimmy Fallon,* Philly's own The Roots still show a heavy amount of love for their hometown. Their annual one-day music festival has attracted A-List talent to Festival Pier at Penn's Landing since 2008. Past acts have included everyone from Erykah Badu and Snoop Dogg to Nas and Vampire Weekend. The Roots, of course, make their way onstage, too. ⊕ *rootspicnic.com*
Late May–Early June	**Philly Beer Week.** Conceived as a way to bring together regional craft breweries and their out-of-town cohorts, Philly Beer Week has blossomed into one of the nation's largest and most ambitious brew-centric events. The schedule comprises hundreds of events (tastings, dinners, rare releases, meet the brewer, etc.) hosted at an equally dizzying array of area bars, restaurants, and venues. A steadily growing tourism draw, Beer Week stretches across a 10-day span from late May to early June. ⊕ *phillybeerweek.org*
July 4	**Wawa Welcome America!** Wawa, the region's best-loved convenience store chain, sponsors this ambitious celebration on Independence Day with a multitude of patriotic happenings, from a massive block party on the Benjamin Franklin Parkway to free museum access and historical tours. It all culminates with a concert and fireworks extravaganza held on the Parkway that is attended by thousands. ⊕ *www.welcomeamerica.com*
Early September	**Made in America.** Held over the long Labor Day weekend, the unofficial end of summer, Made in America is a multi-day musical festival founded by the brewery Budweiser and Jay-Z. The event, which takes over the Benjamin Franklin Parkway, typically features world-renowned acts; past installments have seen Beyoncé, Pearl Jam, Drake, Calvin Harris, and Run-DMC grace the stage. ⊕ *a.madeinamericafest.com*
FALL	
Mid-September	**FringeArts and FEASTIVAL.** Taking place every autumn, FringeArts is a celebration of cutting-edge and avant garde theater and performance art. Inspired by the comparable approach taken by Fringe Festival organizers in cities like Edinburgh, Philly's Fringe has grown into a formidable cultural and artistic force, attracting talent from around the world to stage shows in Philly over a 17-day stretch each September. The

	artistic community links up with the culinary at FEASTIVAL, FringeArts' annual fund-raising soiree, featuring top restaurants commingling with performers and patrons. FringeArts' headquarters, also the home of FEASTIVAL, is located at Columbus Boulevard and Race Street. ⊕ *fringearts.com, www.phillyfeastival.com*
Late October	**Philadelphia International Film Festival.** Organized by the Philadelphia Film Society, the city's annual film fest screens titles both high-profile and under-the-radar every fall. First established in 1991, the fest brings together a diverse slate of entries, with categories such as "World Narratives" (for global cinema), "Documentary," "Graveyard Shift" (horror and sci-fi), and "Filmadelphia" (films shot locally, and/or with a local connection). Screenings are held at theaters throughout the city. ⊕ *filmadelphia.org*
November–February	**The Rothman Institute Ice Rink.** This picturesque ice rink, sponsored by the local medical orthopedic center, is centrally located in Dilworth Park, on the northwest side of City Hall. A seasonal attraction running from November to February, it offers affordable admission as well as skate rentals ($9). ⊕ *www.ccdparks.org/dilworth-park/rothmanicerink*

EXPLORING
PHILADELPHIA

Updated by
Adam Erace

Philadelphia continues on its upward trend of development in terms of new construction, a restaurant renaissance, and a cultural revival. The city rests its heels on an impressive past, and thanks to aggressive civic leadership and a close-knit local community, it continues to push toward an exciting future. And in many ways, it's only started to realize its potential.

Philadelphia is a place of contrasts: Grace Kelly and Rocky Balboa; Vetri—one of the nation's finest Italian haute-cuisine restaurants—and the fast-food heaven of Jim's Steaks; Independence Hall and the modest Mario Lanza Museum; 18th-century national icons with 21st-century–style skyscrapers soaring above them. The Philadelphia Orchestra performs in a stunning concert hall—the focal point of efforts to transform Broad Street into a multicultural Avenue of the Arts. Along the same street, 25,000 Mummers dressed in outrageous sequins and feathers historically have plucked their banjos and strutted their stuff in a parade every New Year's Day. City residents include descendants of the staid Quaker Founding Fathers, the self-possessed socialites of the Main Line, and the unrestrained sports fans, who are as vocal as they are loyal.

Philadelphia has a population of just over 1.5 million, but is known as a city of neighborhoods (some say there are 109). Shoppers haggle over the price of tomatoes in South Philly's Italian Market; families picnic in the parks of Germantown; street vendors hawk soft pretzels in Logan Circle; and all around the city vendors sell local produce and other goods at farmers' markets. There's also a strong sense of neighborhood loyalty: ask a native where he's from and he'll tell you: Fairmount, Fishtown, or Frankford, rather than Philadelphia.

Today you can find Philadelphia's compact 5-square-mile downtown (William Penn's original city) between the Delaware and the Schuylkill (pronounced *skoo*-kull) rivers. Thanks to Penn's grid system of streets—laid out in 1681—the downtown area is a breeze to navigate. The traditional heart of the city is Broad and Market streets (Penn's Center Square), where City Hall now stands. Market Street divides the city north and south; 130 South 15th Street, for example, is in the second block south of Market Street. North–south streets are numbered, starting with Front (1st) Street, at the Delaware River, and increasing to the west. Broad Street is the equivalent of 14th Street. The diagonal Benjamin Franklin Parkway breaks the rigid grid pattern by leading from City Hall out of Center City into Fairmount Park, which straddles the Schuylkill River and Wissahickon Creek for 10 miles.

Although Philadelphia is the sixth-largest city in the nation (about 1.5 million people live in the city, more than 6 million in the metropolitan area), it maintains a small-town feel. It's a cosmopolitan, exciting, but not overwhelming city, a town that's easy to explore on foot yet big enough to keep surprising even those most familiar with it.

HE HISTORIC DOWNTOWN

dor's Choice
★

Any visit to Philadelphia, whether you have one day or several, should begin in the city area that comprises Independence National Historical Park. Philadelphia was the birthplace of the United States, the home of the country's first government, and nowhere is the spirit of those miraculous early days—the boldness of conceiving a brand-new nation—more palpable than along the cobbled streets of the city's most historic district.

In the late 1940s, before civic-minded citizens banded together to save the area and before the National Park Service stepped in, the Independence Hall neighborhood was crowded with factories and run-down warehouses. Then the city, state, and federal government took interest. Some buildings were restored, and others were reconstructed on their original sites; several attractions were built for the 1976 Bicentennial celebration. In recent years a flurry of construction has again transformed the area, with several notable buildings—including an expanded visitor center, a more attractive home for the Liberty Bell, and national museums to celebrate the U.S. Constitution and the contributions of Jewish-Americans. Today the park covers 42 acres and holds close to 40 buildings. Urban renewal in Independence Mall plaza and in Society Hill have ensured that Independence Hall will never again keep unsightly company. The city's most historic area is now also one of its loveliest.

PLANNING YOUR TIME

If you've put on your walking shoes and are good at negotiating the cobblestones, you can wander through this compact area in about two hours. But the city's atmospheric historic district warrants a slower pace.

If possible, set aside four or five hours on a Sunday for your visit to Old City. You could attend the 9 am service at Christ Church, as George and Martha Washington did, and then join the 10:30 Quaker meeting at the Arch Street Friends Meeting House, where William Penn worshipped. If you detour to the Poe House, allow another two hours.

TOURS

Ride the Ducks. Take 80-minute surf-and-turf tours of Philadelphia's historic district, Penn's Landing, and the Delaware River using military-designed land-sea vehicles. You'll board the "ducks"—amphibious open-air vehicles that replicate circa-1945 Army DUKW trucks with watertight hulls—across from the Liberty Bell. On land you'll proceed through the historic district, Old City, and South Street before taking a 20-minute plunge into the Delaware River via a specially constructed ramp just south of the Ben Franklin Bridge. On the water, you'll have close-up views of the USS *Olympia* and the battleship *New Jersey,* and panoramic views of the skyline and the bridge. ⊠ *6th and Chestnut Sts., Old City* ☎ *877/887–8225* ⊕ *philadelphia.ridetheducks.com* ✉ *$29* ☉ *Mid-Mar.–Nov., schedule varies.*

OLD CITY

In Colonial days the rich folks in residential Society Hill whispered of those who lived "north of Market," for this area, between Front and 5th streets and Chestnut and Vine streets, was the city's commercial district for industry and wholesale distributors, filled with wharves and warehouses and taverns. It also held the modest homes of craftsmen and artisans. Old City (as it became known more than 40 years ago, to distinguish it from the national park area around Independence Hall) is aptly named: it's one of the city's oldest and most historic neighborhoods, home to Elfreth's Alley; the Betsy Ross House; and Christ Church, where George Washington and John Adams came (across the tracks!) to worship at services. There's evidence of the Quaker presence here, too, in the Arch Street Meeting House.

Today the Old City neighborhood is Philadelphia's version of New York's SoHo. Many cast-iron building facades remain, though the old warehouses, with telltale names such as the Sugar Refinery and the Hoopskirt Factory, now house well-lighted loft apartments popular with artists and architects. There are small theaters—the Painted Bride, the Arden Theatre Company—and numerous art galleries and boutiques. The Old City Arts Association hosts a festive, popular event the first Friday of each month—known, appropriately enough, as First Friday—when the galleries throw open their doors during evening hours.

TOP ATTRACTIONS

FAMILY **Betsy Ross House.** It's easy to find this little brick house with the gabled roof: just look for the 13-star flag displayed from its second-floor window. Whether Betsy Ross, also known as Elizabeth Griscom Ross Ashbourn Claypoole (1752–1836) actually lived here and whether she really made the first Stars and Stripes is debatable. Nonetheless, the house, built around 1740, is a splendid example of a Colonial Philadelphia home and is fun to visit. Owned by the city and maintained by the nonprofit Historic Philadelphia Inc., the eight-room house overflows with artifacts such as a family Bible and Betsy Ross's chest of drawers and reading glasses. The small rooms hold period pieces that reflect the life of this hardworking Quaker (who died at the age of 84, outliving three husbands). You may have to wait in line, as this is one of the city's most popular attractions. The house, with its winding narrow stairs, is not accessible to people with disabilities. Alongside the house is a courtyard with a fountain, as well as the graves of Betsy Ross and her third husband, John Claypoole. Visitors can meet Betsy in her upholstery shop (the only working Colonial upholstery shop in the country) and enjoy free, interactive historical programming in the courtyard from May to September. ✉ *239 Arch St., Old City* ☎ *215/686–1252* ⊕ *www. historicphiladelphia.org/betsy-ross-house/what-to-see* 🎟 *$5, $7 with Audio Guide* ◷ *Mar.–Nov., daily 10–5; Dec.–Feb., Tues.–Sun. 10–5.*

Fodor'sChoice **Elfreth's Alley.** This alley is the oldest continuously occupied residential
★ street in America, dating back to 1702. Much of Colonial Philadelphia resembled this area, with its cobblestone streets and narrow two- or three-story brick houses. These were modest row homes, most built for rent, and lived in by craftsmen, such as cabinetmakers, silversmiths,

and pewterers, and their families. They also housed sea captains and others who made their living in the city's busy shipping industry. The earliest houses (two stories) have pent eaves; taller houses, built after the Revolution, show the influence of the Federal style. The Elfreth's Alley Museum includes two homes that have been restored by the Elfreth's Alley Association: No. 124, home of a Windsor chair maker, and No. 126, a Colonial dressmaker's home, with authentic furnishings and a Colonial kitchen. In early June residents celebrate Fete Day, when some of the 30 homes are open to the public for tours hosted by guides in Colonial garb. On the second Friday evening in December, residents again welcome visitors for a candlelight holiday tour. Both of these special events require advance tickets. ⊠ *Front and 2nd Sts. between Arch and Race Sts., 124–126 Elfreth's Alley, Old City* ☎ *215/627–8680* ⊕ *www.elfrethsalley.org* ⊠ *Alley free; museum $5* ⊗ *Fri.–Sun. noon–5; hrs may be extended for holiday seasons.*

FAMILY **Franklin Court [The Benjamin Franklin Museum].** This highly interactive and informative museum built on the site that was Benjamin Franklin's first permanent home in Philadelphia was thoroughly updated and renovated in 2013 and reopened as The Benjamin Franklin Museum. The new exhibits combine the latest in touch-screen displays and computer-generated animation with a chess set, eyeglasses, and other items actually used by this Renaissance man. Franklin's multifaceted roles as scientist and inventor (of bifocals and the lightning rod), philosopher and writer, savvy politician, and successful businessman, are represented in various rooms through the help of interactive displays. Franklin, publisher of *Poor Richard's Almanac*, helped draft the Declaration of Independence and negotiate the peace with Great Britain. He also helped found Pennsylvania Hospital, the University of Pennsylvania, the Philadelphia Contributionship, and the American Philosophical Society.

In the courtyard adjacent to the museum, architect Robert Venturi erected a steel skeleton of Franklin's former home. You can peek through "windows" into cutaways to see wall foundations, outdoor privy wells, and other parts of his home that were uncovered during excavations. At the Market Street side are several houses, now exhibition halls, that Franklin had rented in addition to his main home. In one, you can see how Franklin fireproofed the building: his interest in fireproofing led him to experiment with kite flying and lightning. Here, too, you can find a restoration of a Colonial-era print shop and a post office. Don't forget to get a letter hand-stamped with a "b. free franklin" cancellation. ⊠ *314–322 Market St., or enter from Chestnut St. walkway, Old City* ☎ *267/514–1522* ⊕ *www.nps.gov* ⊠ *$5* ⊗ *Daily 9–5; summer hrs (approximately Memorial Day–Labor Day) daily 9–7.*

Fodor's Choice **Independence Hall.** The birthplace of the United States, this redbrick
★ building with its clock tower and steeple is one of the nation's greatest icons. America's most historic building was constructed in 1732–56 as the Pennsylvania State House. What happened here between 1775 and 1787 changed the course of American history—and the name of the building to Independence Hall. The delegates to the Second Continental Congress met in the hall's Assembly Room in May 1776, united in anger over the blood that had been shed when British troops fired on

CLOSE UP

Visiting Independence National Historical Park

Your first stop should be the Independence Visitor Center, where you can buy tickets for tours and pick up maps and brochures. From here you can easily explore the park on your own; in each building a park ranger can answer all your questions. In summer more than a dozen storytellers wander through the park, perching on benches to tell tales of the times. Special paid guided tours are also available through the Independence Visitor Center.

Hours and Fees: The Independence Visitor Center is open daily 8:30–6, and Independence Hall and the Liberty Bell Pavilion are open daily year-round 9–5. In summer the closing times are often later. Other park buildings are also open daily, although their hours may vary from season to season. Call *800/537–7676*, the 24-hour hotline, for current hours plus a schedule of park programs; or visit ⊕ *www. nps.gov/inde*. Except as noted, all attractions run by the park are free.

When to Go: The best time to visit America's birthplace is on America's

birthday; just expect big crowds. The city throws the weeklong Wawa Welcome America! party. From June 27 to July 4 there are more than 50 free events, including parades (the Mummers and an illuminated boat procession), outdoor concerts, historical reenactments, and eye-popping fireworks. The rest of the summer is filled with plays, musicals, and parades.

How Long to Stay: Budget a full day here. An early start lets you reserve timed tickets for a tour of the Todd and Bishop White houses and adjust your schedule to catch some of the special events on the visitor center's daily schedule. Allow about 40 minutes for the Independence Hall tour and another hour each at Franklin Court and the Todd and Bishop White houses. Allow 30 minutes each at Declaration House and the visitor center, where it's a good idea to see the film *Independence* before you set out. You might want to dine in the area before wrapping up for the day.

citizens in Concord, Massachusetts. In this same room George Washington was appointed commander in chief of the Continental Army, Thomas Jefferson's eloquent Declaration of Independence was signed, and later the Constitution of the United States was adopted. Here the first foreign minister to visit the United States was welcomed; the news of Cornwallis's defeat was announced, signaling the end of the Revolutionary War; and, later, John Adams and Abraham Lincoln lay in state. The memories this building holds linger in the collection of polished muskets, the silver inkstand used by delegates to sign the Declaration of Independence, and the "Rising Sun" chair in which George Washington sat. (After the Constitution was adopted, Benjamin Franklin said about the sun carving on the chair, "I have the happiness to know that it is a rising and not a setting sun.")

In the **East Wing**—attached to Independence Hall by a short colonnade—you can embark on free tours that start every 15 to 20 minutes and last 35 minutes. Admission is first-come, first-served; pick up free, timed tickets from the visitor center to avoid waiting in line. The **West Wing** of Independence Hall contains an exhibit of the national historical park's collection of our nation's founding documents: the final draft of the Constitution, a working copy of the Articles of Confederation, and the first printing of the Declaration of Independence.

In front of Independence Hall, next to the statue of George Washington, note the plaques marking the spots where Abraham Lincoln stood on February 22, 1861, and where John F. Kennedy delivered an address on July 4, 1962. With Independence Hall in front of you and the Liberty Bell behind you, this is a place to stand for a moment and soak up a sense of history. From March through December and on major holidays, free, timed tickets from the Independence Visitor Center are required for entry. Tickets also can be reserved online (⊕ *www. recreation.gov*). ⊠ *520 Chestnut St., between 5th and 6th Sts., Old City* ☎ *215/965–2305, 877/444–6777 advance tickets* ⊕ *www.nps.gov/inde* 🖃 *Free* ☉ *Daily 9–5; some extended hrs in summer and on holidays.*

Independence Visitor Center. This is the city's official visitor center as well as the gateway to Independence National Historical Park. Here, you'll find a fully staffed concierge-and-trip-planning desk, which provides information on the Park, the Philadelphia Museum of Art, the Philadelphia Zoo, and other attractions, as well as a reservation and ticketing service. Before you set off on a walking tour, acquaint yourself with Colonial American history by watching the Founding Fathers come to life in the 30-minute movie *Independence,* one of the films shown in the center's two theaters. There's also a coffee bar with sandwiches, salads, and desserts, and an excellent bookstore, where you can stock up on books, videos, brochures, prints, wall hangings, and souvenirs of historic figures and events. An atrium connects the visitor center to a renovated underground parking area. The outdoor café, Independence Mall Cafe, on the east side of the visitor center, is open May through October.

To see two of the city's famous historic homes—the Bishop White and Todd houses—you'll need to stop at the information desk to get a free, timed ticket, and reserve a spot on one of the tours, each of which takes about an hour. ⊠ *1 N. Independence Mall W, 6th and Market Sts., Old City* ☎ *215/965–7676, 800/537–7676* ⊕ *www. independencevisitorcenter.com* ☉ *Sept.–May, daily 8:30–6; June–Aug., daily 8:30–7* ☞ *Hrs may be extended during holidays and peak seasons.*

●dor's Choice ★ **Liberty Bell Center.** The bell fulfilled the words of its inscription when it rang to "proclaim liberty throughout all the land unto all the inhabitants thereof," beckoning Philadelphians to the State House yard to hear the first reading of the Declaration of Independence. Ordered in 1751 and originally cast in England, it cracked during testing and was recast in Philadelphia by Pass and Stow two years later. To keep it from falling into British hands during the Revolution—they would have melted it down for ammunition—it was spirited away by horse and wagon to Allentown, 60 miles to the north. The Liberty Bell is the subject of much legend; one story says it cracked when tolled at the funeral of Chief Justice John Marshall in 1835. Actually, the bell cracked slowly over a period of years. It was repaired but cracked again in 1846 and

Historic Downtown

Delaware River

Camden

NEW
JERSEY

Benjamin Franklin Bridge

0   500 M

0   1,000 ft

Philadelphia's Place in American History

William Penn founded the city in 1682, and chose to name it Philadelphia—Greek for "brotherly love"—after an ancient Syrian city, site of one of the earliest and most venerated Christian churches. Penn's Quakers settled on a tract of land he described as his "greene countrie towne." After the Quakers, the next waves of immigrants to arrive were Anglicans and Presbyterians (who had a running conflict with the "stiff Quakers" and their distaste for music and dancing). The new residents forged traditions that remain strong in parts of Philadelphia today: united families, comfortable houses, handsome furniture, and good education. From these early years came the attitude Mark Twain summed up as: "In Boston, they ask: 'What does he know?' In New York, 'How much does he make?' In Philadelphia, 'Who were his parents?'"

The city became the queen of the English-speaking New World from the late 1600s to the early 1800s. In the latter half of the 1700s Philadelphia was the largest city in the colonies, a great and glorious place. So when the delegates from the colonies wanted to meet in a centrally located, thriving city, they chose Philadelphia. They convened the First Continental Congress in 1774 at Carpenters' Hall. The rest, as they say, is history. It is here that the Declaration of Independence was written and adopted, the Constitution was framed, the capital of the United States was established, the Liberty Bell was rung, the nation's flag was sewn by Betsy Ross (though scholars debate this), and George Washington served most of his presidency.

was then forever silenced. It was called the State House Bell until the 1830s, when a group of abolitionists adopted it as a symbol of freedom and renamed it the Liberty Bell.

After more than 200 years inside Independence Hall, the bell was moved to a glass-enclosed pavilion for the 1976 Bicentennial, which for many seemed an incongruous setting for such a historic object. In mid-2003 it once again moved to another glass-enclosed pavilion with redbrick accents. This time, great care was taken to improve access and viewing of its former home at Independence Hall, which is seen against the backdrop of the sky—rather than 20th-century buildings. The Liberty Bell complex houses a bell chamber, an interpretive exhibit area with historic displays and memorabilia, and a covered area for waiting in line.

During construction for the bell's current home, the foundation and other archaeological remains of The President's House, the home of the nation's chief executives before the capital shifted to Washington, D.C., were discovered, as well as evidence of slaves owned by President George Washington who lived there during his time in office. A new permanent installation includes a series of video panels focusing on the stories of the nine enslaved African Americans, as well as glass panels through which you can view the remains of the structure's foundation. ⊠ *6th and Chestnut Sts., 526 Market St., Old City* ☎ *215/965–2305* ⊕ *www.nps.gov/inde/liberty-bell-center.htm* ⊠ *Free* ☉ *Daily 9–5; hrs may be extended during peak visitor periods.*

★dor's Choice
★

National Constitution Center. This 160,000-square-foot museum brings the U.S. Constitution alive through a series of highly interactive exhibits tracing the development and adoption of the nation's landmark guiding document. The heart of the sprawling museum, The Story of We the People, takes you from the American Revolution through the Constitution's ratification to major events in the nation's constitutional history, including present-day events like the inauguration of President Barack Obama, Hurricane Katrina, and the recent economic crisis. Later, you can play the role of a Supreme Court justice deciding an important case, and walk among the framers in Signers' Hall, where you can decide whether to add your signature to the list of Founding Fathers. The facility has 100-plus exhibits, plays host to many events with major historians, authors, and political figures, and also houses the Annenberg Center for Education and Outreach, a hub for constitutional education efforts that is not open to the public. ⊠ *525 Arch St., Independence Mall, Old City* ☎ *215/409–6700* ⊕ *www.constitutioncenter.org* ☐ *$14.50 (with extra charges for some special exhibits)* ⊙ *Weekdays 9–5, Sat. 9–6, Sun. noon–5* Ⓜ *SEPTA; the Market-Frankfurt subway line stops 1 block from the Center at 5th and Market Sts.*

The President's House. This site commemorates the location of the home to U.S. presidents George Washington and John Adams from 1790 to 1800, as well as nine enslaved Africans who worked as household staff. The outdoor monument, which is open 24 hours a day, shows video clips that bring the house's history alive. Inside, take note of the bow window, which is thought to have inspired the shape of the Oval Office at the White House, as well as the remains of a passage torn down in 1832 that connected the main house to the slave quarters. ⊠ *6th and Market Sts., Old City* ☎ *800/537–7676* ☐ *Free* ⊙ *Daily 9–5. Hrs may be extended during peak visitor seasons* ☞ *The outdoor site is accessible at all times, but the interactive exhibits run concurrent with the Liberty Bell Pavilion hrs.*

QUICK
BITE

✕ **Bourse. Enter the Bourse and you're in another century. The skylighted Great Hall, with its Corinthian columns, marble, wrought-iron stairways, and Victorian gingerbread details, has been magnificently restored. Built in 1895 as a stock exchange, it now houses shops and a food court, where you can grab a cup of cappuccino or a Philly cheesesteak. The food court at the Bourse offers a voucher program and box lunch options for large groups or tours which make arrangements ahead of time.** ⊠ *5th St. across from Liberty Bell Pavilion, 111 S. Independence Mall E, Old City* ☎ *215/625–0300* ⊕ *www.bourse-pa.com* ⊙ *Closed Sun. Dec.–Feb. No dinner.*

United States Mint. The first U.S. mint was built in Philadelphia at 16th and Spring Garden streets in 1792, when the Bank of North America adopted dollars and cents instead of shillings and pence as standard currency; the current mint was built in 1971. During a self-guided tour you can see blank disks being melted, cast, and pressed into coins, which are then inspected, counted, and bagged. Historic artifacts such as the Key to the First Mint and the gold medal awarded to General Anthony Wayne for his capture of Stony Point during the Revolutionary War are displayed. Seven Tiffany glass tile mosaics depict coin making in ancient Rome. A shop in the lobby sells special coins and medals—in mint condition. ⊠ *5th and Arch Sts., 151 N. Independence Mall E, Old City* ☎ *215/408–0112* ⊕ *www.usmint.gov* ✉ *Free* ⊙ *Weekdays 9–4:30* ☞ *The mint is subject to U.S. Homeland Security rules. If the Homeland Security threat is raised to "orange," no public tours will be allowed.*

WORTH NOTING

African American Museum in Philadelphia. The centerpiece of this museum is "Audacious Freedom: African Americans in Philadelphia 1776–1876," a permanent exhibit that uses video and touch-screen monitors to tell the stories of pioneers in the freedom movement. The list includes Frances Ellens Watkins Harper, a conductor on the Underground Railroad and suffragist; Thomas Morris Chester, a journalist and lawyer who was the first black to argue a case before the U.S. Supreme Court; and Elizabeth Taylor Greenfield, a renowned singer who performed for Queen Victoria. The museum's gift shop stocks one of the area's widest selection of books on black culture, history, fiction, poetry, and drama, along with African textiles and sculpture and African-American jewelry, prints, and tiles. Opened in the Bicentennial year of 1976, this is the first museum of its kind funded and built by a city. ⊠ *701 Arch St., Old City* ☎ *215/574–0380* ⊕ *www.aampmuseum.org* ✉ *$14* ⊙ *Thurs.–Sat. 10–5, Sun. noon–5.*

Arch Street Meeting House. Constructed in 1804 for the Philadelphia Yearly Meeting of the Society of Friends, this building of simple lines is still used for that purpose, as well as for weekly services. Among the most influential members in the 19th century was Lucretia Mott (1793–1880), a leader in the women's suffrage, antiwar, and antislavery movements. A small museum in the building presents a series of dioramas and a 14-minute slide show depicting the life and accomplishments of William Penn (1644–1718), who gave the land on which the meeting house sits to the Society of Friends. Quaker guides give tours year-round. ⊠ *320 Arch St., at 4th St., Old City* ☎ *215/627–2667* ⊕ *www. archstreetmeetinghouse.org* ✉ *$2 suggested donation* ⊙ *Tues.–Sat. 10–4; worship Wed. at 7 pm and Sun. at 10:30 am.*

OFF THE BEATEN PATH

Benjamin Franklin Bridge. When the bridge opened in 1926, its 1,750-foot main span made it the longest suspension bridge in the world. Paul Cret, architect of the Rodin Museum, was the designer. The bridge has been having some rust problems of late, but a massive, multiyear project has restored its glorious blue paint job. The bridge is most impressive when it's lighted at night. Start the 1¾-mile walk (one-way) from either the Philadelphia side, two blocks north of the U.S. Mint, or the Camden, New Jersey, side. ⊠ *5th and Vine Sts., Old City* ☎ *215/218–3750* ⊕ *www.drpa.org* ✉ *Free* ⊙ *Pedestrian walkway open daily Oct.–Apr. 6 am–8 pm; May–Sept. 6 am–9 pm, weather permitting* ☞ *Weather and construction conditions may restrict access to the walkway. For updates call 856/968–2255 or 215/218–3750 Ext. 2255 (weekdays 9–5). All other times call DRPA Police Radio at 856/968–3301 or 215/218–3750 Ext 3301.*

Bishop White House. Built in 1786, this restored upper-class house embodies Colonial and Federal elegance. It was the home of Bishop William White (1748–1836), rector of Christ Church, first Episcopal bishop of Pennsylvania, and spiritual leader of Philadelphia for 60 years. White, a founder of the Episcopal Church after the break with England, was chaplain to the Continental Congress and entertained many of the country's first families, including Washington and Franklin. The second-floor study contains much of the bishop's own library. The house tour is not recommended for small children. Free tickets are required to tour the house and are available at the Independence Visitor Center for one-hour tours that include the Todd House. ⊠ *309 Walnut St., Old City* ☎ *215/965–2305* ⊕ *www.nps.gov/inde/learn/historyculture/places-bishopwhitehouse.htm* 🖃 *Free* ⊗ *Tours are available daily when the visitor center is open at 11, 12:30, 1:30, and 3 with ticket and include a tour of Todd House* ☞ *Tickets are required for tours and available on a first-come, first-served basis at the Independence Visitor Center daily; tours are limited to 10 adults at a time.*

Carpenters' Hall. This handsome, patterned red-and-black brick building dating from 1770 was the headquarters of the Carpenters' Company, a guild founded to support carpenters, who were both builders and architects in this era, and to aid their families. In September 1774 the First Continental Congress convened here and addressed a declaration of rights and grievances to King George III. Today re-creations of Colonial settings include original Windsor chairs and candle sconces and displays of 18th-century carpentry tools. The Carpenters' Company still owns and operates the building. ⊠ *320 Chestnut St., Old City* ☎ *215/925–0167* ⊕ *www.carpentershall.org* 🖃 *Free; donations accepted* ⊗ *Jan. and Feb., Wed.–Sun. 10–4; Mar.–Dec., Tues.–Sun. 10–4.*

Christ Church. The Anglicans of the Church of England built a wooden church on this site in 1697. When they outgrew it, they erected a new church, the most sumptuous in the colonies, probably designed by Dr. John Kearsley and modeled on the work of famed English architect Sir Christopher Wren. The symmetrical, classical facade with arched windows, completed in 1754, is a fine example of Georgian architecture; the church is one of the city's treasures. The congregation included 15 signers of the Declaration of Independence. The bells and the soaring 196-foot steeple, the tallest in the colonies, were financed by lotteries run by Benjamin Franklin. Brass plaques mark the pews of George and Martha Washington, John and Abigail Adams, Betsy Ross, and others. Two blocks west of the church is Christ Church Burial Ground. Guided tours are available throughout the day. ⊠ *20 N. American St., 2nd St. north of Market St., Old City* ☎ *215/922–1695* ⊕ *www.christchurchphila.org* 🖃 *$3 suggested donation* ⊗ *Mar.–Dec., Mon.–Sat. 9–5, Sun. 1–5; Jan. and Feb., Wed.–Sat. 9–5, Sun. 1–5; services year-round Sun. at 9 and 11, Wed. at noon* Ⓜ *2nd and Market Sts.*

Christ Church Burial Ground. Weathered gravestones fill the resting place of five signers of the Declaration of Independence and other Colonial patriots. The best-known is Benjamin Franklin; he lies alongside his wife, Deborah, and their son, Francis, who died at age four. According to local legend, throwing a penny onto Franklin's grave will bring you good luck. The burial ground is open to the public—except in December, January, and February—for regular visits. Guided tours may be available with advanced reservations in the winter months, weather permitting. ⊠ *5th and Arch Sts., Old City* ☎ *215/922–1695* ⊕ *www. christchurchphila.org* ⊡ *$2, $7 with guided tour* ۞ *Mar.–Nov., Mon.–Sat. 10–4, Sun. noon–4, weather permitting; guided tours available 11–3:30 daily.*

Congress Hall. Formerly the Philadelphia County Courthouse, Congress Hall was the meeting place of the U.S. Congress from 1790 to 1800—one of the most important decades in our nation's history. Here the Bill of Rights was added to the Constitution; Alexander Hamilton's proposals for a mint and a national bank were enacted; and Vermont, Kentucky, and Tennessee became the first new states after the original colonies. On the first floor you can find the House of Representatives, where President John Adams was inaugurated in 1797. On the second floor is the Senate chamber, where in 1793 George Washington was inaugurated for his second term. Both chambers have been authentically restored. ⊠ *520 Chestnut St., at 6th St., Old City* ☎ *215/965–2305* ⊕ *www.nps.gov/inde* ⊡ *Free* ۞ *Daily 9–5; some extended hrs in summer and on holidays* ☞ *Admission is on a first-come, first-served basis.*

Curtis Center. The lobby of the Curtis Publishing Company building has a great treasure: a 15-by-50-foot glass mosaic mural, *The Dream Garden,* based on a Maxfield Parrish painting. It was executed by the Louis C. Tiffany Studios in 1916. The work's 260 colors and 100,000 pieces of opalescent hand-fired glass laced with gold leaf make it perhaps the finest Tiffany mural in the world. The mural was also designated a "historic object" by the Philadelphia Historical Commission after its owner, the estate of a local art patron, put it up for sale for $9 million in 1998; the designation, the first in the city's history, stopped the sale and the mural remains in public view, under the auspices of the Pennsylvania Academy of the Fine Arts. ⊠ *601–45 Walnut St., at 6th St., Old City* ☎ *215/627–7280* ⊡ *Free* ۞ *Weekdays 6–6* ☞ *The mural is open to the public whenever the building is open.*

Declaration House. In a second-floor room that he had rented from bricklayer Jacob Graff, Thomas Jefferson (1743–1826) drafted the Declaration of Independence in June 1776. The home was reconstructed for the Bicentennial celebration; the bedroom and parlor in which Jefferson lived that summer were re-created with period furnishings. The first floor has a Jefferson exhibition. The display on the Declaration of Independence shows some of the changes Jefferson made while writing it. You can see Jefferson's original version—which would have abolished slavery had the passage not been stricken by the committee that included Benjamin Franklin and John Adams. ⊠ *701 Market St., at 7th St., Old City* ☎ *215/965–2305* ⊕ *www.nps.gov/inde* ⊡ *Free* ۞ *May–Nov., guided tours at 1:30 and 4 daily.*

William Penn and His Legacy

William Penn was a rebel with a cause. Born in London in 1644 into a nobleman's family, he attended Oxford University, studied law, and tried a military career (in emulation of his father, an admiral in the British Navy). It was at Oxford that Penn first heard Quaker preachers professing that each life is part of the Divine spirit, and that all people should be treated equally. At age 23, Penn joined the Religious Society of Friends (Quakers), who at the time were considered religious zealots.

Penn was imprisoned in the Tower of London for his heretical pamphlets, but he was spared worse persecution because of his father's support of King Charles II. He petitioned the king to grant him land in the New World for a Quaker colony; he was given a 45,000-square-mile tract along the Delaware River in payment of a debt Charles owed to his late father. Indeed, the king named the land Pennsylvania in honor of the admiral.

On Penn's first visit to his colony, from 1662 to 1664, he began his "Holy Experiment," establishing his haven for Quakers. His laws guaranteed religious freedom and an elected government. He bought land from the Native Americans and established a peace treaty that lasted for 70 years.

Penn was called back to England in 1684 and remained there until 1699, caring for his ill wife, Gulielma Maria Springett, who would die without seeing his beloved Pennsylvania. Penn was suspected of plotting with the former Catholic king, James II, to overthrow the Protestant monarchy of William and Mary, who revoked his charter in 1692 for 18 months.

Penn made his second trip to America with his second wife, Hannah Callowhill Penn, in 1699. The couple moved into Pennsbury Manor along the upper Delaware River, where, while preaching about a life of simplicity, he lived in luxury. Penn issued a new frame of government, the Charter of Privileges, which became a model for the U.S. Constitution. He had to return to England yet again in 1701; there he was consumed by the political and legal problems of his colony, a term in prison for debt, and then illness. Penn died before he could return to Pennsylvania. After his death, his wife honored him by assuming the governorship for nine years.

Although Penn spent only 4 of his 74 years in Pennsylvania, his legacy is profound. As a city planner, he mapped out a "greene countrie towne" with broad, straight streets. He positioned each house in the middle of its plot, so that every child would have play space; he named its streets—Walnut, Spruce, Chestnut—for trees, not for men. His original city plan has survived. As a reformer, Penn replaced dungeons with workhouses; established the right of a jury to decide a verdict without harassment by a judge; provided schools where boys—and girls—could get a practical education; and limited the death penalty to two offenses—murder and treason—rather than the 200 mandated by English criminal law.

2

QUICK
BITE ✕ **Farmicia Restaurant.** You'll find a wide range of lunch and dinner dishes, as well as a tantalizing array of brownies and cookies, along with coffee and other beverages. On weekends there are both breakfast and brunch services, and there's a substantial bar menu for late-afternoon and late-night cravings. ✉ *15 S. 3rd St., Old City* ☎ *215/627–6274* ⊕ *www.farmiciarestaurant.com* ⊗ *Closed Mon.* Ⓜ *2nd and Market Sts.*

FAMILY **Fireman's Hall Museum.** Housed in an authentic 1876 firehouse, this museum traces the history of firefighting, from the volunteer company founded in Philadelphia by Benjamin Franklin in 1736 to the professional departments of the 20th century. The collection includes early hand- and horse-drawn fire engines, such as an 1796 hand pumper, an 1857 steamer, and a 1907 three-horse Metropolitan steamer; fire marks (18th-century building signs marking them as insured for fire); uniforms; other memorabilia; and a 9/11 memorial. There is also a gift shop on-site and online. ✉ *147 N. 2nd St., Old City* ☎ *215/923–1438* ⊕ *www.firemanshall.org* 🎟 *Free; donations requested* ⊗ *Tues.–Sat. 10–4:30, 1st Fri. of each month 10–9.*

First Bank of the United States. A fine example of Federal architecture, the oldest bank building in the country was headquarters of the government's bank from 1797 to 1811. Designed by Samuel Blodget Jr. and erected in 1795–97, the bank was an imposing structure in its day, exemplifying strength, dignity, and security. Head first to the right, to the north side of the structure, to find a wrought-iron gateway topped by an eagle. Pass through it into the courtyard, and you magically step out of modern-day Philadelphia and into Colonial America. Before you do so, check out the bank's pediment. Executed in 1797 by Clodius F. Legrand and Sons, its cornucopia, oak branch, and American eagle are carved from mahogany—a late-18th-century masterpiece that has withstood acid rain better than the bank's marble pillars. ✉ *120 S. 3rd St., Old City* ⊗ *Interior closed to public.*

Franklin Square. One of five squares William Penn placed in his original design, this park is now a family-friendly destination. There are two modern playgrounds (for younger and older kids) open year-round. From April through December the square also features a carousel; a food stand with burgers, salads, shakes, and ice cream operated by famed local restaurateur Stephen Starr; and an 18-hole miniature-golf course, whose holes boast scale models of Independence Hall, the Philadelphia Museum of Art, Ben Franklin Bridge, and other local landmarks. While the park remains open year-round, the attractions are closed in January and February. ✉ *200 N. 6th Street, at Race St., Old City* ☎ *215/629–4026* ⊕ *www.historicphiladelphia.org* 🎟 *Park free; attraction prices vary* ⊗ *Park daily 10–10.*

Free Quaker Meeting House. This was the house of worship for the Free "Fighting" Quakers, a group that broke away from the Society of Friends to take up arms against the British during the Revolutionary War. The building was designed in 1783 by Samuel Wetherill, one of the original leaders of the group, after they were disowned by their pacifist brothers. Among the 100 members were Betsy Ross (then Elizabeth

Griscom) and Timothy Matlack, colonel in Washington's Army and assistant secretary of the Continental Congress. After the Free Quaker group dissolved (many left to become Episcopalian), the building was used as a school, library, and warehouse. The meetinghouse, built in the Quaker plain style with a brick front and gable roof, has been carefully restored. ⊠ *500 Arch St., at 5th St., Old City* ☎ *215/965–2305* ⊕ *www. nps.gov/inde/free-quaker.htm* ⊞ *Free* ⊙ *Mar.–Nov., weekends 11–4.*

Independence Square. On July 8, 1776, the Declaration of Independence was first read in public here. Although the square is not as imposing today, it still has great dignity. You can imagine the impact the reading had on the colonists. ⊠ *Bounded by Walnut and Chestnut Sts. and 5th and 6th Sts., Old City* ⊕ *www.nps.gov/inde* ⊞ *Free* ⊙ *Daily 9–5; hrs may be extended during summer and peak tourist seasons* ⌫ *Visitors may have to pass through a security checkpoint at 5th and Chestnut Sts.*

Library Hall. This 20th-century building is a reconstruction of Franklin's Library Company of Philadelphia, the first public library in the colonies. The American Philosophical Society, one of the country's leading institutions for the study of science, has its library here. The vaults contain such treasures as a copy of the Declaration of Independence handwritten by Thomas Jefferson, William Penn's 1701 Charter of Privileges, and journals from the Lewis and Clark expedition of 1803–06. The library's collection also includes first editions of Newton's *Principia Mathematica*, Franklin's *Experiments and Observations*, and Darwin's *On the Origin of Species*. The APS also offers a small, rotating exhibit of its rare books and manuscripts in the lobby of its first floor. ⊠ *105 S. 5th St., Old City* ☎ *215/440–3400* ⊕ *www.amphilsoc.org* ⊞ *Free* ⊙ *Weekdays 9–4:45* Ⓜ *5th and Market Sts.*

Lights of Liberty. This 15-minute, 3-D film called *Liberty 360* is narrated by "Benjamin Franklin," telling the story of the founding of the nation and the meaning of its symbols in an indoor theater-in-the-round. Although the narrative offers little new information for history buffs, kids of all ages will enjoy wearing the 3-D glasses and getting a unique perspective on the nation's founding history. ⊠ *Historic Philadelphia Center PECO Theater, 6th and Chestnut Sts., Old City* ☎ *215/629–5801* ⊕ *www.historicphiladelphia.org/lights-of-liberty/ what-to-see* ⊞ *$6* ⊙ *Mon.–Sat. 10–6, Sun. 11–5. Hrs may vary seasonally; call to verify.*

Loxley Court. One of the restored 18th-century houses in this lovely court was once home to Benjamin Loxley, a carpenter who worked on Independence Hall. The court's claim to fame, according to its residents, is as the spot where Benjamin Franklin flew his kite in his experiment with lightning; the key tied to it was the key to Loxley's front door. ⊠ *321–323 Arch St., Old City* ⊙ *Closed to public* ⌫ *The residences are gated and privately owned. There is no admittance for the public.*

Mikveh Israel. Nathan Levy, a Colonial merchant whose ship, the *Myrtilla*, brought the Liberty Bell to America, helped found this Jewish congregation in 1740, making it the oldest in Philadelphia and the second oldest in the United States. The original synagogue was at 3rd and Cherry streets; the congregation's current space, where it has been since

1976, is in the Sephardic style (following Spanish and Portuguese Jewish ritual). The synagogue's Spruce Street Cemetery (about eight blocks away, beyond Old City) dates from 1740 and is the oldest surviving Jewish site in Philadelphia. It was the burial ground for the Spanish-Portuguese Jewish community. Guided tours of the cemetery, arranged through the synagogue, are given mid-June through mid-August, Tuesday to Friday and Sunday 10 to 3, and by appointment the rest of the year. ⊠ *44 N. 4th St., Old City* ☎ *215/922–5446* ⊕ *www.mikvehisrael.org* ✉ *Free; donations accepted* ⊙ *Mon.–Thurs. 10–4, Fri. and Sun. 10–1, but no docents are available* ☞ *The daily minyan (7:30 weekdays, 8:30 Sun. and holidays) and Shabbat services (Fri. 7:15 pm, Sat. 9 am) are open to all* ⊠ *Cemetery, Spruce St. between 8th and 9th Sts., Old City* ☎ *215/922–5446* ⊕ *www. ushistory.org/mikvehisrael* ✉ *Free; donation suggested* ⊙ *Mid-June–mid-Aug., Sun. and Tues.–Fri. 10–3* ☞ *Private tours may be arranged through the synagogue Sept.–May with advanced notice.*

National Liberty Museum. Using interactive exhibits, video, and works of art, the museum aims to combat bigotry in the United States by putting a spotlight on the nation's rich traditions of freedom and diversity. Galleries celebrate outstanding Americans and contemporary heroes from around the world. The Live Like a Hero exhibit celebrates everyday heroes, including teachers, first responders, and extraordinary children working to better their communities. The museum's collection of glass art is symbolic of the fragility of peace; its highlight is Dale Chihuly's 20-foot-tall red glass sculpture *Flame of Liberty*. Sandy Skoglund's colorful *Jelly Bean People* are a reminder that many of our differences are only skin deep. ⊠ *321 Chestnut St., Old City* ☎ *215/925–2800* ⊕ *www.libertymuseum. org* ✉ *$7; $2 children 2–17 accompanied by an adult; children under 2 free; $15 Family Admission includes 2 adult family members and all accompanying children* ⊙ *Daily 10–5; hrs may vary on holidays.*

National Museum of American Jewish History. Established in 1976, this museum in 2011 moved to a new, $150-million, contemporary building on a high-profile corner near Independence Hall. The 100,000-square-foot facility, via multimedia displays, historic objects, and ephemera, traces the history of American Jews from 1654 to the present. Highlights include "Only in America," a showcase of the accomplishments of 18 famed Jewish Americans, including polio-vaccine inventor Jonas Salk, actress-singer-director Barbra Streisand, and Broadway composer Irving Berlin; a three-level timeline covering everything from immigration, the formation of Israel, and the civil rights movement to the westward migration, suburban life, and *Seinfeld*; a Contemporary Issues Forum, where you can share your views on various issues on Post-it-style notes that are scanned electronically and displayed; and "It's Your Story," where you can record clips about your family history. The museum's exterior offers two contrasting sculptures symbolizing how American Jewish history is intertwined with the nation's story: one is a 19th-century marble monument dubbed *Religious Liberty*; the other, an LED torch atop the corner of the facility's glass facade. ⊠ *5th and Market Sts., 101 S. Independence Mall E, Old City* ☎ *215/923–3811* ⊕ *www.nmajh.org* ✉ *$12 (pay-what-you-wish after 5)* ⊙ *Tues.–Fri. 10–5, weekends 10–5:30; Memorial Day–Labor Day, Wed. 10–8.*

New Hall Military Museum. The original of this reconstructed 1790 building briefly served as headquarters for the U.S. Department of War. On display are Revolutionary War uniforms, medals, and authentic weapons, including powder horns, swords, and a blunderbuss. Dioramas depict highlights of the Revolutionary War, and there are several scale models of warships and frigates. ⊠ *320 Chestnut St., east of 4th St., Old City* ☎ *215/965–2305* ⊕ *www.nps.gov/inde/learn/historyculture/places-newhallmilitarymuseum.htm* ☒ *Free* ⊙ *Late May–Oct., daily noon–5.*

Old City Hall. Independence Hall is flanked by Congress Hall to the west and Old City Hall to the east: three distinctive Federal-style buildings erected to house the city's growing government. But when Philadelphia became the nation's capital in 1790, the just-completed city hall was lent to the federal government. It housed the U.S. Supreme Court from 1791 to 1800; John Jay was the Chief Justice. Later, the boxlike building with a peaked roof and cupola was used as the city hall. Today an exhibit presents information about the early days of the federal judiciary. ⊠ *5th and Chestnut Sts., Old City* ☎ *215/965–2305* ⊕ *www.nps.gov/inde/old-city-hall.html* ☒ *Free* ⊙ *Daily 9–5; hrs may be extended during summer and peak visitor seasons.*

Philadelphia History Museum at the Atwater Kent. Formerly known as the Atwater Kent Museum, this museum chronicling the city's 300-year-long history reopened in spring 2012 following an extensive renovation. Started in 1938 by A. Atwater Kent, a wealthy inventor, radio magnate, and manufacturer, the museum contains more than 100,000 objects—everything from textiles to toys—that illustrate what everyday life was like for generations of Philadelphians. It occupies an elegant 1826 Greek Revival building designed by John Haviland, who was also the architect of the Eastern State Penitentiary. Exhibits include the interactive "City Stories: An Introduction to Philadelphia" which explores the city's history from the 1680s to today; "Made in Philadelphia," which has hanging displays on different industries; and "The Ordinary, The Extraordinary and the Unknown: The Power of Objects." Among the eclectic items on show are a 17th-century wampum belt given to William Penn by the Lenape people, George Washington's presidential desk, and boxing gloves worn by former heavyweight champion Joe Frazier. ⊠ *15 S. 7th St., Old City* ☎ *215/685–4830* ⊕ *www.philadelphiahistory.org* ☒ *$10* ⊙ *Tues.–Sat. 10:30–4:30.*

Philadelphia Merchant's Exchange. Designed by the well-known Philadelphia architect William Strickland and built in 1832, this impressive Greek Revival building served as the city's commercial center for 50 years. It was both the stock exchange and a place where merchants met to trade goods. In the tower a watchman scanned the Delaware River and notified merchants of arriving ships. The exchange stands behind Dock Street, a cobblestone thoroughfare. The building houses a small exhibit on its history and now serves as the headquarters for Independence National Park. ⊠ *143 S. 3rd St., Old City* ☎ *215/965–2305* ☒ *Free* ⊙ *Weekdays 8–4:30.*

Philosophical Hall. This is the headquarters of the American Philosophical Society, founded by Benjamin Franklin in 1743 to promote "useful knowledge." The members of the oldest learned society in America have included Washington, Jefferson, Lafayette, Emerson, Darwin, Edison, Churchill, and Einstein. Erected between 1785 and 1789 in what has been called a "restrained Federal style" (designed to complement, not outshine, adjacent Independence Hall), Philosophical Hall is brick with marble trim, has a handsome arched entrance, and houses the Society's museum, open to the public. The society's library is across the street in Library Hall. ✉ *104 S. 5th St., Old City* ☎ *215/440–3400* ⊕ *www. apsmuseum.org* 🖃 *$2 suggested donation* ⊙ *Thurs.–Sun. 10–4.*

Todd House. Built in 1775 by John Dilworth, Todd House has been restored to its 1790s appearance, when its best-known resident, Dolley Payne Todd (1768–1849), lived here. She lost her husband, the Quaker lawyer John Todd, to the yellow fever epidemic of 1793. Dolley later married James Madison, who became the fourth president. Her time as a hostess in the White House was quite a contrast to her years in this simple home. There's an 18th-century garden next to Todd House. Free tickets are required to tour the house and are available at the Independence Vsitor Center for one-hour tours that include the Bishop White House. ✉ *400 Walnut Street, at 4th St., Old City* ☎ *215/965–2305* ⊕ *www.nps.gov/inde/learn/historyculture/ places-dolleytoddhouse.htm* 🖃 *Free* ⊙ *Tours are available daily when the visitor center is open at 11, 12:30, 1:30, and 3 with ticket and include a tour of the Bishop White House* ☞ *Tickets are required for tours and available on a first-come, first-served basis at the Independence Visitor Center; limited 10 adults per tour.*

Welcome Park. A scale model of the Penn statue that tops City Hall sits on a 60-foot-long map of Penn's Philadelphia, carved in the pavement of Welcome Park. (The *Welcome* was the ship that transported Penn to America.) The wall surrounding the park displays a time line of William Penn's life, with information about his philosophy and quotations from his writings. The park was the site of the slate-roof house where Penn lived briefly and where he granted the Charter of Privileges in 1701. Written by Penn, the Charter of Privileges served as Pennsylvania's constitutional framework until 1776; the Liberty Bell was commissioned to commemorate the charter's 50th anniversary. The City Tavern, across the street, marks the site where George Washington once dined. It's still open for historically accurate lunches and dinners. ✉ *2nd St. just north of Walnut St. at Samson St. Alley, Old City* ⊕ *www.ushistory.org/tour/ welcome-park.htm* 🖃 *Free.*

SOCIETY HILL

During the 18th century Society Hill was Philadelphia's showplace. A carefully preserved district, it remains the city's most photogenic neighborhood, filled with hidden courtyards, delightful decorative touches such as chimney pots and brass door knockers, wrought-iron foot scrapers, and other remnants from the days of horse-drawn carriages and

2

muddy, unpaved streets. Here time has not quite stopped but meanders down the cobblestone streets, whiling away the hours.

A trove of Colonial- and Federal-style brick row houses, churches, and narrow streets, Society Hill stretches from the Delaware River to 8th Street, south of Independence National Historical Park. Those homes built before 1750 in the Colonial style generally have 2½ stories and a dormer window jutting out of a steep roof. The less heavy, more graceful houses built after the Revolution were often in the Federal style, popularized in England during the 1790s.

Here lived the "World's People," wealthier Anglicans who arrived after William Penn and loved music and dancing—pursuits the Quakers shunned when they set up their enclave in Old City, north of Market Street, in a less desirable commercial area. The "Society" in the neighborhood's moniker refers, however, to the now-defunct Free Society of Traders, a group of business investors who settled here on William Penn's advice.

Today many Colonial homes in this area have been lovingly restored by modern pioneers who moved into the area nearly 50 years ago and rescued Society Hill from becoming a slum. Inspired urban renewal efforts have transformed vast empty factory spaces into airy lofts; new town houses were carefully designed to blend in with the old. As a result, Society Hill is not just a showcase for historic churches and mansions but a living, breathing neighborhood.

PLANNING YOUR TIME

You'll need about one hour to walk through Society Hill, more if you tour the Powel and Physick houses. If walking is your main interest, save this excursion for a warm day, because it can be quite windy along the waterfront. On summer weekends revitalized Penn's Landing bustles with festivals and pop-up parks, and Headhouse Square turns into a farmers' market with locally grown products and baked goods.

TOP ATTRACTIONS

Fodor's Choice ★ **Headhouse Square.** This open-air Colonial marketplace, extending from Pine Street to Lombard Street, is a reminder of the days when people went to central outdoor markets to buy food directly from farmers. It was first established as New Market in 1745. George Washington was among those who came here to buy butter, eggs, meat, fish, herbs, and vegetables. The Head House, a boxy building with a cupola and weather vane, was built in 1803 as the office and home of the market master, who tested the quality of the goods. Today, every Sunday from May through December, it is the site of a farmers' market, featuring about two dozen vendors selling everything from honey and flowers to pickles and pastries. On some summer weekends the square also is home to a crafts-and-fine-arts fair featuring the work of more than 30 Delaware Valley artists. ⊠ *2nd and Pine Sts., Society Hill* ☎ *215/413–3713* ☽ *May–Dec., Sat. 10–5 (the Franklin Flea Market); Sun. 10–2 (the Headhouse Square Farmers Market).*

Physick House. Built in 1786, this is one of two remaining freestanding houses from this era in Society Hill (you will see plenty of the famous Philadelphia row houses here), with elegantly restored interiors and some of the finest Federal and Empire furniture in Philadelphia. Touches of Napoléon's France are everywhere: the golden bee motif woven into upholstery; the magenta-hue Aubusson rug (the emperor's favorite color); and stools in the style of Pompeii, the Roman city rediscovered at the time of the house's construction. Upstairs in the parlor, note the inkstand that still retains Benjamin Franklin's fingerprints. The house's most famous owner was Philip Syng Physick, the "Father of American Surgery" and a leading physician in the days before anesthesia. His most celebrated patient was Chief Justice John Marshall. The garden planted on three sides of the house is filled with plants common during the 19th century: complete with an Etruscan sarcophagus, a natural grotto, and antique cannon, it is considered to be the city's loveliest. ⊠ *321 S. 4th St., Society Hill* ☏ *215/925–7866* ⊕ *www.philalandmarks.org/ physick-house* ⊠ *$8 adult, $6 students and seniors; children under 6 free* ⊙ *Mar.–Dec., Thurs.–Sat. noon–4, Sun. 1–5; closed Jan. and Feb.* ☞ *Tours by appointment only Jan. and Feb.*

Powel House. The 1765 brick Georgian house purchased by Samuel Powel in 1769 remains one of the most elegant homes in Philadelphia. Powel—the "Patriot Mayor"—was the last mayor of Philadelphia under the Crown and the first in the new republic. The lavish home, a former wreck saved from demolition in 1931, is furnished with important pieces of 18th-century Philadelphia furniture. A mahogany staircase from Santo Domingo embellishes the front hall, and there is a signed Gilbert Stuart portrait in the parlor. In the second-floor ballroom Mrs. Powel—the city's hostess-with-the-mostest—served floating islands and whipped syllabubs to distinguished guests (including Adams, Franklin, and Lafayette) on Nanking china that was a gift from George and Martha Washington. Today the ballroom can be rented for parties and special events. ⊠ *244 S. 3rd St., Society Hill* ☏ *215/627–0364* ⊕ *www. philalandmarks.org/powel-house-1* ⊠ *$8* ⊙ *Mar.–Dec., Thurs.–Sat. noon–4, Sun. 1–5; by appointment only Jan. and Feb.*

WORTH NOTING

Athenaeum. Housed in a national landmark Italianate brownstone dating from the mid-1800s and designed by John Notman, the Athenaeum is a research library specializing in architectural history and design. Its American Architecture Collection has close to a million items. The library, founded in 1814, contains significant materials on the French in America and on early American travel, exploration, and transportation. Besides books, the Athenaeum has notable paintings and period furniture; changing exhibits are presented in the gallery. ⊠ *219 S. 6th St., Society Hill* ☏ *215/925–2688* ⊕ *www.philaathenaeum.org* ⊙ *Weekdays 9–5; Sept.–June, also Sat. 11–3* ☞ *Tours are self-guided or guided by appointment* Ⓜ *4 blocks from the 5th and Market stop.*

Bouvier's Row. Three of the Victorian brownstones on a stretch of 3rd Street near Spruce Street, often called Bouvier's Row, were once owned by the late Jacqueline Kennedy Onassis's ancestors. Michel Bouvier, her greatgreat-grandfather—the first of the family to come from France—and many of his descendants lie in the family vault at Old St. Mary's Church, a few blocks away on 4th Street. ⊠ *258–262 S. 3rd St., Society Hill.*

Mother Bethel African Methodist Episcopal Church. Society Hill holds a notable landmark in the history of African Americans in the city. In 1787 Richard Allen led fellow blacks who left St. George's Methodist Church as a protest against the segregated worship. Allen, a lay minister and former slave who had bought his freedom from the Chew family of Germantown, purchased this site in 1791. It's believed to be the country's oldest parcel of land continuously owned by African Americans. When the African Methodist Episcopal Church was formed in 1816, Allen was its first bishop. The current church, the fourth on the site, is an example of the 19th-century Romanesque Revival style, with broad arches and a square corner tower, opalescent stained-glass windows, and stunning woodwork. The earlier church buildings were the site of a school where Allen taught slaves to read and also a stop on the Underground Railroad. Allen's tomb and a small museum are on the lower level. ⊠ *419 Richard Allen Ave., S. 6th St. between Pine and Lombard Sts., Society Hill* ☏ *215/925–0616* ⊕ *www.motherbethel.org* ▤ *Donation requested* ⊙ *Museum Tues.–Sat. 10–3; after services on Sun. until 3.*

Old Pine Street Presbyterian Church. Designed by Robert Smith in 1768 as a simple brick Georgian-style building, Old Pine is the only remaining Colonial Presbyterian church and churchyard in Philadelphia. Badly damaged by British troops during the Revolution, it served as a hospital and then a stable. In the mid-19th century its exterior had a Greek Revival face-lift that included Corinthian columns. In the 1980s the interior walls and ceiling were stenciled with thistle and wave motifs, a reminder of Old Pine's true name—Third, Scots, and Mariners Presbyterian Church, which documented the congregation's mergers. The beautifully restored church is painted in soft shades of periwinkle and yellow. In the churchyard are the graves of 100 Hessian soldiers from the Revolution—and of Eugene Ormandy, former conductor of the Philadelphia Orchestra. ⊠ *412 Pine St., Society Hill* ☏ *215/925–8051* ⊕ *www.oldpine.org* ▤ *Free; donations accepted* ⊙ *Churchyard open daily dawn–dusk; church open weekdays 8:30–4 when an attendant is available; Sun. worship at 10:30* ☞ *Call the church office to arrange docent-led tours of the churchyard and church building.*

Old St. Joseph's Church. In 1733 a tiny chapel was established by Jesuits for Philadelphia's 11 Catholic families. It was one of the first places in the English-speaking colonies where Catholic mass could be legally celebrated, a right granted under William Penn's 1701 Charter of Privileges, which guaranteed religious freedom. But freedom didn't come easy; on one occasion Quakers had to patrol St. Joseph's to prevent a Protestant mob from disrupting the service. The present church, built in 1839, is the third on this site. The late-19th-century stained-glass windows are notable. ⊠ *321 Willings Alley, Society Hill* ☏ *215/923–1733* ⊕ *www.oldstjoseph.org* ▤ *Free* ⊙ *Daily 9:30–4:30; mass Mon.–Sat. 12:05, Sat. 5:30, Sun. 7:30, 9:30, 11:30, 6:30* ☞ *A free, self-guided audio tour is available for download on the church's website.*

Old St. Mary's Church. The city's second-oldest Catholic church, circa 1763, became its first cathedral when the archdiocese was formed in 1810. A Gothic-style facade was added in 1880; the interior was redone in 1979. The stained-glass windows, a ceiling mural of St. Mary, and brass chandeliers that hung in the Founders Room of Independence Hall until 1967 are highlights. Commodore John Barry, a Revolutionary War naval hero, and other famous Philadelphians are buried in the small churchyard. ✉ *252 S. 4th St., Society Hill* ☎ *215/923–7930* ⊕ *www.oldstmary.com* 🖃 *Free* ⊙ *Daily 9–4; mass Sat. 4:30, Sun. 10.*

**OFF THE
BEATEN
PATH**

Pennsylvania Hospital. Inside the fine 18th-century original buildings of the oldest hospital in the United States are the nation's first medical library and first surgical amphitheater (an 1804 innovation, with a skylight). The hospital also has a portrait gallery, early medical instruments, art objects, and a rare-book library with items dating from 1762. The artwork includes the Benjamin West painting *Christ Healing the Sick in the Temple.* Today Pennsylvania Hospital is a full-service modern medical center four blocks southwest of the Athenaeum. There are self-guided tours weekdays and guided tours if you call ahead for times and reservations. The suggested donation is $4 per person. ✉ *800 Spruce St., at 8th St., Society Hill* ☎ *215/829–3370* ⊕ *www.uphs.upenn. edu/paharc/tours* 🖃 *$4 suggested donation* ⊙ *Weekdays 9–4.*

Philadelphia Contributionship for the Insurance of Houses from Loss by Fire. The Contributionship, the nation's oldest fire insurance company, was founded by Benjamin Franklin in 1752; the present Greek Revival building with fluted marble Corinthian columns dates from 1836 and has some magnificently elegant salons (particularly the boardroom, where a seating plan on the wall lists Benjamin Franklin as the first incumbent of seat Number One). The architect, Thomas U. Walter, was also responsible for the dome and House and Senate wings of the U.S. Capitol in Washington, D.C. This is still an active business, but a small museum is open to the public by appointment. ✉ *212 S. 4th St., Society Hill* ☎ *215/627–1752 Ext. 1286 to arrange a tour* ⊕ *www.contributionship. com* 🖃 *Free* ⊙ *Weekdays 9–4 (museum by appointment only).*

St. Peter's Episcopal Church. Founded by members of Christ Church in Old City who were living in newly settled Society Hill, St. Peter's has been in continuous use since its first service on September 4, 1761. William White, rector of Christ Church, also served in that role at St. Peter's until his death in 1836. The brick Palladian-style building was designed by Scottish architect Robert Smith, who was responsible for Carpenters' Hall and the steeple on Christ Church. William Strickland's simple steeple, a Philadelphia landmark, was added in 1842. Notable features include the grand Palladian window on the chancel wall, high-back box pews that were raised off the floor to eliminate drafts, and the unusual arrangement of altar and pulpit at either end of the main aisle. The design has been called "restrained," but what is palpable on a visit is the silence and grace of the stark white interior. In the churchyard lie Commodore John Hazelwood, a Revolutionary War hero, painter Charles Willson Peale, and seven Native American chiefs who died of smallpox on a visit to Philadelphia in 1793. A guide may be on hand Saturday from 11 to 3 and on Sunday after services from 1 to 3 to answer questions. Call ahead for tours. ✉ *313 Pine St., Society Hill* ☎ *215/925–5968* ⊕ *www.stpetersphila.org* 🖃 *Free; donations accepted* ⊙ *Daily 8–4, the churchyard is often open 8 am–7 pm in the summer months; services Sun. 9 and 11* ☞ *There is a free* *audio tour of the church interior and churchyard accessible by phone at 215/554–6161. Cell charges may apply* Ⓜ *SEPTA buses 12, 40, and 57 all stop alongside St. Peter's campus.*

Thaddeus Kosciuszko National Memorial. A Polish general who later became a national hero in his homeland, Kosciuszko came to the United States in 1776 to help fight in the Revolution; he distinguished himself as one of the first foreign volunteers in the war. The plain three-story brick house, built around 1776, in 2009 launched a series of new exhibits that feature a rotating collection of artifacts from six museums in Poland to help depict Kosciuszko's life in his homeland as well as some of his original possessions. An eight-minute film (in English and Polish) portrays the general's activities during the Revolution. ✉ *301 Pine St., Society Hill* ☎ *215/597–9618* ⊕ *www.nps.gov/thko* 🔖 *Free* ⊗ *Apr.–Oct., weekends noon–4.*

Washington Square. This leafy area resembling a London park has been through numerous incarnations since it was set aside by William Penn. From 1705 until after the Revolution, the square was lined on three sides by houses and on the fourth by the Walnut Street Prison. The latter was home to Robert Morris, who went to debtors' prison after he helped finance the Revolution. The square served as a burial ground for victims of the 1793 yellow fever epidemic and for 2,600 British and American soldiers who perished during the Revolution. The square holds a Tomb of the Unknown Soldier, erected to the memory of unknown Revolutionary War soldiers. By the 1840s the square had gained prestige as the center of the city's most fashionable neighborhood. It later became the city's publishing center. ✉ *Bounded by 6th and 7th Sts. and Walnut and Locust Sts., Society Hill* ⊕ *www.nps.gov/inde/washington-square.htm* 🔖 *Free.*

ENN'S LANDING

The spot where William Penn stepped ashore in 1682 is the hub of a 37-acre riverfront park that stretches from Market Street south to Lombard Street. Walk along the waterfront for a view of pleasure boats moored at the marina and cargo ships chugging up and down the Delaware River. Philadelphia's harbor, which includes docking facilities in New Jersey and Delaware, is one of the world's largest freshwater ports. Attractions at Penn's Landing include historic vessels like the world's largest four-masted tall ship, the *Moshulu,* which doubles as a restaurant. The waterfront is also the scene of July 4 fireworks, as well as jazz and big-band concerts, ethnic festivals, and children's events. Recent years have moved the on-again, off-again development of the waterfront forward in a positive direction. Race Street Pier Park, designed by the architects behind New York's High Line, is a great place to stroll, jog and take in views of the Ben Franklin Bridge stretching overhead, while pop-ups like Spruce Street Harbor Park and the Lodge at Winterfest are insanely popular with locals for snacking, sipping, and lounging.

GETTING HERE AND AROUND

Penn's Landing is within easy walking distance of the Historic Area, Old City, and Society Hill, or can be accessed by SEPTA. To reach Penn's Landing, cross the Walnut Street Bridge at Front Street, which deposits you at the Independence Seaport Museum. The RiverLink Ferry connects Penn's Landing to Camden, New Jersey.

Riverlink Ferry. This passenger ferry makes a 10-minute trip across the Delaware River; it travels back and forth between the Independence Seaport Museum at Penn's Landing and Camden's waterfront attractions, including the New Jersey State Aquarium, the Camden Children's Museum, and the battleship *New Jersey*. On summer weekends, you can also take a 30-minute water-shuttle tour, departing hourly between noon and 6 pm, departing from the Spruce Street Harbor Park dock. You can get a picturesque view of Philadelphia's skyline and the Ben Franklin Bridge. It runs daily from June through August and then weekends only in May and September. Besides its daytime schedule, the ferry runs express service before and after Susquehanna Bank Center concerts and Camden Riversharks baseball games. Round-trip tickets cost $7. ⊠ *Penn's Landing, Columbus Blvd. and Walnut St., Penn's Landing* ✢ *Near Independence Seaport Museum* ☎ *215/625–0221* ⊕ *www.delawareriverwaterfront.com/places/riverlink-ferry.*

PLANNING YOUR TIME

You could easily spend a whole day here. If your kids are in tow, allow an hour and a half for the Independence Seaport Museum and its historic boats and another two or three hours for the ferry ride and visit to the aquarium, followed by a tour of the battleship *New Jersey*.

TOP ATTRACTIONS

FAMILY **Adventure Aquarium.** This high-tech, hands-on science education center is the home of "Shark Realm," a 550,000-gallon tank stretching two stories high and thick with sharks, stingrays, and sawfish. The daring can "swim with the sharks" by snorkeling along the tank's perimeter under the careful supervision of aquarium staff. In the "Hippo Haven" hippopotamuses cohabit with birds, crocodiles, and porcupines. There are also daily "animal experiences," penguin feedings, live animal talks, and "4-D" theater presentations, in which the 3-D on-screen action is choreographed to motion in the theater's seats. To get here, drive or take the ferry from Penn's Landing. ⊠ *1 Riverside Dr., Camden Waterfront, Camden* ☎ *856/365–3300* ⊕ *www.adventureaquarium.com* ◨ *$25.95* ☺ *Daily 10–5.*

FAMILY **Independence Seaport Museum.** Philadelphia's maritime museum houses many nautical artifacts, figureheads, and ship models, as well as interactive exhibits that convey just what the Delaware and Schuylkill rivers have meant to the city's fortunes over the years. You can climb in the gray, cold, wooden bunks used in steerage; unload cargo from giant container ships with a miniature crane; or even try your hand at designing your own boat. Enter the museum by passing under the three-story replica of the Benjamin Franklin Bridge, and be sure to check out the Ship Model Shack, where members of the Philadelphia Ship Model Society Society put together scale-model ships in front of visitors' eyes. Admission to the museum includes the USS *Becunia* and USS *Olympia*. ⊠ *211 S. Columbus Blvd., at Walnut St., Penn's Landing* ☏ *215/925–5439* ⊕ *www.phillyseaport.org* 🖃 *$15, includes admission to USS Becuna and USS Olympia* ⊙ *Daily 10–5; Memorial Day–Labor Day, Thurs.–Sat., ships stay open until 7 pm.*

Race Street Pier. The first in a planned series of pocket parks along the Delaware River, this green space offers dramatic views of the adjacent Ben Franklin Bridge and allows you to get up-close views of the river itself. Designed by the same firm behind New York's popular High Line, the two-level promenade features lush plantings, including some three dozen trees and many perennials, as well as amphitheater-style seating near the river's edge and plenty of benches and green lawns for relaxing and free yoga classes (BYO mat) daily during the summer months. ⊠ *N. Columbus Blvd. and Race St., Penn's Landing* ☏ *215/922–2386* ⊕ *www.delawareriverwaterfront.com/places/race-street-pier* 🖃 *Free* ⊙ *Daily 7 am–11 pm.*

WORTH NOTING

FAMILY **Battleship *New Jersey*.** The World War II–era USS *New Jersey*, one of the most decorated battleships in the history of the U.S. Navy, is now a floating museum. It's docked in Camden, New Jersey, south of the Susquehanna Bank Center. A 2½-hour guided tour takes you around the upper and lower decks of the ship, or you can explore on your own. Families with at least one child between 6 and 18 can arrange for a sleepover on the ship. ⊠ *62 Battleship Pl., Camden Waterfront, Camden* ☏ *866/877–6262* ⊕ *www.battleshipnewjersey.org* 🖃 *$21.95* ⊙ *Mid-Feb.–Mar. and Nov.–Dec. 24, weekends 9:30–3; Apr. and Labor Day–Nov. 1, daily 9:30–3; May–Labor Day and Dec. 26–31, daily 9:30–5.*

FAMILY **USS *Becuna*.** You can tour this 307-foot-long "guppy class" submarine, which was commissioned in 1944 and conducted search-and-destroy missions in the South Pacific. The guides—some of whom are World War II vets—tell amazing stories of what life was like for a crew of 88 men, at sea for months at a time, in these claustrophobic quarters. Then you can step through the narrow walkways, climb the ladders, and glimpse the torpedoes in their firing chambers. Children love it, and it's fascinating for adults, too. Tickets must be purchased at the Independence Seaport Museum and include admission to the museum and the USS *Olympia*. ⊠ *211 S. Columbus Blvd., at Walnut St., Penn's Landing* ☏ *215/413–8655* ⊕ *www.phillyseaport.org/becuna* 🖃 *$15, includes admission to USS Olympia and the Independence Seaport Museum* ⊙ *Daily 10–5.*

FAMILY **Camden Children's Garden.** Located adjacent to the Adventure Aquarium on the Camden waterfront, this delightful 4-acre garden is an interactive horticultural playground with theme exhibits. You can smell, hear, touch, and even taste some of the elements in the Dinosaur, Cityscapes, Picnic, and Storybook exhibits, as well as in the gardens and the Butterfly House. Other attractions include Amaze, Carousel, Train Ride, Tree House, and more. To get here, drive or take the ferry from Penn's Landing. ⊠ *3 Riverside Dr., Camden Waterfront, Camden* ☏ *856/365–8733* ⊕ *www.camdenchildrensgarden.org* 🖃 *$6* ⊙ *Wed.–Sun. 10–5; group reservations Apr.–Dec., Tues.–Fri.*

Gazela of Philadelphia. Built in 1883 and formerly named *Gazela Primeiro,* this 177-foot square-rigger is the last of a Portuguese fleet of cod-fishing ships. Still in use as late as 1969, it's the oldest and largest wooden square-rigger still sailing. As the Port of Philadelphia's ambassador of goodwill, the *Gazela* sails up and down the Atlantic coast from May to October to participate in harbor festivals and celebrations. It's also a ship school and a museum. An all-volunteer crew of 35 works on ship maintenance from November to April, while it's in port. ⊠ *Penn's Landing at Market St., Penn's Landing* ☎ *215/238–0280* ⊕ *phylashipguild.org* ⊙ *By appointment only.*

FAMILY **USS Olympia.** Commodore George Dewey's flagship at the Battle of Manila in the Spanish-American War is the only remaining ship from that war. Dewey entered Manila Harbor after midnight on May 1, 1898. At 5:40 am he told his captain, "You may fire when ready, Gridley," and the battle began. By 12:30 the Americans had destroyed the entire Spanish fleet. The *Olympia* was the last ship of the "New Navy" of the 1880s and 1890s, the beginning of the era of steel ships. You can tour the entire restored ship, including the officers' staterooms, galley, gun batteries, and pilothouse, while "behind the scenes" tours are offered the first Saturday of the month from April through November. Tickets must be purchased at the Independence Seaport Museum and include admission to the USS *Becuna* and the museum. ⊠ *211 S. Columbus Blvd., at Walnut St., Penn's Landing* ☎ *215/413–8655* ⊕ *www.phillyseaport.org/olympia* 🎟 *$15, includes admission to USS Becuna and Independence Seaport Museum* ⊙ *Daily 10–5.*

CENTER CITY

For a grand introduction to the heart of the downtown area, climb the few steps to the plaza in front of the Municipal Services Building at 15th Street and John F. Kennedy Boulevard. You'll be standing alongside a 10-foot-tall bronze statue of the late Frank L. Rizzo waving to the people. Rizzo, nicknamed the "Big Bambino," was the city's police commissioner, two-term mayor (in the 1970s), and a five-time mayoral candidate. He shaped the political scene just as the structures that surround you—City Hall, the Philadelphia Saving Fund Society Building, the Art Museum, the skyscrapers at Liberty Place, Oldenburg's Clothespin, and more—shape its architectural landscape.

The story behind this skyline begins with Philadelphia's historic City Hall, which reaches to 40 stories and was the tallest structure in the metropolis until 1987. No law prohibited taller buildings, but the tradition sprang from a gentleman's agreement not to build higher. In May 1984, when a developer proposed building two office towers that would break the 491-foot barrier, it became evident how entrenched this tradition was: the proposal provoked a public outcry. The traditionalists contended that the height limitation had made Philadelphia a city of human scale, given character to its streets and public places, and showed respect for tradition. The opposing camp thought that a dramatic new skyline would shatter the city's conservative image and encourage economic growth. After painstaking debate the go-ahead was granted. In short order the midtown area became the hub of the city's commercial center, Market Street west of City Hall became a district of high-rise office buildings, and the area became a symbol of the city's ongoing transformation from a dying industrial town to a center for service industries. Here, too, are a number of museums, the excellent Reading Terminal Market and the convention center, and Chinatown.

GETTING HERE AND AROUND

The heart of Center City is an easy 10- to 15-minute stroll from the Historic Area, or about a 20- to 25-minute walk from Penn's Landing. To orient yourself, Broad Street (the name for what would be 14th Street) serves as a delineation for Center City East and Center City West, while City Hall, located at Broad and Market streets, is the diving line for north–south addresses on the numbered streets. You also can use SEPTA bus lines on Market or Walnut streets, or the underground Blue line on Market Street, to reach points west of the Historic Area or take the PHLASH, which runs seasonally. The City Hall SEPTA station is a major hub that includes connections for the north–south Orange Line, as well as the east–west Blue and Green lines.

PLANNING YOUR TIME

To get a feel for the city at work, save this neighborhood for a weekday, when the streets are bustling, but even on weekends you'll encounter plenty of people strolling and shopping. Besides, the City Hall Observation Tower is open weekdays only, and the Masonic Temple is closed on Sundays and Mondays. You could walk through the neighborhood in 45 minutes, but reserve about half a day, with an hour each at the Masonic Temple, City Hall Tower, and the Pennsylvania Academy of the Fine Arts. If you get an early start, you can finish with lunch at the Reading Terminal Market.

CENTER CITY EAST

Though geographically accurate, Center City East is not the name Philadelphians use to refer to this zone bounded by Broad Street to the west and Old City to the east. Instead you might hear them name-drop the sub-neighborhoods within the area, like Midtown Village, a dining-and-shopping juggernaut that has grown up along formerly derelict 13th Street. Or the Gayborhood, the historic HQ for LGBTQ Philly where the street signs are etched in rainbows. Or Washington Square West, a larger catchall for the area.

There's a lot of overlap between the interloping districts of Center City East, but no matter what you call it, its core is leafy Washington Square, the eastern mirror to Rittenhouse Square across Broad. Jefferson Hospital has claimed a lot of real estate here, so it's not uncommon to see flocks of eds and meds buzzing around the area in teal scrubs. This is also the home to Jewelers' Row, a generations-deep ecosystem of gem setters, diamond brokers, and gold salesmen; many Philadelphians still come here to buy their engagement rings.

TOP ATTRACTIONS

Fodor's Choice **City Hall.** Topped by a 37-foot bronze statue of William Penn, City
★ Hall was Philadelphia's tallest building until 1987; you can study the
trappings of government and also get a panoramic view of the city
here. With 642 rooms, it's the largest city hall in the country and the
tallest masonry-bearing building in the world: no steel structure supports it. Designed by architect John McArthur Jr., the building took 30
years to build (1871–1901) and cost taxpayers more than $23 million.
The result has been called a "Victorian wedding cake of Renaissance
styles." Placed about the facade are hundreds of statues by Alexander
Milne Calder, who also designed the statue of William Penn at the top.
Calder's 27-ton cast-iron statue of Penn is the largest single piece of
sculpture on any building in the world.

Not only the geographic center of Penn's original city plan, City Hall
is also the center of municipal and state government. Many of the
magnificent interiors—splendidly decorated with mahogany paneling,
gold-leaf ceilings, and marble pillars—are patterned after the Second
Empire salons of part of the Louvre in Paris. On a tour each weekday at
12:30 you can see the Conversation Hall, the Supreme Court of Pennsylvania, the City Council chambers, and the mayor's reception room.
You can attend the frequently heated City Council meetings, held each
Thursday morning at 10.

To top off your visit, take the elevator from the seventh floor up the
tower to the observation deck at the foot of William Penn's statue
for a 30-mile view of the city and surroundings. The elevator holds
only six people per trip and runs every 15 minutes; the least crowded
time is early morning. The 90-minute building tour, including a trip
up the tower, steps off weekdays at 12:30. The tour office is in Room
121. ⊠ *Broad and Market Sts., Center City East* ☎ *215/686–2840,
215/686–2840 tour information* ⊕ *www.visitphilly.com* ✉ *$12 for tour
and tower visit; $6 for tower only* ☺ *Building weekdays 9–4:30; tower
weekdays 9:30–4:15; 2–3 pm reserved for 12:30 tour participants.*

Fodor's Choice **Macy's.** The former John Wanamaker department store, this building
★ is almost as prominent a Philadelphia landmark as the Liberty Bell.
Wanamaker began with a clothing store in 1861, and became one of
America's most innovative and prominent retailers. The massive building, which occupies a city block with grace, was designed by the noted
Chicago firm of D. H. Burnham and Company. Its focal point is a 2,500-
pound statue of an eagle, a remnant of the 1904 Louisiana Purchase
Exposition in St. Louis. "Meet me at the Eagle" remains a popular way
for Philadelphians to arrange a rendezvous. The store's 30,000-pipe
organ—the largest ever built—is used for free concerts Monday, Tuesday, Thursday, and Saturday at noon and 5:30, and Wednesday and Friday at noon and 7. They offer a spectacular holiday light show between
Thanksgiving and New Year as well. ⊠ *1300 Market St., at 13th St.,
Center City East* ☎ *215/241–9000* ⊕ *www.macys.com* ☺ *Weekdays
9–9, Sat. 10–9, Sun. 11–7.*

Fodor's Choice ★ **Reading Terminal Market.** The market is nothing short of a histori sure, and a food heaven to Philadelphians and visitors alike. On beneath the former Reading Railroad's 1891 train shed, the spr market has more than 75 food stalls and other shops, selling items from hooked rugs and handmade jewelry to South American and African crafts. Here, amid the local color, you can sample Bassett's ice cream, Philadelphia's best; down a cheesesteak, a hoagie, a bowl of snapper soup, or a soft pretzel; or nibble Greek, Mexican, Thai, and Indian specialties. From Wednesday through Saturday the Amish from Lancaster County cart in their goodies, including Lebanon bologna, shoofly pie, and scrapple. Many stalls have their own counters with seating; there's also a central eating area. An open kitchen offers regular demonstrations by some of the region's top chefs. You can also take a guided Market Tour on Wednesdays and Saturdays at 10 am. The entire building is a National Historic Landmark, and the train shed is a National Engineering Landmark. The market is easily accessible by SEPTA's Blue Line subway, regional rail, and bus. ⊠ *51 N. 12th St., at Arch St., Center City East* ☎ *215/922–2317* ⊕ *www.readingterminalmarket.org* ⊗ *Mon.–Sat. 8–6, Sun. 9–5.*

WORTH NOTING

Avenue of the Arts. Broad Street, the city's main north–south thoroughfare, has been reinvented as a performing arts district. Although most of the cultural institutions are situated along South Broad Street from City Hall to Spruce Street, the avenue's cultural, education, and arts organizations reach as far south as Washington Avenue in South Philadelphia and as far north as Dauphin Street in North Philadelphia. The main venue is the Kimmel Center for the Performing Arts, at Broad and Spruce streets, which includes a 2,500-seat concert hall designed for the Philadelphia Orchestra. The newest addition is the Suzanne Roberts Theatre, a 365-seat facility that is home to the Philadelphia Theatre Company. ⊠ *408 S. Broad St., Center City East* ☎ *215/731–9668* ⊕ *www.avenueofthearts.org.*

Masonic Temple. The temple is one of the city's architectural jewels, but it remains a hidden treasure even to many Philadelphians. Historically, Freemasons were skilled stoneworkers of the Middle Ages who relied on secret signs and passwords. Their worldwide fraternal order—the Free and Accepted Masons—included men in the building trades, plus many honorary members; the secret society prospered in Philadelphia during Colonial times. Brother James Windrim designed this elaborate temple as a home for the Grand Lodge of Free and Accepted Masons of Pennsylvania. The ceremonial gavel used here at the laying of the cornerstone in 1868, while 10,000 brothers looked on, was the same one that Brother George Washington used to set the cornerstone of the U.S. Capitol. The temple's ornate interior consists of seven lavishly decorated lodge halls built to exemplify specific styles of architecture: Corinthian, Ionic, Italian Renaissance, Norman, Gothic, Oriental, and Egyptian. The Egyptian hall, with its accurate hieroglyphics, is the most famous. The temple also houses an interesting museum of Masonic items, including Benjamin Franklin's printing of the first book on Freemasonry published in America and George Washington's Masonic

Apron. ✉ *1 N. Broad St., Center City East* ☎ *215/988–1900* ⊕ *www. pagrandlodge.org/tour/onsite.html* ✉ *$7 for library and museum only; tours $13* ☉ *Tours Tues.–Fri. 10, 11, 1, 2, and 3; Sat. 10, 11, and noon.*

Pennsylvania Convention Center. It's big: a massive expansion completed in 2011 covers 20 acres of central Philadelphia. And it's beautiful: the 2.3 million square feet of space are punctuated by the largest permanent collection of contemporary art in a building of its kind. Many city and state artists are represented in the niches, nooks, and galleries built to house their multimedia works. To see the architectural highlight of the building—the Reading Terminal's magnificently restored four-story-high Victorian train shed, which has been transformed into the Convention Center's Grand Hall—enter the building through the century-old Italian Renaissance Headhouse structure on Market Street between 11th and 12th streets and ride up the escalator. ✉ *1101 Arch St., Center City East* ☎ *800/428–9000* ⊕ *www.paconvention.com* ✉ *Free* ☉ *Tours by appointment only.*

QUICK BITE

✗ **10 Arts Lounge.** For a most civilized break from touring, enter the luxurious world of the Ritz-Carlton's soaring rotunda, now the site of the 10 Arts Lounge (in the Bistro breakfast is available daily). Here the stately marble columns and classical architecture nicely contrast with modern, upholstered furniture and other contemporary design touches. You can take it all in with a cool drink or cocktail and a gourmet Philly-style snack, like housemade soft pretzel bites with cheddar sauce, Dijon mustard, and jalapeño jam. The lounge also offers afternoon tea and happy hour at different times of the year. Call ahead for reservations. ✉ *10 S. Broad St., Center City East* ☎ *215/523–8273* ⊕ *www.10arts.com.*

Sir John Temple Heritage Center at the Union League of Philadelphia. An elegant double staircase sweeps from Broad Street up to the entrance of this 1865 French Renaissance–style building, which was added to the National Historic Register in 1979, while within lies a bastion of Philadelphia conservatism. The Union League is a private social club founded during the Civil War to support the Union—in a big way. The club contributed hundreds of millions of dollars to the Union war effort, then a huge sum, as well as troops and other material support. While the club remains strictly private, the Heritage Center welcomes visitors a few hours every week. Tours of the full facilities are available only for groups of 20 or more. ✉ *140 S. Broad St., Center City East* ☎ *215/563–6500* ⊕ *www.unionleague.org* ✉ *Free* ☉ *Tues. and Thurs. 3–6, 2nd Sat. 1–4* ☞ *Visitors are expected to abide by the League's dress code for members, which includes a jacket and tie for men and appropriate business attire or the equivalent for women.*

CENTER CITY WEST

Stretching from the eastern banks of the Schuylkill River to Broad Street, Center City West is Philly's entertainment and business hub. Oriented around leafy Rittenhouse Square (the name of the park as well as the posh surrounding neighborhood), this side of Center City is where you can expect to do a bulk of shopping and dining. You'll find big brands and luxury labels along Walnut Street and Chestnut Street, with independent boutiques on the little sides streets that fan out to the south, and restaurants follow suit. This is also where most hotels set up shop in Philly.

TOP ATTRACTIONS

odor's Choice ★ **The Comcast Center.** Now Philadelphia's tallest building, the 975-foot Comcast Center is also one of its most eco-friendly: the 58-story design by Robert A.M. Stern Architects uses 40% less water than a traditional office building and also deploys its glass-curtain-wall facade to reduce energy costs significantly. Not to be missed is *The Comcast Experience*, a 2000-square-foot high-definition video "wall" in the building's "winter garden" lobby, which also features "Humanity in Motion," an installation of 12 life-size figures by Jonathan Borofsky that appear to be striding along girders 110 feet above. The building is also the site of an upscale food court, a steak house, and a seasonal, outdoor café. ⊠ *1701 John F. Kennedy Blvd., Center City West* ⊙ *Mon.–Fri. 8–7, Sat. 8–5.*

odor's Choice ★ **Pennsylvania Academy of the Fine Arts.** This High Victorian Gothic structure is a work of art in itself. Designed in 1876 by the noted, and sometimes eccentric, Philadelphia architects Frank Furness and George Hewitt, the multicolor stone-and-brick exterior is an extravagant blend of columns, friezes, and Richardsonian Romanesque and Moorish flourishes. The interior is just as lush, with rich hues of red, yellow, and blue and an impressive staircase. The nation's first art school and museum (founded in 1805) displays a fine collection that ranges from the Peale family, Gilbert Stuart, Benjamin West, and Winslow Homer to Andrew Wyeth and Red Grooms. *Fox Hunt* by Winslow Homer, and *The Artist in His Museum* by Charles Willson Peale, are just a few notable works. The academy faculty has included Thomas Sully, Charles Willson Peale, and Thomas Eakins. The latter painted what is now the museum's most prized work, *The Gross Clinic,* a dramatic depiction of Samuel D. Gross, a celebrated 19th-century surgeon, presiding over an operation under a skylighted roof; the masterwork is co-owned with the Philadelphia Museum of Art, and is displayed for six months at a time at each institution.

Supplementing the permanent collection are constantly changing exhibitions of sculptures, paintings, and mixed-media artwork in the adjacent Samuel M. V. Hamilton Building; the 11-story facility, which opened for the academy's 200th anniversary, is also the home to the Sculpture Study Center, which offers changing displays from the permanent collection, classrooms, group and private studios for more than 300 students, and Portfolio, the museum's gift shop. The 1400 block of Cherry Street, which runs between the two buildings, is a pedestrian plaza featuring *Paint Torch,* a 53-foot-tall sculpture of a paintbrush by Claes Oldenburg, a three-part serpentine bench, and outdoor seating. ⊠ *118–128 N. Broad St., at Cherry St., Center City West* ☎ *215/972–7600* ⊕ *www.pafa.org* ⊑ *$15* ⊙ *Tues., Thurs., and Fri. 10–5; Wed. 10–9; weekends 11–5.*

WORTH NOTING

Clothespin. Claes Oldenburg's 45-foot-high, 10-ton steel sculpture stands in front of the Center Square Building, above one of the entrances to SEPTA's City Hall subway station. Lauded by some and scorned by others, this pop-art piece contrasts with the traditional statuary so common in Philadelphia. ⊠ *1500 Market St., at 15th St., Center City West.*

Historical Society of Pennsylvania. Following a merger with the Balch Institute for Ethnic Studies in 2002 and the Genealogical Society of Pennsylvania in 2006, this superlative special-collections library now contains more than 500,000 books, 300,000 graphic works, and 19 million manuscript items; the emphasis is on Colonial, early national, and Pennsylvania history, as well as immigration history and ethnicity. Founded in 1824, the society also owns one of the largest family history libraries in the nation. This is the place to go to trace your family roots. Notable items from the collection include the Penn family archives, President James Buchanan's papers, a printer's proof of the Declaration of Independence, and the first draft of the Constitution. ⊠ *1300 Locust St., Center City West* ☎ *215/732–6200* ⊕ *www.hsp.org* ⊠ *$8* ☉ *Tues. and Thurs. 12:30–5:30, Wed. 12:30–8:30, Fri. 10–5:30.*

Library Company of Philadelphia. Founded in 1731, this is one of the oldest cultural institutions in the United States and the only major Colonial American library that has survived virtually intact, despite having moved from building to building. From 1774 to 1800 it functioned as the de facto Library of Congress, and until the late 19th century it was the city library. Ten signers of the Declaration of Independence were members, among them Benjamin Franklin, Robert Morris, Benjamin Rush, and Thomas McKean. The 500,000-volume collection includes 200,000 rare books. Among the first editions—many acquired when they were first published—are Herman Melville's *Moby-Dick* and Walt Whitman's *Leaves of Grass.* The library is particularly rich in Americana up to 1880, black history to 1915, the history of science, and women's history. Changing exhibits showcase the library's holdings. ⊠ *1314 Locust St., Center City West* ☎ *215/546–3181* ⊕ *www.librarycompany. org* ⊠ *Free* ☉ *Weekdays 9–4:45.*

QUICK BITE

✕ **The Shops at Liberty Place Food Court.** The Shops at Liberty Place houses a large international food court on the second level, above the upscale stores. You can find anything from salad to sushi to those familiar Philly cheesesteaks. ⊠ *1625 Chestnut St., between Liberty One and Liberty Two, Center City West* ☎ *215/851–9055* ⊕ *www.shopsatliberty.com* ☉ *No breakfast Sun.* Ⓜ *Suburban Station.*

CHINATOWN

Centered on 10th and Race streets two blocks north of Market Street, Chinatown serves as the residential and commercial hub of the city's Chinese community. Chinatown has grocery stores, souvenir and gift shops, martial arts studios, a fortune cookie store, bilingual street signs, and more than 50 restaurants. Over the past 20 years Chinatown's population has become more diverse, reflecting the increase in immigration from Vietnam, Cambodia, Thailand, and Myanmar. One striking Chinatown site is the Chinese Friendship Gate, straddling 10th Street at Arch Street. This intricate and colorful 40-foot-tall arch—the largest authentic Chinese gate outside China—was created by Chinese artisans, who brought their own tools and construction materials. The citizens of Tianjin, Philadelphia's sister city in China, donated the building materials, including the ornamental tile.

RITTENHOUSE SQUARE

Rittenhouse Square has long been one of the city's swankiest addresses. The square's entrances, plaza, pool, and fountains were designed in 1913 by Paul Cret, one of the people responsible for the Benjamin Franklin Parkway. The square was named in honor of one of the city's 18th-century stars: David Rittenhouse, president of the American Philosophical Society. The first house facing the square was erected in 1840, soon to be followed by other grand mansions. Almost all the private homes are now gone, replaced by hotels, apartments, and cultural institutions, and elegant restaurants and stylish cafés dot the neighborhood. The area south and west of the square is still largely residential and lovely, with cupolas and balconies, hitching posts and stained-glass windows. Peek in the streets behind these homes or through their wrought-iron gates and into well-tended gardens.

Four blocks east of the square is the Avenue of the Arts, also known as Broad Street. "Let us entertain you" could be the theme of the ambitious cultural development project that has transformed North and South Broad Street from a commercial thoroughfare to a performing arts district. Dramatic performance spaces have been built, old landmarks have been refurbished, and South Broad Street has been spruced up with landscaping, cast-iron lighting fixtures, special architectural lighting of key buildings, and decorative sidewalk paving.

PLANNING YOUR TIME

This is one of the city's loveliest neighborhoods for strolling. Two hours would allow you enough time to wander through the Rittenhouse Square area and visit the Rosenbach Museum and Library. Add at least another hour for a stroll along South Broad Street, including a cool drink or snack at the Ritz-Carlton's tony 10 Arts lounge.

TOP ATTRACTIONS

Fodor's Choice ★ **Academy of Music.** The only surviving European-style opera house in America is the current home of the Opera Company of Philadelphia and the Pennsylvania Ballet; for the past century, it was home to the Philadelphia Orchestra. Designed by Napoleon Le Brun and Gustav Runge, the 1857 building has a modest exterior; the builders ran out of money and couldn't put marble facing on the brick, as they had intended. The lavish interior, modeled after Milan's La Scala, has elaborate carvings, murals on the ceiling, and a huge Victorian crystal chandelier. ⊠ *Broad and Locust Sts., Rittenhouse Square* ☎ *215/893–1999 box office* ⊕ *www.academyofmusic. org* ☐ *Free* ☉ *Tours are available on select dates, arranged through the Kimmel Center* ☞ *Call 215/790–5886 for information/reservations.*

Philadelphia Flower Show

It takes one week; 7,000 Belgian blocks; 3,500 volunteers; thousands of plumbers, carpenters, and electricians; more than a million plants; and 50 tractor-trailer loads of mulch to transform the Pennsylvania Convention Center into the annual Philadelphia Flower Show (⊕ www.theflowershow.com), the world's largest indoor horticultural event. But the exhibitors—nursery owners, landscapers, and florists from the region and from Africa, Japan, and Europe—spend the better part of a year planning their displays. Each year the show has a theme, and the show's designers think big—very big. The astonishing, fragrant results of their efforts arrive in the city as a touch of spring in early March.

It's a fitting tribute to William Penn that Philadelphia hosts this extravaganza, for this was Penn's "greene countrie town," which he laid out on a grid punctuated with tree-lined streets, pocket parks, small squares, and large public parks. It's also appropriate that this city gave root to the Pennsylvania Horticultural Society, the nation's first such organization. In 1829, two years after its founding, the society hosted its first show at the Masonic Hall in an 82-by-69-foot exhibition space; 25 society members showed off their green thumbs.

Today the show fills 10 acres of exhibition space at the convention center and spills throughout the area as local restaurants, hotels, and attractions offer special deals. (The show's website may have discounts and coupons.) Along with the more than 50 major exhibits, amateur gardeners contribute more than 2,000 entries in 330 competitive categories—from pressed plants and miniature settings to spectacular jewelry designs that use flowers. There are free cooking and gardening demonstrations, lectures, and an area where you can try out the latest gardening gadgets. Hundreds of vendors sell plants, birdhouses, topiaries, watering systems, botanical prints, and more.

Many people plan trips to Philadelphia during the run of the flower show, so be sure to make reservations early. Wear good walking shoes, check your coat, and bring spending money for the many horticultural temptations. To avoid crowds, which can be daunting, arrive after 4 on weekdays and stay until the 9 pm closing, or show up when the doors open on weekend mornings at 8.

If you've made reservations, you can rest your weary feet during Garden Tea at the Flower Show, a proper English tea served at 12:30 and 3:45.

Hyatt Philadelphia at the Bellevue. Though its name has been changed many times, this building will always be "the Bellevue" to Philadelphians. The hotel has had an important role in city life, much like the heroine of a long-running soap opera. The epitome of the opulent hotels characteristic of the early 1900s, the Bellevue Stratford was the city's leading hotel for decades. It closed in 1976 after the first outbreak of Legionnaires' disease, which spread through the building's air-conditioning system during an American Legion convention. The hotel has reopened several times since then, and now includes upscale shops and restaurants and a food court in its basement, but its character seems to have remained the same. ✉ *200 S. Broad St., at Walnut St., Rittenhouse Square* ☎ *215/893–1776* ⊕ *www.philadelphiabellevue. hyatt.com/en/hotel/home.html.*

Kimmel Center for the Performing Arts. Intended to make a contemporary design statement, the Kimmel Center for the Performing Arts has some architectural oomph with its dramatic vaulted glass roof. The 450,000-square-foot venue by architect Rafael Viñoly includes the 2,500-seat Verizon Hall, the more intimate 650-seat Perelman Theater, Jose Garces's restaurant Volvér, a café, a gift shop, and a rooftop terrace. Making their home at the Kimmel are the Philadelphia Orchestra, Philadanco, Philadelphia Chamber Music Society, Chamber Orchestra of Philadelphia, and the Philly Pops. Free performances are given before some performances and on many weekends in the center's Commonwealth Plaza. ✉ *Broad and Spruce Sts., Rittenhouse Square* ☎ *215/790–5800, 215/893–1999 call center/tickets, 215/790–5886 tour info* ⊕ *www.kimmelcenter.org* ☑ *Free* ☉ *Daily 10–6; general tour Tues.–Sun. at 1; art and architecture tour Sat. at 10:30.*

Rittenhouse Square. Once grazing ground for cows and sheep, Philadelphia's most elegant square is reminiscent of a Parisian park. One of William Penn's original five city squares, the park was named in 1825 to honor David Rittenhouse, 18th-century astronomer, clock maker, and the first director of the United States Mint. Many of Philadelphia's celebrities have lived here. Extra paths were made for Dr. William White, a leader in beautifying the square, so he could walk directly from his home to the exclusive Rittenhouse Club across the square and lunch with author Henry James. Until 1950 town houses bordered the square, but they have now been replaced on three sides by swank apartment buildings and hotels. Some great houses remain, including the former residence of Henry P. McIlhenny on the southwest corner. If you want to join the office workers who have lunch-hour picnics in the park, you can find many eateries along Walnut, Sansom, and Chestnut streets east of the square. Or you can dine alfresco at one of several upscale open-air cafés across from the square on 18th Street between Locust and Walnut. The term "Rittenhouse Row" describes the greater Rittenhouse Square area, bordered by Pine, Market, 21st, and Broad streets. ✉ *Walnut St. between 18th and 19th Sts., Rittenhouse Square.*

✕ **Di Bruno Bros.** This two-level gourmet shop has a dazzling array of prepared foods, mouthwatering pastries, and creamy gelato. Sampling the wares can make for a good snack, but if you require something more substantial, head to the café upstairs. ✉ *1730 Chestnut St., Rittenhouse Square* ☎ *215/665–9220* ⊕ *www.dibruno.com.*

Rosenbach Museum and Library. This 1863 three-floor town house and an adjoining building are filled with Persian rugs and 18th-century British, French, and American antiques (plus an entire living room that once belonged to poet Marianne Moore), but the real treasures are the artworks, books, and manuscripts here. Amassed by Philadelphia collectors Philip H. and A. S. W. Rosenbach, the collection includes paintings by Canaletto, Sully, and Lawrence; drawings by Daumier, Fragonard, and Blake; book illustrations ranging from medieval illuminations to the works of Maurice Sendak, author of *Where the Wild Things Are*; the only known copy of the first issue of Benjamin Franklin's *Poor Richard's Almanack*; and the library's most famous treasure, the original manuscript of James Joyce's *Ulysses*. The Rosenbach celebrates "Bloomsday" on June 16 with readings from *Ulysses* by notable Philadelphians. The library has more than 130,000 manuscripts and 30,000 rare books. ⊠ *2008–10 Delancey Pl., Rittenhouse Square* ☎ *215/732–1600* ⊕ *www.rosenbach.org* ⊠ *$10* ⊙ *Tues. and Fri. noon–5, Wed. and Thurs. noon–8, weekends noon–6; guided tours on the hr.*

WORTH NOTING

QUICK BITE

✕ **Capogiro.** Capogiro is Italian for "swooning," so be sure to grab a chair before tasting the gelato at this popular spot. The daily list of flavors ranges from the trendy (rosemary-honey goat's milk, Thai iced tea) to the classic (pistachio, chocolate). ⊠ *119 S. 13th St., Rittenhouse Square* ☎ *215/351–0900* ⊕ *capogirogelato.com* ⊙ *Hrs may vary by season; open daily during summer months.*

Curtis Institute of Music. Graduates of this tuition-free school for outstanding students include Leonard Bernstein, Samuel Barber, Ned Rorem, and Anna Moffo. The school occupies four former private homes; the main building is in the mansion that belonged to banker George W. Childs Drexel. Built in 1893 by the distinguished Boston firm of Peabody and Stearns, it's notable for Romanesque and Renaissance architectural details. Free student and faculty concerts are given from October through May, usually at 8 pm on Monday, Wednesday, and Friday. ⊠ *1726 Locust St., Rittenhouse Square* ☎ *215/893–5261 recital hotline, 215/893–7902 ticket office* ⊕ *www.curtis.edu* ⊙ *Call recital hotline for dates and times of public performances* Ⓜ *Walnut/Locust stop; Broad Street Line.*

Delancey Place. At No. 2010 is the **Rosenbach Museum and Library.** Cypress Street, north of Delancey Place, and Panama Street (especially the 1900 block, one block south of Delancey) are two of the many intimate streets lined with trees and town houses characteristic of the area. ⊠ *Rittenhouse Square.*

Mütter Museum. Skulls, antique microscopes, and a cancerous tumor removed from President Grover Cleveland's mouth in 1893 form just part of the unusual medical collection in the Mütter Museum, in the College of Physicians of Philadelphia. The museum has hundreds of anatomical and pathological specimens, medical instruments, and organs removed from patients, including a piece of John Wilkes Booth's neck tissue. The collection contains 139 skulls; items that belonged to Marie Curie, Louis Pasteur, and Joseph Lister; and a 7-foot, 6-inch skeleton, the tallest on public exhibition in the United States. ⊠ *19 S. 22nd St., Rittenhouse Square* ☎ *215/560–8564* ⊕ *www.collphyphil.org* ⊠ *$16* ⊙ *Daily 10–5.*

ENJAMIN FRANKLIN PARKWAY
ND FAIRMOUNT

Alive with colorful flowers, flags, and fountains, the Benjamin Franklin Parkway stretches northwest from John F. Kennedy Plaza to the Kelly (East) and MLK Jr. (West) River drives. This 250-foot-wide boulevard is crowned by the Philadelphia Museum of Art, as well as where the Barnes Foundation has built its new home. French architects Jacques Greber and Paul Cret designed the Parkway in the 1920s. Today a distinguished assemblage of museums, institutions, hotels, and apartment buildings line the street, competing with each other in grandeur.

The Parkway district leads to the residential Fairmount neighborhood named for Fairmount Park, which encompasses natural areas—woodlands, meadows, rolling hills, two scenic waterways, and a forested 5½-mile gorge. It also contains tennis courts, ball fields, playgrounds, trails, exercise courses, several celebrated cultural institutions, and some historic Early American country houses that are operated by the Philadelphia Museum of Art and open to visitors. Philadelphia has more works of outdoor art than any other city in North America, and more than 200—including statues by Frederic Remington, Jacques Lipchitz, and William Rush—are scattered throughout Fairmount Park. Some sections of the park that border depressed urban neighborhoods are neglected; it's better maintained along the Schuylkill.

GETTING HERE AND AROUND

The Parkway is easily reached on foot from Rittenhouse Square, but it's a 30-minute walk from the far eastern sections of the Historic Area. SEPTA or the PHLASH also are good options to reach this neighborhood. If you have a car, it's also fairly easy to find parking on metered spaces along the Parkway or north of the museum on Pennsylvania Avenue. The museum also has a parking structure with hundreds of spaces.

PLANNING YOUR TIME

The Parkway is at its most colorful in spring, when the trees and flowers are in bloom. Start early in the morning and plan to spend an entire day—and possibly the evening—in this area. On Wednesdays and Fridays you can cap off your day of culture with dinner and entertainment at the Philadelphia Museum of Art. If it's a Friday or Saturday, save the Franklin Institute for mid-afternoon, head out to dinner in the neighborhood, and return for a film on the giant screen of the IMAX theater, which usually has a final show close to midnight. How much time you spend at each museum depends on your interests; be aware that the Philadelphia Museum of Art is closed on Monday and the Rodin Museum is closed on Tuesday.

ENJAMIN FRANKLIN PARKWAY

Modeled after the Champs-Élysées in Paris, the Benjamin Franklin Parkway (or simply, the Parkway, as locals call it) is the Philadelphia's grand boulevard. Stretching from City Hall to the Art Museum and lined with international flags, the Parkway is where you'll find many of the city's major museums and institutions, from the Franklin Institute to the Barnes Foundation. On a beautiful day, it's the most majestic stroll in town. Or, grab a bike and ride the Parkway past the Art Museum (watch out for the *Rocky* runners) into Fairmount Park.

TOP ATTRACTIONS

Fodor's Choice ★ **Barnes Foundation.** Nearly sequestered from public view for a century in Lower Merion, Pennsylvania, this legendary collection of 19th- and 20th-century masterpieces made world headlines when it relocated to this spectacular new home in May 2012. While the statistics are impressive—81 Renoirs, 69 Cézannes, 59 Matisses, 46 Picassos, 7 Van Goghs, 6 Seurats (and many more)—almost more inspiring is this soaring marble-and-glass museum. Largely thanks to a brilliant modernist setting, the greatness of this collection of art is only now revealed, due to a new design that lends a sense of intimacy between viewer and object, while at the same time increasing one's appreciation of capital-A art.

The collection was amassed (in the 1920s and 1930s) thanks to the millions Dr. Albert C. Barnes made in pharmaceuticals. As a theorist, he wanted to help people "see as an artist saw" and to do this, he created for each gallery wall an "ensemble" of mirror-like symmetry: a Matisse could hang side-by-side with a Goya, above an African sculpture, and below a Old Master sketch and a French tin shoe buckle. As his will decreed that nothing could be changed, everything had to be transported—lock, stock, and Modigliani—to this new showcase.

Warmed by walls of tawny-colored Negev sandstone, centered around an enormous "Light Court"—the perfect place for gallery-goers to reflect on art—and entered through a narrow "mood tube" of reflecting pools and tall trees, the design of architects Tod Williams and Billy Tsien may be minimalist in style but remains mellow in impact. Inside, an interior garden, art library, restaurant, two classrooms, and café are winningly used as buffer zones to the rooms hung with the core collection.

Highlights include some of the most fabled paintings of Impressionist, Post-Impressionist, and Modern art, including Cézanne's *The Card Players*, Georges Seurat's *Models*, Van Gogh's *Postman Roulin*, Monet's *Studio Boat*, Matisse's *Joy of Life* and *La Danse* mural, Renoir's *The Artist's Family*, and Picasso's *Acrobat and Young Harlequin*. Thanks to a new lighting system, the art looks so fresh that it seems the artists had just put down their palettes. It is safe to say that most museumgoers will find this new Barnes Foundation a work of art in itself. For information about the museum's packed calendar of classes, lectures, and concerts, see the website. It's wise to make a reservation in advance. ⊠ *2025 Benjamin Franklin Pkwy., Benjamin Franklin Parkway* ☎ *215/278–7000* ⊕ *www.barnesfoundation.org* ☑ *$22 weekdays, $25 weekends; some special exhibits require additional fees* ☉ *Wed.–Mon. 10–5; 1st Fri. of the month, also open 6 pm–9 pm.*

FAMILY Fodor's Choice ★ **The Franklin Institute.** Founded more than 175 years ago to honor Benjamin Franklin, this science museum is as clever as its namesake, thanks to an abundance of dazzling hands-on exhibits. To make the best use of your time, study the floor plan before exploring. You can sit in the cockpit of a T-33 jet trainer, trace the route of a corpuscle through

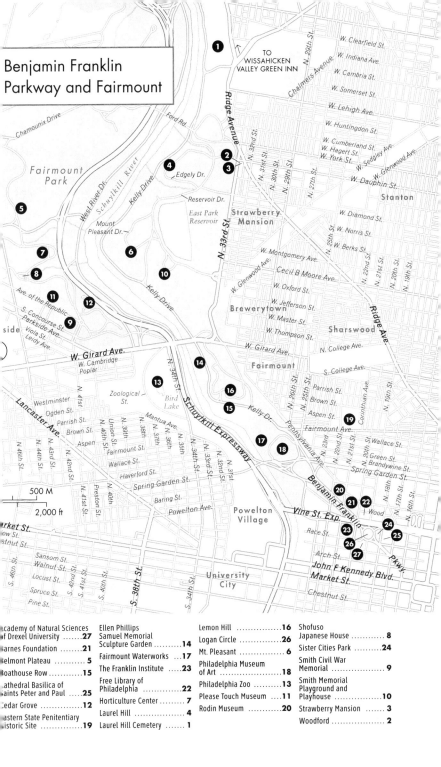

Benjamin Franklin Parkway and Fairmount

TO WISSAHICKEN VALLEY GREEN INN

Fairmount Park

Schuylkill River

Strawberry Mansion

Stanton

Brewerytown

Sharswood

Fairmount

Powelton Village

University City

500 M
2,000 ft

the world's largest artificial heart (15,000 times life size), and ride to nowhere on a 350-ton Baldwin steam locomotive. Most visitors flock to a pair of exhibitions: **Electricity**, which focuses on sustainable energy and includes Franklin's famous lightning rod; and **Changing Earth.** One don't-miss is the 30-ton white-marble statue of Franklin; you can see the likeness (and an accompanying hourly multimedia presentation) without paying admission.

The **Franklin Air Show** celebrates powered flight with the Wright Model B Flyer. **The Sports Zone** conveys the physics, physiology, and material science behind your favorite sport by simulating surfing, testing your center of mass and reaction time, and more. The **Fels Planetarium**—which has a state-of-the-art aluminum dome, lighting and sound systems, and a related astronomy exhibit, "Space Command"—has shows about the stars, space exploration, comets, and other phenomena. The Tuttleman IMAX Theater, with a 79-foot domed screen and a 56-speaker sound system, screens recent Hollywood films and special documentaries. ⊠ *271 N. 21st St., at Benjamin Franklin Pkwy., Benjamin Franklin Parkway* ☎ *215/448–1200* ⊕ *www.fi.edu* ⊠ *$19.95– $34.95 adult; some exhibitions require additional fees* ⊙ *Daily 9:30–5.*

Fodor's Choice   **Philadelphia Museum of Art.** The city's premier cultural attraction is one
★   of the country's leading museums. One of the greatest treasures of the museum is the building itself. Constructed in 1928 of Minnesota dolomite, it's modeled after ancient Greek temples but on a grander scale. The museum was designed by Julian Francis Abele, the first African-American to graduate from the University of Pennsylvania School of Architecture. You can enter the museum from the front or the rear; choose the front and you can run up the 99 steps made famous in the movie *Rocky.*

Once inside, you'll see the grand staircase and Saint-Gaudens's statue *Diana;* she formerly graced New York's old Madison Square Garden. The museum has several outstanding permanent collections: the John G. Johnson Collection covers Western art from the Renaissance to the 19th century; the Arensberg and A. E. Gallatin collections contain modern and contemporary works by artists such as Brancusi, Braque, Matisse, and Picasso. Famous paintings in these collections include Van Eyck's *St. Francis Receiving the Stigmata,* Rubens's *Prometheus Bound,* Benjamin West's *Benjamin Franklin Drawing Electricity from the Sky,* van Gogh's *Sunflowers,* Cézanne's *The Large Bathers,* and Picasso's *Three Musicians.* The museum has the world's most extensive collection of works by Marcel Duchamp, including the world-famous *Nude Descending a Staircase* and *The Bride Stripped Bare by Her Bachelors, Even.* Among the American art worth seeking out is a fine selection of works by 19th-century Philadelphia artist Thomas Eakins, including *The Gross Clinic,* which the museum co-owns with the Pennsylvania Academy of the Fine Arts.

Perhaps the most spectacular objects in the museum are entire structures and great rooms moved lock, stock, and barrel from around the world: a 12th-century French cloister, a 16th-century Indian temple hall, a 16th-century Japanese Buddhist temple, a 17th-century Chinese palace hall, and a Japanese ceremonial teahouse. Among the other collections are costumes, Early American furniture, and Amish and Shaker crafts. An unusual touch—and one that children especially like—is the Kienbusch Collection of Arms and Armor.

The Ruth and Raymond G. Perelman Building, across the street in the former Reliance Standard Life Insurance Building, is home to the museum's permanent collection of photography, costume, and contemporary design.

Friday evenings feature live jazz and world music performances in the Great Hall. The museum has a fine restaurant and a surprisingly good cafeteria now under the management of well-known restaurateur Stephen Starr. A short stroll away is the Fairmount Waterworks and Boathouse Row, as well as a path well used by bikers and joggers that connects the museum to Center City's Fitler Square neighborhood. ⊠ *26th St. and Benjamin Franklin Pkwy., Benjamin Franklin Parkway* ☎ *215/763–8100* ⊕ *www.philamuseum.org* ⊠ *$20; 1st Sun. of each month and every Wed. after 5 pm, pay what you wish* ⊙ *Tues., Thurs., and weekends 10–5; Wed. and Fri. 10–8:45.*

Fodor's Choice
★
Rodin Museum. This jewel of a museum holds the biggest collection outside France of the work of sculptor Auguste Rodin (1840–1917). Occupying a 20th-century building designed by French architects Jacques Greber and Paul Cret, it reopened in June 2012 after a brief closing for interior renovations; the idea is to honor Cret's original idea that inside and out offer a "unified setting" for the presentation of sculpture. Entering the museum, you pass through a re-landscaped courtyard to reach Rodin's *Gates of Hell*—a 21-foot-high sculpture with more than 100 human and animal figures. In the exhibition hall, the sculptor's masterworks are made even more striking by the use of light and shadow. Here are *The Kiss, The Burghers of Calais,* and *Eternal Springtime.* A small room is devoted to one of Rodin's most famous sitters, the French novelist Balzac. Photographs by Edward Steichen showing Rodin at work round out the collection. ⊠ *2154 Benjamin Franklin Pkwy., at 22nd St., Benjamin Franklin Parkway* ☎ *215/763–8100* ⊕ *www.rodinmuseum. org* ⊠ *$10 suggested donation; $20 2-day ticket with access to the Philadelphia Museum of Art and Perelman Building, and historic houses Mt. Pleasant and Cedar Grove* ⊙ *Wed.–Mon. 10–5.*

WORTH NOTING

FAMILY **Academy of Natural Sciences of Drexel University.** The dioramas of animals from around the world displayed in their natural habitats give this natural history museum an old-fashioned charm. The most popular attraction is Dinosaur Hall, with reconstructed skeletons of a Tyrannosaurus rex and some 30 others of its ilk, as well as the "Big Dig," where you can hunt for real fossils, and "Outside-In," an interactive area where kids can crawl through a log, investigate a real beehive, and touch a legless lizard. Another draw is "Butterflies!," where colorful, winged creatures take flight in a tropical garden setting. Founded in 1812, the academy is considered the oldest science-research institution in the western hemisphere and a world leader in the fields of natural-science research, education, and exhibition; the present building dates from 1876. That history is celebrated in the Ewell Sale Stewart Library, a trove natural-history books and artworks. ⊠ *1900 Benjamin Franklin Pkwy., at 19th St., Benjamin Franklin Parkway* ☎ *215/299–1000* ⊕ *www.ansp.org* ☜ *$17.95* ☽ *Weekdays 10–4:30, weekends 10–5.*

QUICK BITE

✕ **Capriccio Café and Espresso Bar at Café Cret.** At the eastern end of the Parkway sits the Capriccio Café and Espresso Bar at Café Cret, which, from its glass-enclosed indoor pavilion or alfresco seating, offers commanding views of the famed LOVE statue and City Hall. On the menu are a range of hot and cold coffee-based drinks, along with breakfast items, pastries, sandwiches, and salads. ⊠ *16th St. and Benjamin Franklin Pkwy., Benjamin Franklin Parkway* ☎ *215/735–9797* ⊕ *www.capricciocafe.com.*

Cathedral Basilica of Saints Peter and Paul. The basilica of the archdiocese of Philadelphia is the spiritual center for the Philadelphia area's 1.4 million Roman Catholics. Topped by a huge copper dome, it was built between 1846 and 1864 in the Italian Renaissance style. Many of the interior decorations are by Constantino Brumidi, who painted the dome of the U.S. Capitol. Several Philadelphia bishops and archbishops are buried beneath the altar. ⊠ *18th and Race Sts., Benjamin Franklin Parkway* ☎ *215/561–1313* ⊕ *cathedralphila.org* ☜ *Free* ☽ *Church: Weekdays 7:30–5, Sat. 9:30–5:15, Sun. 8–6:30. Mass: Sept.–May, weekdays 7:15 and 12:05; Sat. 12:05 and 5:15; Sun. 7:30, 12:05, and 12:35; Jun.–Aug., Sat. 12:30 and 5:15; Sun. 8, 9:30, 11, 12:30 (Spanish-language), and 6:30.*

Free Library of Philadelphia. Philadelphia calls its vast public-library system the Fabulous Freebie. Founded in 1891, the central library has more than 1 million volumes. With its grand entrance hall, sweeping marble staircase, and enormous reading rooms, this Greek Revival building looks the way libraries should. It's also the site of regular author readings and other book-related fairs and events. With more than 12,000 musical scores, the Edwin S. Fleisher collection is the largest of its kind in the world. The department of social science and history has nearly 100,000 charts, maps, and guidebooks. The rare-book department is a beautiful suite housing first editions of Dickens, ancient Sumerian clay tablets, illuminated medieval manuscripts, and more modern manuscripts, including the only known handwritten copy of Poe's "The Raven." The children's department houses the city's largest collection of children's books in a made-for-kids setting. The library is in the midst of renovations in preparation for a 130,000-square-foot addition designed by acclaimed architect Moshe Safdie that will house a new children's department, an area for teens, a self-publishing center, exhibition galleries, and a 550-seat auditorium. ⊠ *1901 Vine St., between 19th St. and Benjamin Franklin Pkwy., Benjamin Franklin Parkway* ☎ *215/686–5322* ⊕ *www.library.phila.gov* ☜ *Free* ☽ *Mon.–Thurs. 9–9, Fri. 9–6, Sat. 9–5, Sun. 1–5; building tours Tues. and Thurs. 10 am, Sat. 10 am and 2 pm; tours of rare book department weekdays at 11.*

Logan Circle. One of William Penn's five squares, Logan Circle was originally a burying ground and the site of a public execution by hanging in 1823. It found a fate better than death, though. In 1825 the square

Benjamin Franklin in Philadelphia

Unlike the bronze statue of William Penn perched atop City Hall, a marble likeness of Benjamin Franklin is within **The Franklin Institute.** Perhaps that's as it should be: noble-born Penn above the people and common-born Franklin sitting more democratically among them.

Franklin (1706–90) was anything but a common man. In fact, biographer Walter Isaacson called him "the most accomplished American of his age." Franklin's insatiable curiosity, combined with his ability to solve problems in his own life, inspired his invention of bifocals, an odometer to measure postal routes, a "long arm" to reach books high on his shelves, and a flexible urinary catheter for his brother who was suffering with kidney stones. His great intellect inspired his launching of the American Philosophical Society, the oldest learned society in America. He was the only Founding Father who shaped and signed all of the nation's founding documents, including the Declaration of Independence, the Constitution, and treaties with France and England. He was a citizen of the world—a representative in the Pennsylvania General Assembly, a minister to France.

It's fortunate for Philadelphians that Franklin spent so many of his 84 years here. That might have been an act of fate or early recognition that "time is money," as he wrote in *Advice to*

a Young Tradesman in 1748. Born in Boston in 1706, Franklin ran away from home and the oppression of his job as a printer's apprentice at his brother's shop. When he couldn't find work in New York, he didn't waste time; he moved on to Philadelphia. Within 10 years Franklin had opened his own printing office. His *Pennsylvania Gazette* was the most successful newspaper in the colonies; his humor propelled his *Poor Richard's Almanack* to best-seller status in the colonies. In Franklin's Print Shop in the **Franklin Court** complex, site of Ben's first permanent home in Philadelphia, you can get a letter hand-stamped with a "B. Free Franklin" cancellation.

Franklin had time and passion for civic duties. As postmaster, he set up the city's postal system. He founded the city's first volunteer fire company and the **Library Company of Philadelphia,** its first subscription library. After his famous kite experiment, he opened the first fire-insurance company, the **Philadelphia Contributionship for the Insurance of Houses from Loss by Fire.** He proposed the idea for the **University of Pennsylvania** and personally raised money to finance **Pennsylvania Hospital,** the nation's first.

Franklin was laid to rest alongside his wife, Deborah, and one of his sons, Francis, in the **Christ Church Burial Ground.**

was named for James Logan, Penn's secretary; it later became a circle and is now one of the city's gems. The focal point of Logan Circle is the **Swann Fountain** of 1920, designed by Alexander Stirling Calder, son of Alexander Milne Calder, who created the William Penn statue atop City Hall. You can find many works by a third generation of the family, noted modern sculptor Alexander Calder, the mobile- and stabile-maker, in the nearby **Philadelphia Museum of Art.** The main figures in the fountain symbolize Philadelphia's three leading waterways: the

Delaware and Schuylkill rivers and Wissahickon Creek. Around Logan Circle are some examples of Philadelphia's magnificent collection of outdoor art, including *General Galusha Pennypacker,* the Shakespeare Memorial (*Hamlet and the Fool,* by Alexander Stirling Calder), and *Jesus Breaking Bread.* ⊠ *Benjamin Franklin Parkway.*

Sister Cities Park. This formerly run-down park marking the city's connections with Florence, Italy; Tel Aviv, Israel; and eight other "sister cities" has been transformed to better suit its prime location near Logan Circle, the Four Seasons Hotel, and the Cathedral of Saints Peter and Paul. The park now features a year-round café, plaza, and fountain and an extensive play area for kids inspired by the local Wissahickon watershed that features a rock-climbing area, discovery garden, and sailboat pond. ⊠ *210 N. 18th St., at Benjamin Franklin Pkwy., Benjamin Franklin Parkway* 🕾 *215/440–5500* ⊕ *www.ccdparks.org/sister-cities-park* 🎟 *Free* ☾ *Daily 6 am–1 am.*

FAIRMOUNT

Located north of the Parkway, Fairmount is a residential district popular with young families and the eds-and-meds crowd. Mature trees and manor-like homes line the sleepy, strollable streets behind the main commercial strip, Fairmount Avenue, which is also home to the bulking Eastern State Penitentiary, a decommissioned prison that becomes a spectacular haunted house at Halloween.

TOP ATTRACTIONS

Eastern State Penitentiary Historic Site. Designed by John Haviland and built in 1829, Eastern State was at the time the most expensive building in America; it influenced penal design around the world and was the model for some 300 prisons from China to South America. Before it closed in 1971, the prison was home to Al Capone, Willie Sutton, and Pep the Dog, who allegedly killed the cat that belonged to a governor's wife. The audio tour of the prison features narration by actor Steve Buscemi. The penitentiary, just a half mile north of the Rodin Museum, hosts changing art exhibitions, haunted house tours around Halloween, and a Bastille Day celebration the Sunday before July 14, with a reenactment of the storming of the Bastille. ⊠ *2027 Fairmount Ave., at 22nd St., Fairmount* 🕾 *215/236–3300* ⊕ *www.easternstate.org* 🎟 *$14 adult, $12 senior, $10 student/child; tickets for the Halloween-themed night tours "Terror Behind the Walls" range $13–$45* ☾ *Daily 10–5; last entry at 4; Sept.–Nov., daily 6:30 pm–12:30 am for Halloween-themed tours* ☞ *Day and evening tours require separate entries and admission prices.*

QUICK BITE

✕ **Mugshots Coffeehouse and Cafe.** Across the street from the brooding Eastern State Penitentiary is a more welcoming spot—Mugshots Coffeehouse and Cafe, a neighborhood hangout offering organic fair-trade coffee, fresh juices, and smoothies, as well as an all-day chalkboard menu of bagel-and-egg sandwiches, soups, salads, veggie wraps, and even an updated tuna melt. ⊠ *1925 Fairmount Ave., Fairmount* 🕾 *267/514-7145* ⊕ *www.mugshotscoffeehouse.com* ☾ *Mon. and Wed.–Fri. 6:30 am–8 pm, Tues. 6:30 am–9 pm, weekends 7–7.*

AIRMOUNT PARK

2

Stretching from the edge of downtown to the city's northwest corner, Fairmount Park is the largest landscaped city park in the world. With more than 8,500 acres and 2 million trees (someone claims to have counted), the park winds along the banks of the Schuylkill River—which divides it into west and east sections—and through parts of the city. On weekends the 4-mile stretch along Kelly Drive is crowded with joggers, bicycling moms and dads with children strapped into kiddie seats atop the back wheel, hand-holding senior citizens out for some fresh air, collegiate crew teams sculling on the river, and budding artists trying to capture the sylvan magic just as Thomas Eakins once did.

GETTING HERE AND AROUND

Boathouse Row on Kelly Drive and portions of West River are easily reached on foot from the Philadelphia Museum of Art. To reach the zoo or the Please Touch Museum, you will need to use a car or take SEPTA or the PHLASH. Both the zoo and Please Touch are less than 15-minutes' drive from Center City West.

PLANNING YOUR TIME

You can tour by car (get a good city map), starting near the Philadelphia Museum of Art. Signs point the way, and the historic houses have free parking.

If you leave the driving to the Philadelphia Trolley Works, your narrated tour will take 40 minutes. If you drive yourself, you'll need about two hours. Add another 20–30 minutes for each historic house you tour. Animal lovers can spend half a day at the Philadelphia Zoo, while parents of children nine and under will want to spend a full morning or afternoon at the Please Touch Museum at Memorial Hall, the hub of a new district celebrating sites that were part of the 1876 Centennial Exhibition.

VISITOR INFORMATION

Fairmount Park Historic Preservation Trust. Before you set out, call the Park's Historic Preservation Trust to find out which historic houses are open that day, There are special walking and trolley tours offered around the winter holidays, as well, coordinated through the Philadelphia Museum of Art. ⊠ *6245 Wissahickon Ave., Fairmount Park* ☎ *215/988–9334* ⊕ *parkcharms.com.*

TOP ATTRACTIONS

Fodor's Choice
★

Boathouse Row. These architecturally varied 19th-century buildings—in Victorian Gothic, Gothic Revival, and Italianate styles—are home to the rowing clubs that make up the Schuylkill Navy, an association of boating clubs organized in 1858. The view of the boathouses from the west side of the river is splendid—especially at night, when they're outlined with hundreds of small lights. The row's newest addition, Lloyd Hall, has a gymnasium, bicycle and skate rentals in season, and a two-story café. ⊠ *Kelly Dr., E. Fairmount Park, Fairmount Park* ⊕ *www.boathouserow.org.*

FAMILY **Philadelphia Zoo.** Opened in 1874, America's first zoo is home to more than 2,000 animals representing six continents. It's small and well landscaped enough to feel pleasantly intimate, and the naturalistic habitats allow you to get close enough to hear the animals breathe. The Amphibian and Reptile House houses 87 species, from 15-foot-long snakes to frogs the size of a dime. The 2½-acre Primate Reserve is home to 11 species from around the world. Notable attractions include Big Cat Falls, where you'll find leopards, jaguars, mountain lions, tigers, and lions; the McNeil Avian Center, the state-of-the-art nest for some 100 birds; and African Plains, stomping ground of giraffes and zebras. The new children's zoo, KidZooU, has a goat bridge, where kids can test their climbing skills against live goats, a duck pond, an outdoor grooming area, a butterfly habitat, and more. You can get a bird's-eye view of the zoo and Fairmount Park on the Channel 6 Zooballoon, a 30-passenger helium balloon anchored by a high-tensile-steel cable. ✉ *34th St. and Girard Ave., W. Fairmount Park, Fairmount Park* 🕾 *215/243–1100* ⊕ *www.phillyzoo.org* 🖃 *$16–$20; some attractions require additional fees/tickets* ◷ *Mar.–Oct., daily 9:30–5; Nov.–Feb., daily 9:30–4.*

FAMILY **Please Touch Museum.** Philadelphia's children's museum occupies one of the city's most stately buildings, a gorgeous example of Beaux Arts–style architecture constructed for the 1876 Centennial Exhibition and one of just two public buildings still standing from the event. The facility, which is aimed at children seven and younger, instills a sense of wonder from the get-go, with its marble-floored Hamilton Hall, which has an 80-foot-high ceiling and a 40-foot-tall sculpture of the torch of the Statue of Liberty as its centerpiece. (The real statue's torch was displayed here for the nation's 100th birthday celebration.) The 38,000-square-foot facility is set up as six engaging exhibits, plus three areas designed for toddlers, where kids can learn through hands-on play at a mock supermarket, a hospital area, a space gallery with a rocket-making station, Alice's Wonderland, and a theater with interactive performances. Children can climb aboard with an interactive exhibit based on the railroad, or head outside to explore the Imagination Playground or Please Touch Garden. Another highlight is a circa-1908 Dentzel Carousel ride with 52 gleaming and colorful horses, pigs, cats, and rabbits that's housed in an adjacent, enclosed glass pavilion; separate tickets can be purchased for carousel rides. There also is a café serving lunch items and snacks. ✉ *4231 Ave. of the Republic, W. Fairmount Park, Fairmount Park* 🕾 *215/581–3181* ⊕ *www.pleasetouchmuseum.org* 🖃 *$17* ◷ *Mon.–Sat. 9–5, Sun. 11–5.*

Fodor's Choice ★ **Shofuso Japanese House.** This replica of a 16th-century guesthouse was reassembled here in 1958 after being exhibited at the Museum of Modern Art in New York City. The architectural setting and the waterfall, gardens, Japanese trees, and pond are a serene contrast with the busy city. The house is called Shofu-So, which means "pine breeze villa," and has a roof made of the bark of the hinoki, a cypress that grows only in the mountains of Japan. There's also 20 murals by acclaimed Japanese contemporary artist Hiroshi Senju here, as well as monthly tea ceremonies, for which reservations are required. ✉ *N. Horticultural Dr. and Lansdowne Dr., W. Fairmount Park, Fairmount Park* 🕾 *215/878–5097*

⊕ *www.shofuso.com* 🖭 *$7* ⊙ *May–Sept., Wed.–Fri. 10–4, weekends 11–5; Apr. and Oct., weekends 11–5* ⊙ *Mon.-Tues.* ☞ *Not wheelchair accessible* Ⓜ *SEPTA 38 bus, Please Touch Museum stop.*

WORTH NOTING

Belmont Plateau. Belmont Plateau has a view from 243 feet above river level, which will literally be the high point of your tour. In front of you is the park, the Schuylkill River winding down to the Philadelphia Museum of Art, and, 4 miles away, the Philadelphia skyline. ⊠ *2000 Belmont Mansion Dr., W. Fairmount Park, Fairmount Park.*

Cedar Grove. Five styles of furniture—Jacobean, William and Mary, Queen Anne, Chippendale, and Federal—reflect the accumulations of five generations of the Paschall-Morris family. The house stood in Frankford, in northeastern Philadelphia, for 180 years before being moved to this location in 1927. ⊠ *Lansdowne Dr. and Cedar Grove Dr., Fairmount Park* ☎ *215/763–8100* ⊕ *www.philamuseum.org/ historichouses* 🖭 *$5 (included in 2-day Philadelphia Museum of Art pass)* ⊙ *Apr.–Dec., Thurs.–Sun. 10–5, guided tours at 1 and 2:30; 1st Sun. of the month, tours 10–4* ☞ *Access is only by guided tour, via the Philadelphia Museum of Art.*

Ellen Phillips Samuel Memorial Sculpture Garden. Bronze and granite sculptures by 16 artists stand in a series of tableaux and groupings on riverside terraces. Portraying American themes and traits, they include *The Quaker,* by Harry Rosen; *Birth of a Nation,* by Henry Kreis; and *Spirit of Enterprise,* by Jacques Lipchitz. ⊠ *Kelly Dr., E. Fairmount Park, Fairmount Park.*

Fairmount Waterworks. Designed by Frederick Graff, this National Historic Engineering Landmark built in 1815 was the first steam-pumping station of its kind in the country. The notable assemblage of Greek Revival buildings—one of the city's most beautiful sights—sits just behind the Philadelphia Museum of Art; it includes an interpretive center with original machinery on display, an art gallery, and an information center. ⊠ *Waterworks Dr., off Kelly Dr., Fairmount Park* ☎ *215/685–0723* ⊕ *www.fairmountwaterworks.org* 🖭 *Free* ⊙ *Interpretive center Tues.–Sat. 10–5, Sun. 1–5* ☞ *Donations suggested for group tours.*

Horticulture Center. On the Horticulture Center's 27 wooded acres are a butterfly garden, a greenhouse where plants and flowers used on city property are grown, and a pavilion in the trees for bird-watching from the woodland canopy. Don't miss the whimsical *Seaweed Girl* fountain in the display house. The center stands on the site of the 1876 Centennial Exposition's Horticultural Hall. ⊠ *N. Horticultural Dr., W. Fairmount Park, Fairmount Park* ☎ *215/685–0096* ⊕ *www.phila.gov/ parksandrecreation* 🖭 *Free* ⊙ *Visitor center and greenhouses daily 9–3. Grounds Apr.–Oct., daily 7–6; Nov.–Mar., daily 7–5.*

Laurel Hill. Built around 1767, this Georgian house on a laurel-covered hill overlooking the Schuylkill River once belonged to Dr. Philip Syng Physick (also owner of Society Hill's Physick House). On some Sunday evenings in summer, Women for Greater Philadelphia sponsors candle-light chamber music concerts here. ⊠ *E. Edgely Dr., E. Fairmount Park,*

2701 N. Randolph Dr., Fairmount Park ☎ *215/235–1776* ⊕ *www.laurelhillmansion.org* ✉ *$5* ☉ *Apr.–Dec., Thurs.–Sun. 10–4; Jan.–Mar. by appointment only.*

OFF THE
BEATEN
PATH

Laurel Hill Cemetery. John Notman, architect of the Athenaeum and many other noted local buildings, designed Laurel Hill in 1836. The cemetery is an important example of an early rural burial ground and the first cemetery in America designed by an architect. Its rolling hills overlooking the Schuylkill River, its rare trees, and its monuments and mausoleums sculpted by Alexander Milne Calder, Alexander Stirling Calder, William Strickland, and Thomas U. Walter made it a popular picnic spot in the 19th century; today it's a great place to stroll on your own, or take a guided tour. Among the notables buried in this 78-acre necropolis are prominent Philadelphians and Declaration of Independence signers. Burials still take place here. ✉ *3822 Ridge Ave., Fairmount Park* ☎ *215/228–8200* ⊕ *www.thelaurelhillcemetery.org* ✉ *Free* ☉ *Weekdays 8–4:30, weekends 9:30–4:30* Ⓜ *SEPTA bus route 61; Regional Rail: East Falls Train Station.*

Lemon Hill. An impressive example of a Federal-style country house, Lemon Hill was built in 1800 on a 350-acre farm. Its most distinctive features are oval parlors with concave doors and the entrance hall's checkerboard floor of Valley Forge marble. ✉ *Poplar Dr., E. Fairmount Park, Sedgeley Dr. and Lemon Hill Dr., Fairmount Park* ☎ *215/232–4337* ⊕ *www.lemonhill.org* ✉ *$5* ☉ *Apr.–mid-Dec., Thurs.–Sun. 10–4; Jan.–Mar. by appointment only.*

Mt. Pleasant. Built in 1761 by John Macpherson, a Scottish sea captain, Mt. Pleasant is one of the finest examples of Georgian architecture in the country. The historically accurate furnishings are culled from the Philadelphia Museum of Art's collection of Philadelphia Chippendale furniture. According to legend, Revolutionary War traitor Benedict Arnold purchased this house as an engagement gift for Peggy Shippen, but he was banished before the deal was signed. ✉ *3800 Mt. Pleasant Dr., E. Fairmount Park, Fairmount Park* ☎ *215/763–8100* ⊕ *www.fairmountparkhouses.org* ✉ *$5 (included in 2-day Philadelphia Museum of Art pass)* ☉ *Apr.–Dec., Thurs.–Sun. guided tours at 1 and 2:30; 1st Sun. of each month, guided tours run 10–4* ☞ *The house is only accessible through guided tours via the Philadelphia Museum of Art.*

Smith Civil War Memorial. Built between 1897 and 1912 with funds donated by wealthy foundry owner Richard Smith, the memorial honors Pennsylvania heroes of the Civil War. Among those immortalized in bronze are generals Meade and Hancock—and Smith himself. At the base of each tower is a curved wall with a bench. If you sit at one end and listen to a person whispering at the other end, you can understand why they're called the Whispering Benches. Unfortunately, litter is a constant problem here. ✉ *N. Concourse Dr., W. Fairmount Park, Fairmount Park.*

Smith Memorial Playground and Playhouse. Founded in 1899, this beloved facility has been completely refurbished in recent years with state-of-the-art, age-specific equipment; the centerpiece of the 6½-acre site is the

A Drive Around Fairmount Park

Start your tour with a walk around **Faire Mount.** Park behind the art museum and walk down the stairs. To your right is the Azalea Garden. Straight ahead, overlooking the Schuylkill, is the elegant, Greek Revival **Fairmount Waterworks.** To the north you'll see the Victorian structures of **Boathouse Row**; watch for rowers on the river here, too. Walking north along Kelly Drive, you soon reach the **Ellen Phillips Samuel Memorial Sculpture Garden.**

And now the actual drive begins. Follow Kelly Drive to the end of Boathouse Row; turn right up the hill to a Federal-style country house, **Lemon Hill.** Head back to Kelly Drive, turn right, pass through the rock archway, and turn right again at the equestrian statue of Ulysses S. Grant. The first left takes you to **Mt. Pleasant,** a Georgian mansion. Continue along the road that runs to the right of the house (as you face it) past Rockland, a handsome Federal house that's currently closed. At the dead end turn left onto Reservoir Drive. You'll pass the redbrick Georgian-style Ormiston, also closed. Take the next left, Randolph Drive, to another Georgian house, **Laurel Hill,** on Edgely Drive, which becomes Dauphin Street. Just about 10 feet before reaching 33rd Street, turn left on Strawberry Mansion Drive, and you're at **Woodford,** which has an interesting collection of household goods. A quarter-mile northwest of Woodford stands the house that gave its name to the nearby section of Philadelphia, **Strawberry Mansion.** It has furniture from three periods of its history.

Visit Laurel Hill Cemetery before you cross the river to West Fairmount Park. Drive back down the driveway of Strawberry Mansion, turn left at the stop sign, and follow the narrow road as it winds right to the light. Turn left onto Ridge Avenue and follow it to the entrance gate, which sits between eight Greek columns.

To skip the cemetery and continue your tour, proceed down the Strawberry Mansion driveway to the stop sign, turn left, and follow the road as it loops down and around to the Strawberry Mansion Bridge. Cross the river and follow the road; when it splits, stay left. You'll come to Chamounix Drive, a long straightaway. Turn left and then left again on Belmont Mansion Drive for a fine view from **Belmont Plateau.** Follow Belmont Mansion Drive down the hill. Where it forks, stay to the left, cross Montgomery Drive, and bear left to reach the **Horticulture Center** with its greenhouse and garden. Loop all the way around the Horticulture Center to visit the serene **Shofoso Japanese House** and its waterfall and gardens.

Drive back around the Horticulture Center and continue through the gates to Montgomery Drive. Turn left and then left again at the first light (Belmont Avenue). Turn left again on North Concourse Drive. On your left is **Memorial Hall,** which now houses the **Please Touch Museum.** The two towers ahead are part of the **Smith Civil War Memorial.** Turn left just past them to see **Cedar Grove.** Just south of Cedar Grove is a Federal mansion, **Sweetbriar.** Continue past the house, make the first left, and turn left again at the stop sign onto Lansdowne Drive. Follow signs to the **zoo.**

Ann Newman Giant Wooden Slide, which measures 40 feet long, 12 feet wide, and 10 feet tall, and can accommodate up to 12 children at a time. ⊠ *Near 33rd and Oxford Sts., 3500 Reservoir Dr., E. Fairmount Park, Fairmount Park* ☏ *215/765–4325* ⊕ *www.smithplayground.org* 🖭 *Free* ⊙ *Playground and Playhouse: Apr.–Sept., Tues.–Fri. 10–4, weekends 10–7; Oct.–Mar., Tues.–Sun. 10–4* Ⓜ *SEPTA bus 32, at 33rd and Oxford Sts.*

Strawberry Mansion. The largest of the Fairmount Park Historic Mansions underwent major structural repairs in 2012, including restoration of the original windows, updated wiring, and the addition of an eco-friendly, geothermal, climate-control system. It has furniture from the three main phases of its history: Federal, Regency, and Empire. In the parlor is a collection of rare Tucker and Hemphill porcelain; it also showcases a large collection of fine antique dolls and toys. ⊠ *2450 Strawberry Mansion Dr., Near 33rd and Dauphin Sts., E. Fairmount Park, Fairmount Park* ☏ *215/228–8364* ⊕ *www.historicstrawberrymansion.org* 🖭 *$5* ⊙ *Tues.–Sun. 10–4; guided tours on the hr, last tour leaves at 3.*

Woodford. The Naomi Wood collection of antique household goods, including Colonial furniture, unusual clocks, and English delftware, and designated her "colonial household gear" in her will, can be seen in this fine Georgian mansion built about 1756. ⊠ *2300 N. 33rd St., at Dauphin St., E. Fairmount Park, Fairmount Park* ☏ *215/229–6115* ⊕ *www.woodfordmansion.org* 🖭 *$5* ⊙ *Tues.–Sun. 10–4.*

SOUTH PHILADELPHIA

Three of the city's most interesting neighborhoods lie south of South Street: Queen Village, Bella Vista, and East Passyunk. Queen Village, stretching from Front to 6th Street and from South Street to Washington Avenue, was the center of the commercial and shipbuilding activity that made Philadelphia the biggest port in the colonies and in the young United States. One of the oldest sections of the city, Queen Village was already settled by the Swedes when the English arrived; the Swedish influence shows in street names such as Swanson, Christian, and Queen.

Directly south of Society Hill, Queen Village is neither as glamorous nor as historically renowned as its neighbor. Chiseled in stone on one facade are these words: "On this site in 1879, nothing happened!" But like Society Hill, Queen Village, Bella Vista, and East Passyunk have been gentrified by young professionals and the creative class; the restoration attracted chic, hip bars, restaurants, and interesting shops.

Through the years South Philadelphia has absorbed boatloads of immigrants—European Jews, Italians, and most recently, Asians and Mexicans. The city's Little Italy is a huge area of identical row houses, many with gleaming white-marble steps, stretching south and west of Queen Village. At the heart of the neighborhood's Bella Vista section, along 9th Street, is the outdoor Italian Market, packed with vendors hawking crabs and octopus, eggplants, and tomatoes. From butcher-shop windows hang skinned animals; cheese shops are crammed with barrels of olives. Sylvester Stallone walked along 9th Street in *Rocky* and *Rocky II,* and almost every campaigning president has visited the market on his swing through Philadelphia. It's a great photo op for them—and for you.

Below Snyder Avenue stretches the rest of South Philadelphia to the south, east, and west. This is the neighborhood that gave the world Mario Lanza, Bobby Rydell, Frankie Avalon, and Fabian, and some area restaurants proudly display gold records earned by these neighborhood celebrities. Plenty of visitors alike head for South Philly's competing culinary shrines, Pat's King of Steaks and Geno's, both at the corner of 9th Street and Passyunk Avenue, but locals go deeper south to John's Roast Pork. One of their titular pig sandwiches (or cheesesteaks) makes a perfect prelude to an evening at the city's sports complexes, at the southern end of South Philadelphia.

GETTING HERE AND AROUND

You can reach the Italian Market on foot from Center City, or you may take SEPTA bus route 47, which runs south on 8th Street and makes a return loop north on 7th Street. There is both free and metered parking available in the neighborhood, at the official Italian Market lot on Carpenter Street between 9th and 10th and in lots just off Washington Avenue between 8th and 9th streets and 9th and 10th.

PLANNING YOUR TIME

It's best to visit this neighborhood Tuesday through Saturday, because the Italian Market is closed Sunday afternoon and Monday, and the Mummers Museum is closed Sunday through Tuesday. Start early— the Italian Market winds down by late afternoon—and allow three to four hours.

OUTH PHILADELPHIA

Outside Bella Vista, Queen Village, and East Passyunk, dozens of mini-neighborhoods comprise the bulk of South Philadelphia. Like historically Irish-American Pennsport, where 2nd Street is called Two Sweet and lined with Mummers Parade clubhouses. Or residential Newbold, home to one of the best beer lists in town at the South Philadelphia Tap Room. Down by the Sports Complex, where you'll go to catch the Phillies, Eagles, Sixers, and Flyers, the decommissioned Navy Yard has become an urban oasis of rolling lawns and slinky canals.

WORTH NOTING

American-Swedish Historical Museum. Near the sports complex in deep South Philly, this neoclassical building with big stone arches in FDR Park celebrates Swedish contributions to American history. The Swedes settled the Delaware Valley in the mid-1600s, and it was a pair of Swedish brothers who owned the land William Penn bought and called Philadelphia. This museum is set amid architectural remnants of the nation's 1926 Sesquicentennial Exposition). Modeled after a 17th-century Swedish manor house, it features galleries that concentrate on a certain era or particularly industrious character. The John Ericsson Room honors the designer of the Civil War ironclad ship the *Monitor,* and the Jenny Lind Room contains memorabilia from the Swedish Nightingale's American tour of 1848–51. One exhibition details Swedish immigration in the

19th century. Other rooms display handmade costumed Swedish peasant dolls, crafts, paintings, and drawings. It's not the most exciting place, but the weird location and building, combined with its examination of forgotten but essential history, make it an interesting visit. You can take the Orange Line subway down Broad Street to Pattison Avenue; when you get out, cross Broad Street and walk five blocks west through the park to the museum. ✉ *1900 Pattison Ave., South Philadelphia* ☎ *215/389–1776* ⊕ *www.americanswedish.org* 💲 *$8* ⊘ *Tues.–Fri. 10–4, weekends noon–4.*

Bartram's Garden. Begun in 1728 by the pioneering botanist John Bartram (1699–1777), this is America's oldest surviving botanical garden. Bartram, with his son William, introduced into cultivation more than 200 native plants from species up and down the East Coast. John became the royal botanist for King George III, and made a fortune selling plants to England. Today the 10-acre historical site along the river has lots of flowering shrubs and trees, including various azaleas, rhododendrons, and magnolias, and the Franklinia, a tree from south Georgia that became extinct in its native habitat and survived only because Bartram gathered it. Although there is almost always something flowering, the best time to come is in May and June, when the gardens are fragrant and filled with the lively chatter of birds. The original 1728 farmhouse still stands, and you can take a tour through its rooms, which have various exhibits, including Native American artifacts from the property dating back 3,000 years. Prince Charles's former gardener David Howard has taken on Bartram's garden as a pet project of sorts. A garden shop is open 10–4 Friday through Sunday. It's tucked down a driveway in an impoverished neighborhood of Southwest Philadelphia; drive or take a cab. ✉ *5400 Lindbergh Blvd., at 54th St., South Philadelphia* ☎ *215/729–5281* ⊕ *www.bartramsgarden.org* 💲 *Garden free, house tour $12 adults, $10 seniors and youth* ⊘ *Garden daily dawn–dusk; self-guided tour maps available in Welcome Center, open Mon.–Thurs. 10–4, Fri.–Sun. 10–6* ☞ *Guided tours available May–Dec., Thurs.–Sun.; private tours may be arranged by appointment Mon.–Wed.; no house tours currently available due to conservation and restoration work* Ⓜ *SEPTA Rte. 36 Trolley.*

OFF THE BEATEN PATH

Fort Mifflin. There are number of strange, forgotten sights in Philadelphia that in any other city would be a major, if not *the* major tourist attraction. Fort Mifflin may be the best of these sights in Southwest Philadelphia. The fort is enormous and nearly always empty. Within its walls, spread out on a huge lawn, are cannons and carriages, officers' quarters, soldiers' barracks, an artillery shed, a blacksmith shop, a bomb shelter, and a museum. The exhibits are dated, but the stories are fascinating, from the 40-day battle in 1777 to hold off British ships coming up the Delaware to the use of the site as a prison during the Civil War. The fort was almost totally destroyed during the Revolution, but was rebuilt in 1798 from plans by French architect Pierre L'Enfant, who also designed Washington, D.C. If you wander off beyond the fort and into the other parts of the 49-acre National Historic Landmark, you will find a long embankment of overgrown and unexcavated battlements from the 1800s. From Penn's Landing it's an easy jaunt on I–95. ✉ *6400 Hog*

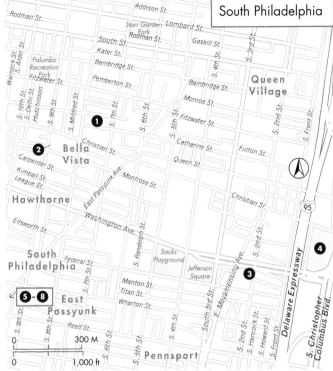

Island Road, at Island Rd., on Delaware River near Philadelphia International Airport, Southwest Philadelphia ☎ *215/685–4167* ⊕ *www.fortmifflin.us* ≊ *$8* ⊗ *Mar.–mid-Dec., Wed.–Sun. 10–4* ☞ *You can call to arrange an appointment or private tour during the off-season.*

OFF THE BEATEN PATH

John Heinz National Wildlife Refuge at Tinicum. Part of the appeal of this refuge is its truly strange location for a nature preserve: it's between the airport and an oil refinery, and visitors seem to really enjoy the oddity of it. More than 280 species of hawks, swallows, herons, egrets, geese, gallinules, eagles, orioles, ducks, and other birds have been spotted at this 1,200-acre preserve, the largest remaining freshwater tidal marsh in Pennsylvania. There are 10 miles of foot trails, an observation deck, and boardwalks through the wet areas. The refuge is also home to fox, deer, muskrat, turtles, and frogs, and you'll likely see large carp and catfish flopping about the lilies. An environmental education center has some explanatory exhibits on wetlands and regional wildlife. There are many guided tours. You can even canoe, kayak, and mountain bike, but there are no rentals here. The refuge is convenient to I–95, which you can pick up from Penn's Landing. Call for directions. ⊠ *8601 Lindbergh Blvd., Southwest Philadelphia* ☎ *215/365–3118* ⊕ *www.fws.gov/refuge/john_heinz* ≊ *Free* ⊗ *Refuge, daily dawn–dusk; visitor center, daily 8:30–4.*

FAMILY **Mummers Museum.** Even if you aren't in Philadelphia on New Year's Day, you can still experience this unique local institution. Famous for extravagant sequin-and-feather costumes and string bands, the Mummers spend the year preparing for the all-day parade up Broad Street. A 45-inch screen shows filmed highlights of past parades.

Early English settlers brought to the colonies their Christmastime custom of dressing in costume and performing pantomimes—the name Mummers derives from the German *Mumme,* meaning "mask" or "disguise." In Philadelphia, families would host costume parties on New Year's Day; on January 1, 1876, the first individual groups paraded informally through the city. The parade caught on, and by 1901 the city officially sanctioned the parade and 42 Mummers' clubs strutted for cash prizes.

These days the Mummers also stage a summer Mummers Parade around July 4 (during the city's Welcome America! celebration). The museum presents free outdoor concerts (weather permitting) on most Thursday evenings 8–10 from May to September. ⊠ *1100 S. 2nd St., at Washington Ave., South Philadelphia* ☎ *215/336–3050* ⊕ *www.mummersmuseum. com* ☞ *$3.50* ☉ *Wed.–Sat. 9:30–4:30; concerts May–Sept., Tues. 8 pm.*

Samuel S. Fleisher Art Memorial. The result of founder Samuel S. Fleisher's invitation to the world "to come and learn art," this school and gallery has offered tuition-free classes since 1898. Fleisher presents regular exhibits of contemporary art, which are selected through its competitive "Challenge" series, as well as works by faculty and students. The Memorial consists of four connected buildings on Catharine Street—including the Sanctuary, a Romanesque Revival Episcopal church designed by the architectural firm of Frank Furness and featuring European art from the 13th to the 15th century—as well as a satellite building at 705 Christian Street dedicated to works on paper. ⊠ *719 Catharine St., South Philadelphia* ☎ *215/922–3456* ⊕ *www.fleisher.org* ☞ *Free* ☉ *Mon.–Thurs. 9–9, Fri. 9–5, Sat. 9–3.*

EAST PASSYUNK

Directly south of Bella Vista, East Passyunk is comprised of two neighborhoods, Passyuk Square and East Passyunk Crossing, that are often conflated. Together they stretch between Washington and Snyder Avenues, Broad Street and 8th Street. The Italian presence is also felt around Passyunk (pronounced pash-unk) but in recent years, the gentrification that altered the DNA of Bella Vista has spilled into this neighborhood. Among the century-old pizza parlors and cheese shops are sushi bars and scooter dealerships, beer boutiques, and restaurants helmed by *Top Chef* winners.

BELLA VISTA

Bella Vista nuzzles against Queen Village, running from 6th Street to Broad Street, though exact boundary is a favorite topic of debate among locals. It is the historic heart of Italian-American Philadelphia, and its centerpiece is the outdoor Italian Market along 9th Street, packed

with vendors hawking crabs and octopus, eggplants, and toma
From butcher-shop windows hang skinned animals; cheese shop
crammed with barrels of olives. Sylvester Stallone walked along 9th
Street in *Rocky* and *Rocky II*, In recent years, Mexican immigrants
have made the Market their own, and the drag is now also the place to
pick up warm-from-the-press tortillas, dozens of different dried chilies,
even festive piñatas.

No trip to South Philly would be complete without a stop at one—or
both—of the city's best-known cheesesteak rivals, Pat's King of Steaks
(⊕ *www.patskingofsteaks.com*) and cross-street competitor Geno's
Steaks (⊕ *www.genosteaks.com*). Both can be found at the intersection
of 9th Street and Passyunk Avenue and are open 24 hours a day. Each
has its loyal fans for what's essentially the same sandwich: thinly sliced
rib-eye steak, grilled onions, cheese—provolone, American, or Cheez
Whiz—all piled on a fresh-baked Italian roll.

TOP ATTRACTIONS

Fodor's Choice **Italian Market.** It's more Naples than Philadelphia: vendors crowd the
★ sidewalks and spill out onto the streets; live crabs wait for the kill,
while it's too late for the lambs and pigs displayed in butcher-shop
windows; fresh, seasonal produce is piled high. The market dates to
the turn of the last century, when it was founded by Italian immigrants.
You'll find fresh pastas, cheeses, spices, meats, fruits and vegetables, and
dry goods and kitchen equipment, as well as junky dollar-stores and
funky boutiques. These days the market has become more diversified,
with the addition of several Mexican grocers, a natural foods grocer,
taquerias, a sandwich shop popular with foodies, and several coffee
spots. ⊠ *9th St. between Washington Ave. and Christian St., Bella Vista*
⊕ *www.phillyitalianmarket.com* ⊙ *Tues.–Sat. 9–5, Sun. 9–2* ☞ *Many
businesses are closed Sun. evenings and all day Mon., but there is no
firm market-wide rule.*

QUICK BITE

✕**Anthony's Italian Coffee House.** When you're ready for an atmospheric
break, stop by Anthony's Italian Coffee House in the heart of the Italian
Market. Here, to the strains of Frank Sinatra, you can sample a fresh panino
with prosciutto and mozzarella or indulge in homemade cannoli or gelato
imported from Italy. ⊠ *903 S. 9th St., Bella Vista* ☎ *215/627–2586*
⊕ *www.italiancoffeehouse.com/anthonysitaliancoffee* ⊙ *Weekdays 7–7,
Sat. 7 am–8 pm, Sun. 7:30–5.*

QUEEN VILLAGE

North of South Street is Society Hill. South of South, Queen Village.
Though there was a time when the former looked down its nose at its
southern neighbor, Queen Village has been a mighty nice place to live for
the last 20 years, home to some of the city's priciest homes, especially at
the northern end closest to Center City. Queen Village is dense, residential
and prettiest on the streets that near the River. Cafés and restaurants dot
the corners, while Fabric Row on 4th Street is where budding designers
go shopping for materials at decades-old cotton and silk houses.

Gloria Dei. One of the few relics of the Swedes who settled Pennsylvania before William Penn, Gloria Dei, also known as Old Swedes' Church, was organized in 1642. Built in 1698, the church has numerous intriguing religious artifacts, such as a 1608 Bible once owned by Sweden's Queen Christina. The carvings on the lectern and balcony were salvaged from the congregation's first church, which was destroyed by fire. Models of two of the ships that transported the first Swedish settlers hang from the ceiling—right in the center of the church. Grouped around the church are the parish hall, the caretaker's house, the rectory, and the guild house. The church sits in the center of its graveyard; it forms a picture that is pleasing in its simplicity and tranquillity. ⊠ *916 Swanson St., near Christian St. and Columbus Blvd., Queen Village* ☎ *215/389–1513* ⊕ *www.nps.gov/glde* ⌨ *Free* ⊘ *Tues.–Sun. 9–4, but call first; worship Sun. 10 am, evensong Tues. 6:30 pm.*

UNIVERSITY CITY AND WEST PHILADELPHIA

University City is the portion of West Philadelphia that includes the campuses of the University of Pennsylvania, Drexel University, and University of the Sciences. It also has the University City Science Center (a leading think tank), the Annenberg Center performing arts complex (part of the University of Pennsylvania), an impressive collection of Victorian houses, and a variety of moderately priced restaurants, movie theaters, stores, and lively bars catering to more than 32,000 students and other residents. The neighborhood stretches from the Schuylkill River west to 44th Street and from the river north to Powelton Avenue.

This area was once the city's flourishing western suburbs, where wealthy Philadelphians built grand estates and established summer villages. It officially became part of the city in 1854. Twenty years later the University of Pennsylvania moved its campus here from the center of the city. The university moved into many of the historic homes, and others were adopted by fraternities.

GETTING HERE AND AROUND
Unless you're a big walker or have access to a bike, you'll want to take either a SEPTA bus or underground Blue or Green trolley to University City. If you're driving, street parking can be easier to find here than in Center City, although it can be tight near the Penn campus when school is in session.

PLANNING YOUR TIME
University City is at its best when college is in session; the students rushing to classes give this area its flavor. Allow half an hour each in the Arthur Ross Gallery and the Institute of Contemporary Art, two hours in the University Museum, and an hour exploring the campus. If your time is limited, skip all but the University Museum, a don't-miss for the archaeologically inclined.

VISITOR INFORMATION

Houston Hall Information Center. The information center is located inside the Perelman Quadrangle at 3417 Spruce Street. ✉ *3417 Spruce St., Room 307, University City* ☎ *215/898–4636* ⊙ *Weekdays 6:30 am–1 am, weekends 7 am–1 am.*

⊃P ATTRACTIONS

FAMILY **University of Pennsylvania Museum of Archaeology and Anthropology.** Rare treasures from the deepest jungles and ancient tombs make this one of the finest archaeological and anthropological museums in the world. The collection of about 1 million objects includes the world's third-largest sphinx from Egypt, a crystal ball once owned by China's Dowager Empress, some of the world's oldest writing—Sumerian cuneiform clay tablets—and the 4,500-year-old golden jewels from the royal tombs at the ancient site of Ur (in modern-day Iraq). The museum's Worlds Intertwined galleries presents its Greek, Roman, and Etruscan collections. Children run to see the Egyptian mummies and to exhibits such as "Imagine Africa." ✉ *33rd and Spruce Sts., University City* ☎ *215/898–4000* ⊕ *www.penn.museum* 🖃 *$15* ⊙ *Tues.–Sun. 10–5, 1st Wed. of each month 10–8* Ⓜ *Market-Frankford Subway Line, 34th and Market Sts.; Blue and Green Line Trolley routes 11, 13, 34, 36.*

ⅤORTH NOTING

A Love Letter To You. You don't have to walk very far to encounter one of Philadelphia's more than 3,000 public murals. But the best way to see what's perhaps the most impressive collection of all is by hopping on the Market-Frankford line. *A Love Letter to You*, a series of 50 works on buildings in West Philadelphia depicting the story of a guy wooing a girl, by artist and Philadelphia native Steve Powers, can mainly be seen from the elevated train line. The murals, which resemble old-fashioned ads, are both witty and touching, with messages like "We share defeats, we share receipts and we share the sheets" and "Miss you too much not to love you." You can download a guide for your own experience or join a Mural Arts Program tour held at 10:30 am on Saturday or 1 pm on Sunday. ✉ *Market St., from 45th to 63rd, University City* ☎ *800/537-7676* ⊕ *www.muralarts.org* 🖃 *Free with SEPTA subway fare, or $20 for Mural Arts guided tour* ⊙ *Jan.–May and Sept.–Dec., Sat. 10:30–noon and Sun. 1–2:30* Ⓜ *SEPTA Market-Frankford Subway Line.*

Arthur Ross Gallery. Penn's official art gallery contains treasures from the university's collections and traveling exhibitions. The gallery shares its historic-landmark building, designed by Frank Furness, with the **Fisher Fine Arts Library.** ✉ *220 S. 34th St., between Walnut and Spruce Sts., University City* ☎ *215/898–2083* ⊕ *www.arthurrossgallery.org* 🖃 *Free* ⊙ *Tues.–Fri. 10–5, weekends noon–5.*

QUICK
BITE

✕ **City Tap House.** A popular hangout for the Penn crowd, this contemporary gastropub keeps five dozen craft beers and other brews running from its extensive tap system, and pairs them with a New American menu offering a little of everything, from burgers, brick-oven-style pizza, and salads to mussels, roasted salmon, and grilled rib eye. You can grab a seat at the huge wraparound bar, sit in the spacious dining room, or hang out on the terrace around one of five stone fire pits. ✉ *3925 Walnut St., University City* ☎ *215/662–0105* ⊕ *www.citytaphouseucity.com.*

Fisher Fine Arts Library. One of the finest examples remaining of the work of Philadelphia architect Frank Furness, this was the most innovative library building in the country when it opened in 1891. It was the first library to separate the reading room and the stacks. Peek into the reading room, dominated by a huge fireplace, and with study alcoves lit from skylights above. The unusual exterior stirred controversy when it was built: note the terra-cotta panels, short heavy columns, and gargoyles on the north end. The mottoes inscribed on many of the surviving leaded-glass windows were chosen by Horace Howard Furness, Frank's older brother and a Shakespeare scholar on the Penn faculty. Energetic visitors should consider making the long, Victorian climb up the main staircase to see the upper half of the tower. The less-energetic can take the modern elevator to the 4th floor. ✉ *220 S. 34th St., University City* ☎ *215/898–8325* ⊕ *www.library.upenn.edu/finearts* ✎ *Free; need photo ID; admittance is more restricted in late evening, weekends, and during exam periods; check website for details* ⊙ *During fall and spring school terms (Sept.–mid-Dec. and mid-Jan.–mid-May), Mon.–Thurs. 8:30 am–midnight, Fri. 8:30–8, Sat. 10–8, Sun. 10–midnight. Between terms (late Dec.–early Jan. and mid-Aug.–early Sept.), weekdays 9–5; closed weekends* ☞ *Library may be closed or restricted to the public during exams and campus events* Ⓜ *34th and Market Sts. (SEPTA Market-Frankford Blue line); 33rd and Market Sts. and 36th and Sansom Sts. (SEPTA subway-surface green lines, routes 11, 13, 34, 36).*

Institute of Contemporary Art. This museum, part of the University of Pennsylvania, has established a reputation for identifying promising artists and exhibiting them at a critical point in their careers. Among the artists who have had shows at ICA and later gone on to international prominence are Andy Warhol, Robert Mapplethorpe, and Laurie Anderson. ✉ *118 S. 36th St., at Sansom St., University City* ☎ *215/898–7108* ⊕ *www.icaphila.org* ✎ *Free* ⊙ *Wed. 11–8, Thurs. and Fri. 11–6, weekends 11–5* Ⓜ *SEPTA Green Line Trolley stop at 36th St. (University of Pennsylvania).*

Penn Park. This 24-acre park stretches along the western side of the Schuylkill River and serves as a new connector between Center City Philadelphia and the University of Pennsylvania campus. The park offers 12 tennis courts for public use, and extensive bike and walking trails, but its most striking feature is an elevated walk that connects to a central plaza and offers panoramic views of the Center City skyline. ✉ *31st St., between Walnut and South Sts., University City* ☎ *215/898–4636* ⊕ *www.upenn.edu* ✎ *Free* ⊙ *Daily 6–midnight.*

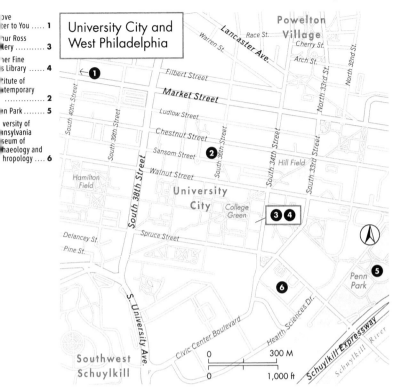

University City and
West Philadelphia

QUICK
BITE

✕ **Pod.** For a pan-Asian fix, grab a stool at the sushi bar at the futuristic Pod, where you can select your favorite raw fish from a conveyor belt. ⊠ *3636 Sansom St., University City* ☎ *215/387–1803* ⊕ *www. podrestaurant.com* ⊙ *No lunch weekends.*

ORTHWESTERN PHILADELPHIA

Chestnut Hill and Mount Airy are very pleasant, predominantly residential neighborhoods. Travel to downtown Philadelphia is easy by car or train. Restaurants and shops run all along Germantown Avenue in Chestnut Hill. Mount Airy is a little more sprawling, but there are a number of good restaurants and bars there as well. Manayunk has little of its history on display, unless you follow the tow path up the Schuylkill to see the last remnants of decaying mills. This predominantly Polish and Irish neighborhood renovated its Main Street in the 1980s into a quaint avenue with restaurants, funky shops, and a few good bars, perfect for a pleasant afternoon.

In 1683, at the founding of Germantown by German settlers, the county encompassed present-day Germantown, Mount Airy, and Chestnut Hill. It played an important role in the nation's founding: during the

American Revolution, it was the sight of the Battle of Germantown, which marked the first attack by American armed forces on the British. Originally intended as a farming community, the land turned out to be too rocky for anything but subsistence farming. Instead the Germans turned to making textiles, milling, and printing.

Germantown became fashionable for wealthy Philadelphians wanting to escape the city's heat in the mid-1700s. There are more than 70 homes dating from the 1700s here, as well as some of the oldest mills in the country. Germantown was also the seat of government for two summers during Washington's presidency, when yellow fever epidemics raged in the city.

Mount Airy and Chestnut Hill came into their own in the 19th century, when they became desirable as the location for summer homes for Philadelphia business owners drawn to Germantown's booming textile industry. Indeed, Philadelphia University had been the Philadelphia College of Textiles from the late 1800s to 1999. Germantown township was incorporated into Philadelphia in 1854, by which point local trains were already servicing the area, making travel to the city convenient.

PLANNING YOUR TIME
Manayunk and the Germantown and Chestnut Hill areas of Northwestern Philadelphia are two separate trips that will occupy the better part of a day. Manayunk has more nightlife, including a couple of bars with decks over the river, so you'll find yourself delayed there longer. Stationing yourself in Chestnut Hill for a weekend and using that as your base for the area and the city is another option.

MANAYUNK

In the mid-1800s, when Philadelphia was one of the nation's leading industrial cities, Manayunk prospered because of its many cotton mills, which provided raw material for the region's thriving paper and textile industries. Today, its Main Street is lined with galleries, antiques shops, boutiques, restaurants, and plenty of bars. Up from Main Street the hill rises steeply and houses are jammed together along twisted streets that are narrow and often end up nowhere near where you thought you were headed. Though it is less pronounced now than in the past, the blue-collar veneer of the rest of Manayunk is still a striking contrast to Main Street, but there is also something of a European hill town to the community.

CHESTNUT HILL

Chestnut Hill is one of the farthest points you can go outside Center City while still being within the city limits. The enclave looks the part with fairy-tale woods, winding drives, and moneyed addresses, but the walkable, family-oriented downtown is true to its streetcar suburb history.

TOP ATTRACTIONS

dor's Choice ★ Valley Green (Wissahickon Park). There are many great sections of Fairmount Park, but the 1,800 acres around Valley Green known as Wissahickon Park may be the most stunning. Miles and miles of trails running along and above the river lead to covered bridges, a statue of an Indian chief, 17th-century caves of a free-love cult, large boulders that drip water, and ducks. Forbidden Drive, on which cars are forbidden, runs from Northwestern Avenue (the westernmost part of Chestnut Hill) all the way to Lincoln Drive, where it connects to a bike and walking path. This leads eventually to Manayunk and Kelly Drive, where there are additional bike paths that can take you to the city or out along the Schuylkill. Admission to the park is free, but permits are required for bicycles and horses along some trails outside the Forbidden Drive, and a fishing license is required for anglers. There are also many miles of surprisingly difficult mountain-bike trails. The Valley Green Inn is a decent restaurant located on Forbidden Drive and Valley Green Road, and there is a refreshment stand there as well. ⊠ *Valley Green Rd., 4301 Henry Ave., Chestnut Hill* ☎ *215/247–0417* ⊕ *www.fow.org* ⊡ *Free* ⊙ *Daily dawn–dusk.*

WORTH NOTING

Historic RittenhouseTown. North America's first paper mill was built here in 1690 by Mennonite minister William Rittenhouse. Over the next 150 years, 10 generations of his family lived on the site and operated the mill. His most famous offspring, born in 1732, was David Rittenhouse, astronomer, statesman, and first president of the U.S. Mint. You can stroll any time through these 30 picturesque acres along the Wissahickon; on summer weekends, the one-hour guided tour of the seven outbuildings gives insight into this self-sufficient industrial village, which is now a National Historic District. Special events include papermaking workshops, cooking demonstrations, and an annual 5K race. ⊠ *206 Lincoln Dr., Chestnut Hill* ☎ *215/438–5711* ⊕ *www. rittenhousetown.org* ⊡ *$5* ⊙ *Tours: June–Sept., weekends noon–4; guided tours available by appointment year-round.*

FAMILY **Morris Arboretum.** This is one of the best arboretums in the country, and makes for a great stroll. Begun in 1887 and bequeathed to the University of Pennsylvania in 1932, this 92-acre arboretum was based on Victorian-era garden and landscape design, with its romantic winding paths, hidden grotto, a fernery, a koi pond, and natural woodland. The highlights are the spectacular rose garden and the swans. Large modern sculptures, some of which are spectacular, are sprinkled throughout the property. The arboretum has 3,500 trees and shrubs from around the world, including one of the finest collections of Asian plants outside Asia. Twice annually, the popular Garden Railway exhibit features an elaborate model railroad surrounded by miniature replicas of historic Philadelphia landmarks and other notable buildings crafted from natural materials. You may want to drive, as it's a good hike from the top of Chestnut Hill and a very hilly but short bike ride. ⊠ *100 E. Northwestern Ave., Chestnut Hill* ☎ *215/247–5777* ⊕ *www.morrisarboretum.org* ⊡ *$16* ⊙ *Apr.–Oct., weekdays 10–4, Sat. 8–5, Sun. 10–5; June–Aug., open until 8 on Wed.; Nov.–Mar., daily 10–4; guided tours weekends at 2.*

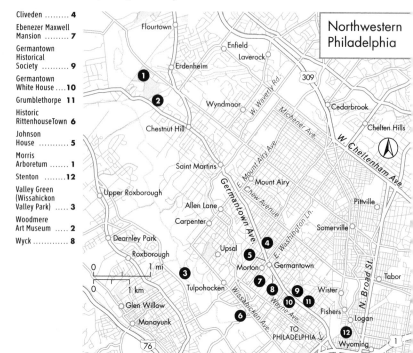

**QUICK
BITE**

✕ **Top of the Hill Cafe.** This small café offers a variety of soups, sandwiches and sides largely culled from the farm-and-fish market it runs next door. Daily specials may include lobster-bundle brioche or a hearty split pea with ham soup. ✉ *186 E. Evergreen Ave., Chestnut Hill* ☎ *215/248–6009.*

Woodmere Art Museum. This modest-sized museum has trouble drawing a crowd due to its location halfway down the other side of the hill from Chestnut Hill's shops and restaurants. You can spend a pleasant half hour here, however, taking in the varied modern, 20th-century and 19th-century art from artists mostly based in the region. Perhaps the best collection is of mid-1900s woodcut and other prints, and the museum has been doing a good job of rotating exhibits and bringing in special exhibitions. There are also some interesting 19th-century Pennsylvania landscapes. The grounds have varied modern outdoor sculpture. ✉ *9201 Germantown Ave., Chestnut Hill* ☎ *215/247–0476* ⊕ *www.woodmereartmuseum.org* ✉ *$10* ⊙ *Tues.–Thurs. and Sun. 10–5, Fri. 10–8:45, Sat. 10–6.*

OUNT AIRY

Like adjacent Germantown and Chestnut Hill, Mount Airy got its start as a vacation village for wealthy Philadelphians in the 1800s. Today, the area is an ideal mix of its neighbors, a blend of Germantown's grit and Chestnut Hill's polish with the same staggeringly gorgeous stock of Victorian and Colonial Revival architecture. Mount Airy is also recognized as one of the first racially integrated neighborhoods in the country, a point of pride among businesses and residents there today.

ERMANTOWN

Germantown, about 6 miles northwest of Center City, has been an integrated, progressive community since 13 German Quaker and Mennonite families moved here in 1683. They soon welcomed English, French, and other European settlers seeking religious freedom. The area has a tradition of free thinking—the first written protest against slavery in America came from its residents. Today it houses a wealth of exceptionally well-preserved architectural masterpieces. The business section of Germantown offers some quirky restaurants and shopping, but is still evolving.

TOP ATTRACTIONS

dor's Choice
★
Cliveden. The grounds take up an entire block, and its unique history, impressive architecture, and the guides who spin a good yarn combine to make Cliveden perhaps the best visiting experience of the historic Germantown homes. The elaborate country house was built in 1767 by Benjamin Chew (1722–1810), a Quaker and chief justice of the colonies, and something of a fence-straddler during the Revolution. Cliveden was at the center of the Battle of Germantown, occupied by British troops, and the walls still bear the marks of American cannon fire. Except for a brief period of time in the late 1700s when it was owned by a privateer (legalized piracy), the house remained in the Chew family until 1972, when it was donated to the National Trust for Historic Preservation. The original house has been completely opened to the public. A shining example of Georgian style, it has Palladian windows and an elegant entrance hall. The family-owned furniture includes a mahogany sofa by Thomas Affleck and looking glasses by James Reynolds. An elaborate reenactment of the Battle of Germantown is held here annually on the first Saturday in October. The house, on 6 acres, can be seen on a 45-minute guided tour. ✉ *6401 Germantown Ave., Germantown* ☎ *215/848–1777* ⊕ *www.cliveden.org* ☜ *$10* ☾ *Apr.–Dec., Thurs.–Sun. noon–4* ☞ *Tours on the hr, last tour at 3 pm.*

WORTH NOTING

Ebenezer Maxwell Mansion. Philadelphia's only mid-19th-century house-museum is a Victorian Gothic extravaganza of elongated windows and arches. This gorgeous 1859 suburban villa is used to illustrate the way Victorian social mores were reflected through its decoration. The downstairs highlights the Rococo Revival (circa 1860), the upstairs is fashioned after the Renaissance Revival (1880s), and the difference is striking, especially the Art Deco–like wall details you may not associate with the time. Also striking is the chamber pot in the dining room that the men used after the ladies retired to the parlor. What makes this house particularly interesting is that it was home to middle-upper-class residents, and so much of the decoration represents the norm of what people in that class strove to be. The house is two blocks from the Tulpehocken stop on SEPTA's Chestnut Hill West line. ⊠ *200 W. Tulpehocken St., at Greene St., Germantown* ☎ *215/438–1861* ⊕ *www.ebenezermaxwellmansion.org* 🗺 *$7* ⊙ *Mid-Jan.–mid-Dec., Thurs.–Sat. noon–4.*

Germantown Historical Society. The headquarters of the society has a historical and genealogical library and a museum showcasing noteworthy furniture, textile, and costume collections, from Colonial highboys and Peale paintings to Quaker samplers and mourning clothes. It's also an orientation point for anyone visiting the Germantown houses. The society doesn't function as well as it should as a gateway to the various sights, but you can collect most of the information that you'll need here. ⊠ *5501 Germantown Ave., Germantown* ☎ *215/844–1683* ⊕ *www.germantownhistory.org* 🗺 *Museum $5, museum and library $10* ⊙ *Tues. 9–1, Thurs. 1–5, 1st Sun. of each month 1–5* ☞ *Call ahead to verify hrs before visit; staff is limited.*

Germantown White House. Formerly called the Deshler-Morris House, the Germantown home was where President Washington lived and held cabinet meetings during the yellow fever epidemic of 1793–94, making it the seat of government of the new republic for a short time, and also the oldest "official" residence of an American president. A major renovation completed in 2009 has put new life into the house. Interpretive exhibits are displayed in the house next door, and the house itself has been restored to the time Washington was there. The emphasis has also shifted to telling the stories of the entire household, from the slaves who worked there to the president and his wife. In October 1777, during the Battle of Germantown, the house was the headquarters for British general Sir William Howe. As one of the many Germantown houses built flush with the road, it has enchanting side and back gardens. The house, which has moved beyond its "Washington slept here" renown into something much more interesting, is part of the Independence National Historical Park. ⊠ *5442 Germantown Ave., near Chelten Ave., Germantown* ☎ *215/597–7130* 🗺 *Free* ⊙ *May.–mid-Sept., Fri.–Sun. 10–4; other times by appointment* ☞ *Open one Sat. in Oct. for Revolutionary Germantown Festival; call for details.*

Grumblethorpe. The blood of General James Agnew, who died after being struck by musket balls during the Battle of Germantown, stains the floor in the parlor of this Georgian house. Built by Philadelphia merchant and wine importer John Wister in 1744, Grumblethorpe is one of Germantown's leading examples of early-18th-century Pennsylvania-German architecture. The Wister family lived here for 160 years, and during the Revolution a teenage Sally Wister kept a diary that has become an important historical source for what that time was like. On display are period furnishings and family mementos, but probably the best part of the house is the large garden. Wisteria, the flowering vine, is named after Charles Wister (John's grandson), who was an avid botanist and amateur scientist, and there is plenty of it in the garden. There are also an enormous hundred-year-old rosebush, a peony alley, a two-story arbor with climbing clematis and a grapevine working its way across its base, and a number of tulips. ✉ *5267 Germantown Ave., Germantown* ☎ *215/843–4820* ⊕ *www.philalandmarks.org* ⏍ *$5; free, 2nd Sat. from Apr.–Oct.* ⊗ *Apr.–Oct., call ahead for appointment, or open 2nd Sat. of month, noon–4.*

Johnson House. After bringing visitors through the hidden back entrance of this 1768 home, guides retrace the experience of slaves who found a haven here when the Johnson House was a key station on the Underground Railroad. They weave the story of the Johnson family, Quakers who worked to abolish slavery, with that of Harriet Tubman, who was sheltered here with runaway slaves and later guided them to freedom. Visitors see hiding places, including the third-floor attic hatch that runaways would use to hide on the roof when the sheriff came by, learn Underground Railroad code words, and view slavery artifacts, such as ankle shackles and collars. The home has contained the gamut of American history; in 1777 the house was in the line of fire during the Battle of Germantown; the shutters still show the impact of the musket rounds. In the early 1900s it was saved from demolition when it became a women's club. The house itself does not amaze, but hearing the stories of the home when you are standing within it is interesting. It's best to call ahead for tours. ✉ *6306 Germantown Ave., Germantown* ☎ *215/438–1768* ⊕ *www.johnsonhouse.org* ⏍ *$8* ⊗ *Sat. 1–4 year-round, Feb.–mid-June and Sept.–Nov. 30, Thurs. and Fri. 10–4* ☞ *Group tours and tours by appointment available year-round. Call for details.*

Stenton. James Logan may not be a household name, but he was a seminal figure in pre-Revolutionary America. He was secretary to William Penn and managed the daily affairs of the colony. Logan, who went on to hold almost every important public office in the colonies, designed the 1730 Georgian manor himself and named it for his father's birthplace in Scotland. He used it to entertain local luminaries and Native American tribal delegates. It was also where he kept one of the area's first libraries, at a time when books were looked upon with suspicion. George Washington was a guest of James's grandson on his way to the Battle of Brandywine, and British General Howe claimed it for his headquarters during the Battle of Germantown. The Stenton mansion is filled with family and period pieces; the site also includes a kitchen wing, barn, and Colonial-style garden. The guided 45-minute tour interprets the life of three generations of the Logan family and the life of the region from the 1720s through the American Revolution. This house has one of the best interiors of any of the Germantown homes. It's best to call ahead for a tour. ✉ *4601 18th St., Germantown* ☎ *215/329–7312* ⊕ *www.stenton.org* ⏍ *$5* ⊗ *Apr.–Dec., Tues.–Sat. 1–4; Jan.–Mar. by appointment only.*

Wyck. Between the 1690s and 1973, Wyck sheltered nine generations of the Wistar-Haines family. Their accumulated furnishings are on display, along with ceramics, children's needlework, dolls, and artifacts generally contemporary with the mid-1800s. On one side is the oldest rose garden of in the United States, dating to the 1820s, which blooms in late May, as well as a magnolia tree from that time. Out back are a large lawn, where you can picnic, and a vegetable garden—the land has been continuously farmed since 1690. Known as the oldest house in Germantown, Wyck was used as a British field hospital after the Battle of Germantown. The home's current form dates to 1824, when William Strickland made alterations. Tours are offered and should be scheduled in advance, but the grounds are open for wandering, and there is a farmers' market offering fruits and produce grown on the grounds on Friday afternoons from May to November. ⊠ *6026 Germantown Ave., Germantown* ☎ *215/848–1690* ⊕ *www.wyck.org* ⊠ *$5* ☾ *Apr.–Nov., Wed.–Sat. noon–4* ☞ *Free self-guided tours on Fri. noon–4 when farmers' market is open.*

NORTHEASTERN PHILADELPHIA

Gentrification continues to transform the Northern Liberties neighborhood from a light industrial area to a hipster artist enclave and popular center for nightlife, restaurants, and shopping. Still, the area has kept its working-class atmosphere—at least for now. One anchor is the Piazza at Schmidt's, a large mixed-used development that incorporates the old Schmidt's Brewery buildings into residential and commercial spaces; it has dozens of galleries and boutiques with a youthful vibe. Northern Liberties is a short taxi ride north of Old City and worth exploring for a look at Philadelphia beyond the city's historic districts.

Gentrification continues to transform Northeastern Philadelphia. The percolation is slow and steady in North Philadelphia and moving at a lightning clip in neighborhoods like Northern Liberties, a once-decrepit part of town that's been a gold mine for real estate developers for more than 10 years, while Fishtown is the place to be these days for charming row homes, neo-pho, and geisha coffee. Beyond stretches the enormity of Northeast Philly just waiting to be discovered and developed next.

NORTH PHILADELPHIA

North Philadelphia makes up a big swath of the city, but the area most pertinent to visitors extends above City Hill, where the eastern edge of Fairmount and the industrial Loft District converge on North Broad Street. The strip has been revitalized in the past couple of years, mainly a credit to chef Marc Vetri, who has two restaurants here. The planned renovation of the historic, long-vacant Divine Lorraine Hotel should keep that energy going.

NORTHEAST PHILADELPHIA

From Port Richmond to Tacony, Bridesburg to Mayfair, Northeast Philly is a patchwork of dense residential communities, each with its own unique personality. The farther north you head along I–95, the larger the houses get (this area was home to some of the city's first suburbs) until you reach Bucks County.

TOP ATTRACTIONS

FAMILY **Insectarium.** In Northeastern Philly, a neighborhood not known for its tourist attractions, is a bug lover's heaven. Revel in this ugly-yet-beautiful collection of thousands of creepy crawlers—tarantulas, giant centipedes, assassin bugs, and metallic beetles that look like pieces of gold jewelry. Started by an exterminator, the museum is home to more than 50 live species and mounted insects from around the world. The 5,000-square-foot space has one of the largest butterfly and moth collections in North America, a working beehive, a man-made (and kid-sized) spider web, and a kitchen teeming with live cockroaches. It's definitely a place for screaming kids, but it's hard not to enjoy at any age. It's easier to drive here than to take public transportation. By public transit, take the Market-Frankford subway to the end (Frankford Transportation Center); transfer to SEPTA bus 66 to Welsh Road. ⊠ *8046 Frankford Ave., Northeast Philadelphia* ☎ *215/335–9500* ⊕ *www.insectariuminstitute. com* ☑ *$9* ⊘ *Mon.–Sat. 10–4* ☞ *Not wheelchair accessible.*

ORTHERN LIBERTIES

Once a postindustrial graveyard, Northern Liberties has been transformed over the last decade into a haven whose hipster edge has faded into a family-friendly neighborhood. At the northern end of the district, the Piazza at Schmidt's redevelopment of the former Schmidt's Brewery draws a postcollegiate crowd.

WORTH NOTING

Edgar Allan Poe National Historic Site. One of America's most original writers, Edgar Allan Poe (1809–49), lived here from 1843 to 1844; it's the only one of his Philadelphia residences still standing. During that time some of his best-known short stories were published: "The Telltale Heart," "The Black Cat," and "The Gold Bug." You can tour the three-story brick house; to evoke the spirit of Poe, the National Park Service displays first-edition manuscripts and other rare books and offers interactive exhibits as well. An adjoining house has exhibits on Poe and his family, his work habits, and his literary contemporaries; there's also an eight-minute film and a small Poe library and reading room. A statue of a raven helps set the mood. The site, easily reached from the African American Museum, is five blocks north of Market Street. SEPTA bus 47 travels on 7th Street to Green Street, where you should disembark. ⊠ *532 N. 7th St., Northern Liberties* ☎ *215/597–8780* ⊕ *www.nps.gov/ edal* ☑ *Free* ⊘ *Fri.–Sun. 9–noon and 1–5.*

SHTOWN

One of Philly's hottest neighborhoods, Fishtown spent the better part of the last century as a working-class enclave for Irish- and Polish-Americans. Longtime residents still live in Fishtown, proud flags fluttering from their tidy row homes, but the area has gotten way more diverse as the creative class took refuge in the affordable real estate, and families and speculators followed. Great independent restaurants and funky boutiques make it a great place to spend a day.

CITY LINE AVENUE

City Line Avenue, a main thoroughfare of Philly's historic old-moneyed Main Line, cuts west from the Schuylkill River and intersects Lancaster Avenue, along which bedroom communities like Bryn Mawr, Ardmore, and Wayne are arranged like pearls on a necklace. Visit for avant-garde breweries, ritzy boutiques, and mansion-gawking.

TOP ATTRACTIONS

Bryn Mawr College. The 1939 film *Philadelphia Story,* a depiction of Main Line society life, starred Katharine Hepburn, a graduate of Bryn Mawr College, the first college for women that offered graduate degrees. Founded in 1885 and modeled after Cambridge and Oxford colleges, Bryn Mawr introduced the "collegiate Gothic" style of architecture to the United States. ⊠ *101 N. Merion Ave., Bryn Mawr* ☎ *610/526–6520* ⊕ *www.brynmawr.edu.*

Chanticleer. At this 35-acre pleasure garden circling a country estate, even the old tennis court has been transformed into a garden. If you enjoy flowers and paths, this is a great stop. It's lavish, but its over-the-top opulence is part of what makes it so enjoyable. ⊠ *786 Church Rd., Wayne* ☎ *610/687–4163* ⊕ *www.chanticleergarden.org* ⊠ *$10* ☉ *Apr.–Nov., Wed.–Sun. 10–5; May–Aug., Fri. 10–8; some 8 am openings scheduled in summer* ☞ *Visitors may be turned away if the parking lot is full.*

WHERE TO EAT

Updated by
Adam Erace

Welcome to the third wave of Philadelphia dining, an era in which locals are more likely to chat you up about their favorite chorizo tacos, wild-yeasted ales, or tasting menu than anything cheesesteak. Yes, the famous sandwich is still around (eat one if you must) but is slowly losing traction to its distant cousin, the roast pork. This is the Philly sandwich to try, be it a traditional rendition at John's or DiNic's in Reading Terminal Market or a new-school take, like the one topped with lacto-fermented broccoli rabe at High Street on Market.

Speaking of Old City's High Street, its chef/partner, Eli Kulp, represents a group of Philadelphia chefs that has had a massive impact on the dining scene in the last few years: the ex–New Yorkers. Like Kulp, Peter Serpico of Serpico, Eli Collins of Pub and Kitchen, Greg Vernick of Vernick Food & Drink and other talented former 212-ers have shifted their careers here from some of NYC's finest kitchens and restaurant groups. Even in East Passyunk and Fishtown, white-hot neighborhoods that are dethroning Center City as Philly's dining nucleus, inflated rents are bargains compared to those in the Big Apple.

The recent influx of out-of-town chefs complements Philly's homegrown talent. This has always been a scene that has fostered and supported its own, and the last several years have seen young chefs rising through the kitchens of Stephen Starr, Marc Vetri, and Georges Perrier and going on to debut compelling, idiosyncratic, solo projects. Like Pierre Calmels, who left the storied (now closed) Le Bec-Fin to open tiny Bibou in Bella Vista, and his LBF successor, Nicholas Elmi, who won Top Chef after opening Laurel on East Passyunk. (To give you an idea of the depth of talent in the 215, Elmi is the second Philly chef to win Top Chef.) And then there's Michael Solomonov, a former Vetri capo who went on to found Zahav, the restaurant that ignited America's passion for Israeli cuisine, and win a James Beard Award. Solo (as he's affectionately known here) is in conscientious empire-building mode with longtime business partner, Steve Cook, and mentoring a new generation of young chefs. You can still catch him working the bread station at Zahav most nights, between annual research trips to Israel and surfing breaks at the Jersey Shore.

The Israeli, Iraqi, Turkish, and Yemenite recipes on the menu at Zahav are just a handful of the cuisines represented in this multiethnic town. Philadelphia has a long history as a city of immigrants, from Western Europeans in the early 20th century to the Vietnamese, Mexicans, and Africans of today. Chinatown reigns as the city's hub of hand-pulled noodles, breakneck dim sum, and siphon coffee before it was cool, while Middle Eastern, Ethiopian, and Senegalese hideaways occupy tree-lined storefronts and old banks in West Philly. Vietnamese pho halls and bakeries congregate along Washington Avenue in South Philly, also home to the city's vibrant Mexican population. In the Italian Market, many of the old businesses have given way to industrious taquerias. You can follow the trail of fresh-pressed tortilla crumbs from Bella Vista down into East Passyunk, a hood where it's not uncommon to hear Spanish, Vietnamese, and five different dialects of Italian just walking down the street.

MEALTIMES

Unless otherwise noted, the restaurants listed in this guide are open daily for lunch and dinner. Philadelphia's starting to keep later hours: restaurants used to close by 10 pm on weekdays and stay open an hour or two later on weekends. As in many other cities, brunch is a weekend ritual and is generally served from 11:30 to 2:30, with Sunday being the big day.

RESERVATIONS AND DRESS

Reservations are noted when they're essential or not accepted. (Many top restaurants are typically booked a month ahead for Saturday night. Vetri is almost always booked two months ahead.)

Most of Philadelphia's restaurants can be classified as business casual, with the exception of inexpensive spots or those in the University City area, where jeans and sneakers are de rigueur. Dress is mentioned in reviews only when men are required to wear a jacket or a jacket and tie.

WINE, BEER, AND SPIRITS

The most popular local beer, Yuengling, is made at one of the oldest breweries in the country. Other area breweries include Victory, Flying Fish, and Yard's.

One happy development to come from Pennsylvania's somewhat arcane alcohol laws is the proliferation of BYOB restaurants—where you can bring your own bottle(s) of wine, beer, or liquor and enjoy them with your meal free of corkage fees. Many different cuisines are available, including Italian, Mexican, Thai, French, and Mediterranean. They are found throughout the city but are perhaps most highly concentrated in the Bella Vista and Queen Village neighborhoods in South Philly.

State-run liquor stores, called state stores, sell wine and other spirits. Beer is sold on a take-out basis by some bars and restaurants, but is otherwise available only by the case from certain distribution centers.

RESTAURANT PRICES

WHAT IT COSTS			
$	$$	$$$	$$$$
Under $15	$15–$19	$20–$24	Over $24

STAURANTS

Restaurant prices are the average cost of a main course at dinner or, if dinner is not served, at lunch.

RESTAURANT REVIEWS

THE HISTORIC DOWNTOWN

You could spend your entire trip to Philadelphia in Old City, Society Hill, and the historic core around Independence National Historic Park and eat *incredibly* well. In these cobblestoned streets, you'll find restaurants regularly mentioned on national best lists (Zahav, High Street on Market) as well as casual pizzerias, great coffee, and cocktail dens.

OLD CITY

$$$$ SPANISH 🍴 **Amada.** Since his debut with Amada in 2005, chef-restaurateur Jose Garces has opened three more restaurants in the city, all of them instant and enduring hits. The young Ecuadorian-American chef has taken Philadelphia by storm, and it was at Amada where he set the stage for his modus operandi of elevating authentic regional cuisine with choice ingredients and a modern touch. On offer are more than 60 tapas, each one worth trying, especially the white-bean stew with escarole and chorizo, and the flatbread topped with fig jam, Spanish blue cheese, and shredded duck. Ingredients—including glorious cheeses—are sourced from northern Spain. The large, festive front room can skew loud; for a quieter meal, ask for a table in the second dining room, beyond the open kitchen. [$] *Average main: $30* ✉ *217–19 Chestnut St., Old City* ☎ *215/625–2450* 🌐 *www.amadarestaurant.com* 🕓 *No lunch weekends.*

$$$$ ASIAN 🍴 **Buddakan.** This post office–turned–stylish restaurant is presided over by a 10-foot-tall gilded Buddha who seems to approve of the sake cocktails and the fusion food that pairs Asian ingredients with various cooking styles. The edamame ravioli appetizer and chocolate bento-box dessert are tasty, but most of the appeal is in the theatrical decor and people-watching also in evidence at Buddakan's outposts in New York City and Atlantic City. A long "community table" provides an opportunity to dine with anyone else fortunate enough to snag this center-stage space. Be prepared for a loud and lively atmosphere as the evening wears on. [$] *Average main: $25* ✉ *325 Chestnut St., Old City* ☎ *215/574–9440* 🌐 *www.buddakan.com* 🕓 *No lunch weekends.*

$$ PIZZA FAMILY 🍴 **Capofitto.** Stephanie and John Reitano have long been known for outstanding gelati and sorbetti at their chain of scoop shops, Capogiro. Now, the couple has set its sights on pizza with Capofitto, a sweet little pizzeria in a former paper factory. Society Hill nannies and roving British tourists pack the dining room's fire-engine-red chairs and rainbow loom banquettes bathed in the glow of the wood-burning oven. Topped with guanciale, Piennolo tomatoes, 'nduja, and other Italian delicacies, the delicious puffy-rimmed pies that 900-degree beast produces follow the Neapolitan style, except for one major difference: a woman is making them. Stephanie successfully infiltrated Naples's notorious pizzaiolo boy's club and trained as an apprentice for an entire summer. The secrets she learned, worked into her own technique, create one of Philly's best pies. [$] *Average main: $17* ✉ *233 Chestnut St., Old City* ☎ *215/897–9999* 🌐 *www.capofittoforno.com.*

$$$$ AMERICAN 🍴 **City Tavern.** You can time-travel to the 18th century at this authentic re-creation of historic City Tavern, where the atmosphere suggests that

Founding Fathers such as John Adams, George Washington, Thoma Jefferson, and the rest of the gang *might* have dined here (they didn't; the restaurant was built under the supervision of the National Park Service in 1994, to the specifications of the original 1773 tavern). The food is heavy and rich—West Indies pepper-pot soup, cornmeal-crusted oysters, and braised rabbit are prepared from enhanced period recipes and served on handsome Colonial-patterned china or pewter. Happily all is not authentic—the restaurant makes good use of refrigeration and electricity. $ *Average main: $26* ⊠ *138 S. 2nd St., Old City* ☎ *215/413–1443* ⊕ *www.citytavern.com.*

$$
ECLECTIC

✕ **Continental Restaurant & Martini Bar.** Light fixtures fashioned like olives pierced with toothpicks are a tip-off to the theme at this cool watering hole. It's installed in a classic diner shell in the center of Old City's action. This is the first of Stephen Starr's trendy restaurants, where he serves lively (but not outré) food in generous portions to people who know how to enjoy it. Don't miss the addictive Szechuan french-fried potatoes with hot-mustard sauce and the crispy calamari salad. $ *Average main: $17* ⊠ *138 Market St., Old City* ☎ *215/923–6069* ⊕ *www.continentalmartinibar.com.*

$$$$
LATIN AMERICAN

✕ **Cuba Libre.** People who have been in Havana swear this place is a dead ringer. In any event, it's lovely, with balconies and fancy streetlights, and even a leaded-glass window—on the interior. An entire menu is devoted to rum from everywhere in the Caribbean and Central and South America, including Cuba Libre's own brand. The appetizers, like lobster empanadas and crab cakes, taste fairly authentic; rice and black beans are served with just about everything, of course, and the mojitos are renowned. $ *Average main: $25* ⊠ *10 S. 2nd St., Old City* ☎ *215/627–0666* ⊕ *www.cubalibrerestaurant.com* ⊗ *No lunch weekends.*

$$$$
AMERICAN
Fodor'sChoice
★

✕ **Fork.** Happy sounds have always emanated from diners in this comfortable, elegant eatery, but the menu of modern American fare went from tasty to transcendental when Eli Kulp took over the kitchen in early 2012. The chef is known for his innovative pastas, love of local meats, and mastery of fermentation. Sit as far back in the restaurant as possible to watch Kulp and his colleagues at work in the open kitchen. $ *Average main: $29* ⊠ *306 Market St., Old City* ☎ *215/625–9425* ⊕ *www.forkrestaurant.com* ⊗ *No lunch Sat.*

$
CAFÉ
FAMILY
Fodor'sChoice
★

✕ **Franklin Fountain.** You can't throw a wet walnut in Philly without hitting an artisanal ice cream maker these days, but brothers Ryan and Eric Berley and their charming Colonial-inspired scoop shop have newcomers beat by 11 years. On summer nights, long lines ripple out the door into the warm Old City night, but the wait (half an hour isn't uncommon in summer) is worth it for the house-made seasonal flavors like fresh peach, brooding black raspberry, and honeycomb made with booty from the Fountain's rooftop hives. $ *Average main: $5* ⊠ *116 Market St., Old City* ☎ *215/627–1899* ⊕ *www.franklinfountain.com* ⊗ *Closed weekdays in winter* ⟟ *Reservations not accepted.*

$$$
AMERICAN
Fodor'sChoice
★

✕ **High Street on Market.** This sunny, clean-cut younger sibling of perennial favorite, Fork, is half clubhouse for its Old City neighbors, half food tourist magnet (thanks to a flood of national press). Open all day, grain-brained High Street will take you from cortados and

Where to Eat in
Central Philadelphia

Map labels:
- Franklin Square
- Wood St.
- Vine St.
- New St.
- 95
- 676
- Benjamin Franklin Bridge
- Race St.
- N. 7th St.
- N. 6th St.
- N. 5th St.
- N. 4th St.
- N. 3rd St.
- N. 2nd St.
- Arch St.
- Historic Downtown
- Market St.
- Chestnut St.
- Independence National Historic Park
- Walnut St.
- ...ington ...uare
- S. 6th St.
- S. 5th St.
- S. 4th St.
- S. 3rd St.
- S. 2nd St.
- S. Front St.
- Delaware Expressway
- N. Christopher Columbus Blvd.
- Delaware River
- Society Hill
- Spruce St.
- Pine St.
- Delancey St.
- Lombard St.
- Gaskill St.
- South St.
- Bainbridge St.
- Monroe St.
- Fitzwater St.
- Queen Village
- Catharine St.
- Fulton St.
- Christian St.
- Queen St.
- 95
- S. 4th St.
- S. 3rd St.
- S. 2nd St.
- S. Front St.
- Washington Ave.
- Jefferson Square
- ...derat St.
- ...arton St.
- 0   500 M
- 0   1,000 ft

kougin-amans in the morning to duck liver meatball sandwiches in the afternoon to creative alt-flour pastas—matcha lasagna anyone?—at night. Eli Kulp is the acclaimed chef and partner, but the secret weapon is bread prodigy Alex Bois, a veteran of Sullivan Street bakery in New York. The James Beard Award Rising Star nominee just got a brand-new, double-deck MIWE oven, and his loaves have never been better. $ *Average main: $23* ⊠ *308 Market St., Old City* ☎ *215/625–0988* ⊕ *www.highstreetonmarket.com.*

$$ ✕ **Karma Restaurant and Bar.** Lots of Old City restaurants are all bark
INDIAN   and no bite, but Karma's the opposite. The interior is nothing more than a good effort, but the food will stick in your memory long after it's unstuck from your chops. Fresh naan, flavorful tikka masala—the menu is full of Indian standards that are done well. $ *Average main: $17* ⊠ *114 Chestnut St., Old City* ☎ *215/925–1444.*

$$$ ✕ **La Peg.** Peter Woolsey, whose tenured Bella Vista bistro, La Minette, is
MODERN FRENCH   beloved by Francophiles, bet big on an out-of-the-way Penn's Landing sequel named for his wife, Peggy. Housed in a former water pumping station, the digs are catnip for engineering and architecture nerds; rivet-studded I-beams crisscross the ceiling like a catwalk, and soaring arched windows overlook the brontosaurus hoof–like supports of the Ben Franklin Bridge. Woolsey's brassiere-inspired menu means plump Burgundy snails, poutine topped with beef Bourgogne, and le hamburger done with triple-crème cheese, onion jam, and brioche. $ *Average main: $20* ⊠ *140 N. Christopher Columbus Blvd., Old City* ☎ *215/375–7744* ⊕ *www.lapegbrasserie.com* ☽ *No lunch weekdays.*

$$$ ✕ **The Olde Bar.** This Jose Garces spot is located in the historic, bally-
SEAFOOD   hooed bones of Old Original Bookbinders, a fish house that catered to politicians, bigwigs, and celebrities in the 1950s. The handsome bar anchors the space in waves of carved mahogany; with nautical caged lights and low pressed-tin ceilings, it creates the vibe of a saloon on a luxurious ocean liner. The menu isn't chef-driven, but manages well with updates on seafood classics like snapper soup and lobster rolls, and the East and West Coast oysters are pristine. But the deep catalog of classic and original cocktails is the real reasons to come: black-peppered mules, elaborate swizzles, sours as foamy as the ocean surf, and an artisanal Grasshopper for a new generation of drinkers. $ *Average main: $20* ⊠ *125 Walnut St., Old City* ☎ *215/253– 3777* ⊕ *www.theoldebar. com* ☽ *No lunch weekdays* ⌸ *Reservations not accepted.*

$$$ ✕ **Plough and the Stars.** The cheery first floor of a renovated bank feels
IRISH   like a genuine Irish pub. A long bar with a dozen spigots is invariably spouting several imported and a few local brews. This is the place to get a Guinness poured the correct way. In winter, patrons crowd around a blazing fireplace on stools set around small tables. It's possible to munch on good Irish smoked salmon on grainy bread while imbibing; you can also head to the upstairs dining room for some respite from the crush and choose from a panoply of worldly appetizers, salads, and main courses. $ *Average main: $20* ⊠ *123 Chestnut St., enter on 2nd St., Old City* ☎ *215/733–0300* ⊕ *www.ploughstars.com.*

$$$ ✕ **Ristorante Panorama.** The name refers to a lovely mural rather than a
ITALIAN window view from this lively spot inside the Penn's View Hotel. The
restaurant has the largest wine cruvinet (storage system) in the country.
Besides more than 120 wines by the glass, there's a huge selection of
well-chosen bottles. You can sip them in Il Bar or in the main dining
room. The food is authentic Italian—simple and hearty. The ambience
is either noisy or animated, depending on your tolerance level. $ *Aver-
age main: $23* ✉ *14 N. Front St., Old City* ☎ *215/922–7800* ⊕ *www.
pennsviewhotel.com* ⊘ *No lunch Sun.*

SOCIETY HILL

$$$ ✕ **Bistro Romano.** Copious portions of regional Italian cuisine are served
ITALIAN in the brick-walled dining room of this early-18th-century granary.
FAMILY Don't miss the acclaimed Caesar salad prepared table-side by the genial
owner, who thoroughly enjoys animated conversations with his guests.
Tuesday-night lobster specials make the trip to the Society Hill area
more than worthwhile. $ *Average main: $24* ✉ *120 Lombard St., Society Hill* ☎ *215/925–8880* ⊕ *www.bistroromano.com* ⊘ *No lunch.*

$$ ✕ **Pizzeria Stella.** Owner Stephen Starr logged mucho hours and miles
PIZZA researching how to make the very best pizza. What's the best dough?
FAMILY The right amount of heat in the oven? The resulting artisanal, 12-inch
rounds with ingredients like black truffle, fresh prosciutto, and earthy
chanterelles are why the cozy 80-seater is always overflowing with neigh-
borhood duos and families. (A no-reservations policy necessitates getting
here very early or very late for no wait.) All tables are good tables—each
has a view of the red-and-white-tiled pizza oven at the restaurant's cen-
ter and of Headhouse Square through plenty of café windows. $ *Aver-
age main: $15* ✉ *420 S. 2nd St., Society Hill* ☎ *215/320–8000* ⊕ *www.
pizzeriastella.net* ⚠ *Reservations not accepted.*

$$$ ✕ **Zahav.** Chef Michael Solomonov has brought great buzz to several
MEDITERRANEAN restaurant locations in Philadelphia. With his latest entry, steeped in the
Fodor's Choice milk and honey and hummus and lamb of his native Israel—as well as
★ the cultures that have left a mark on that Promised Land—he's done it
again. Taking advantage of its dramatic perch above one of the city's
oldest streets, the stripped-down Zahav relies on architectural features
such as picture windows and soaring ceilings to create spectacle. The
open kitchen, on view behind leaded glass, is the true stage. There, a
small staff mixes and matches a melting pot of flavors for a modern
Israeli menu whose highlights include house-baked *laffa* (flatbread),
kebabs of impossibly tender chicken cooked over hot coals and served
with sumac onions and Israeli couscous, and addictive florets of fried
cauliflower served with a lemon-and-dill-spiked *lebneh* (yogurt cheese).
The legendary smoked and pomegranate juice-braised lamb shoulder
should be reserved in advance. $ *Average main: $23* ✉ *237 St. James
Pl., Society Hill* ☎ *215/625–8800* ⊕ *www.zahavrestaurant.com* ⊘ *No
lunch* ⚠ *Reservations essential.*

CENTER CITY

In Center City East (meaning the blocks east of Broad Street), most restaurants are near Washington Square and a few blocks west, along the bustling 13th Street corridor.

CENTER CITY EAST

$$ ⨉ **Amis.** The opening of this hip, industrial-chic trattoria by chef Marc
ROMAN Vetri rendered his talents more accessible to those who don't have the foresight to make reservations months in advance at his celebrated eponymous restaurant nearby. The small plates of Roman comfort food by longtime chef Brad Spence feature interesting elevated takes on Roman classics like *tonarelli cacio e pepe, trippa alla Romana,* and rigatoni *all'amatriciana.* Try to grab one of the six first-come, first-served stools at the chef's counter to watch the James Beard–award-winning action. Ⓢ *Average main: $18* ⊠ *412 S. 13th St., Center City East* ☎ *215/732–2647* ⊕ *www.amisphilly.com* ⊘ *No lunch* ⌂ *Reservations essential.*

$$ ⨉ **Barbuzzo.** This buzzing Mediterranean tapas joint has inspired an
MEDITERRANEAN almost religious devotion among nearly every demographic of Philadelphian. Diners happily stuff themselves into the cramped tables at this long, narrow eatery for a fix of the goat-cheese board, the egg-and-truffle pizza, and the house-made charcuterie. But above all, the salted caramel *budino* (a classic Italian pudding)—with so much demand, chef Marcie Turney figured out how to sell it online in a six-pack and turn it into ice cream pops in the summer—is heavenly. If you don't have a reservation, try and snag the bar and chef's counter, which are first-come, first-served. Ⓢ *Average main: $15* ⊠ *110 S. 13th St., Center City East* ☎ *215/546–9300* ⊕ *www.barbuzzo.com* ⊘ *No lunch Sun.*

$$$$ ⨉ **Capital Grille.** It's only fair to question whether Capital Grille is a
STEAKHOUSE restaurant or an art gallery. When you first enter the stunning dining room, you'll find walls covered with exquisitely framed paintings and pedestals bearing bronze statues. Steaks and chops for the power crowd come in two sizes: large and larger. A baby lobster (about a pound) makes an excellent appetizer along with the requisite green salad and shrimp cocktail. The wine cellar is ample and fairly priced for a selection of excellent bottles. Ⓢ *Average main: $32* ⊠ *1338 Chestnut St., Center City East* ☎ *215/545–9588* ⊕ *www. thecapitalgrille.com* ⊘ *No lunch weekends.*

$$ ⨉ **Effie's.** This restaurant doesn't get the attention it deserves, probably
GREEK because it's been here so long. The Greek taverna in a 19th-century brownstone in the middle of Pine Street's Antique Row serves casual country Greek basics that are consistently satisfying. There's always a selection of fresh fish that can be simply grilled and seasoned with olive oil and lemon. Ask for a seat in the courtyard if the weather's nice. Ⓢ *Average main: $18* ⊠ *1127 Pine St., Center City East* ☎ *215/592–8333* ⊕ *www.effiesrestaurant.com* ⊘ *No lunch.*

$$$ ⨉ **Garces Trading Company.** What started out as a Spanish-themed spe-
EUROPEAN cialty store selling Iberico jam, fancy honey, and rare cheeses has evolved into a full-service restaurant over the years. Chef Jose Garces's one-stop shop is a cheese and dessert counter, an olive oil and vinegar tasting bar,

and a 75-seat café rolled into one. The fare includes excellent pizza, pastas, and familiar plats du jour like paella and steak frites. $ *Average main: $22 ⊠ 1111 Locust St., Center City East* ☎ *215/574–1099* ⊕ *www.garcestradingcompany.com* ⚑ *Reservations essential.*

$$
MEXICAN
✕ **Lolita.** Lolita's recent 10-year anniversary brought a slew of changes and updates to the restaurant that kicked off the birth of Midtown Village district (not to mention chef Marcie Turney's career. The cantina now has a liquor license, lower prices, a credit card machine, crisp decor, and a menu that leaves behind the fusion clichés of the early aughts for house-made corn tortillas, duck-fat tamales, and nightly roasts cooked on a vertical spit. $ *Average main: $15 ⊠ 106 S. 13th St., Center City East* ☎ *215/546–7100* ⊕ *www.lolitaphilly.com* ⊘ *No lunch Sun.*

$$$
ITALIAN
✕ **Mercato.** This BYOB in a former corner food market is noisy, cramped, and cash-only. They have, however, started taking reservations and keep packing them in. Why? It's the Italian/New American bistro's attention to detail, visible in the exquisite artisanal cheese plate, the perfectly seared scallops, whole grilled artichoke, and the homemade triangle-shaped pasta. $ *Average main: $23 ⊠ 1216 Spruce St., Center City East* ☎ *215/985–2962* ⊕ *www.mercatobyob.com* ▭ *No credit cards* ⊘ *No lunch.*

$$
⚞IN AMERICAN
✕ **Mixto.** Latin American and Caribbean cuisine mix in an airy, two-story space on historic Antique Row, a few blocks below Broad Street. The place feels like a well-loved neighborhood joint, with its friendly vibe, heaping portions of slightly greasy food, and Latin music that sets the mood for some of the city's best mojitos. Occasionally the food reaches new heights, as with their paella Valenciana and some solid brunch offerings, including a delicious smoked salmon frittata. $ *Average main: $17 ⊠ 1141–43 Pine St., Center City East* ☎ *215/592–0363* ⊕ *www.mixtorestaurante.com* ⊘ *No lunch Mon. and Tues.*

$$$$
JAPANESE
✕ **Morimoto.** Stunningly expensive dishes created by celebrity chef Masaharu Morimoto (of the Food Network's *Iron Chef*) are served in an elegant, slightly futuristic setting. White plastic tables and benches glow beneath multicolored lights; the ceiling is undulating bamboo. *Omakase* (tasting menus), which run $100 to $150, are well worth the expense, as is the sushi, sliced with special knives Morimoto has handcrafted in Japan. Authentic and creative à la carte dishes include *toro* (tuna) with caviar and wasabi and tempura with Gorgonzola sauce. Reservations are recommended. $ *Average main: $37 ⊠ 723 Chestnut St., Center City East* ☎ *215/413–9070* ⊕ *www.morimotorestaurant.com* ⊘ *No lunch weekends.*

$$$$
AMERICAN
⚞dor's Choice
★
✕ **Talula's Garden.** Aimee Olexy's Talula's Table in Kennett Square was an unlikely phenomenon—the little country market had a months-long backlog of reservations for its lone farmhouse table. Olexy's urban extension of that runaway success has no market and plenty of tables inside a sprawling, high-ceilinged space decorated with Alice Waters quotations printed on the walls. A charming outdoor courtyard with a garden glows under twinkly lights. A game of musical chefs has not diminished the seasonal menu (dandelion greens Caesar, smoked summer corn ravioli), and the knowledgeable servers do a great job explaining interesting cheese boards with names like "Not Your Granny's" and "Secret Stash." $ *Average main: $27 ⊠ 210 W. Washington Sq., Center City East* ☎ *215/592–7787* ⊕ *www.talulasgarden.com* ⊘ *No lunch Mon.–Sat.*

$$ MODERN AMERICAN 🍴 **Vedge.** Less a restaurant than a roving dinner party spread among several rooms in a tony Center City brownstone, Vedge marked a shift for chefs Rich Landau and Kate Jacoby. At their longtime vegan spot, Horizons, the focus was on making non-meat look and taste like meat. Here, it's a celebration of vegetables, many of them sourced from nearby farms. Which is not to say you won't find tofu or seitan; you will, but they'll be starring as themselves, in landscapes of gorgeous produce touched by spices, smoke, and fermentations. Jacoby's ethereal desserts are can't-miss. [$] *Average main: $15* ✉ *1221 Locust St., Center City East* ☎ *215/320–7500* 🌐 *www.vedgerestaurant.com* 🕒 *No lunch.*

$$$$ ITALIAN 🍴 **Vetri.** When he's not opening new restaurants around the region (and most recently, in Austin, Texas), Philadelphia's foremost practicioner of Italian cooking, Marc Vetri, can be found at his eponymous ristorante just off Broad Street. In this lovely, sepia-toned town house (the original home of the late Le Bec-Fin) you can expect exquisite but superexpensive custom-built tasting menus that may involve freshly milled alt-grain pastas, quivering buffalo-milk mozzarella flown in from Campania, and long-standing classics like the golden onion crepe and roasted suckling goat. Don't try to eat here if you haven't made reservations. As an alternative, try booking one of Vetri's popular interactive classes or special dinners in the new upstairs dining room. [$] *Average main: $155* ✉ *1312 Spruce St., Center City East* ☎ *215/732–3478* 🌐 *www.vetriristorante.com* 🕒 *No lunch* ✍ *Reservations essential.*

CENTER CITY WEST

$$$$ AMERICAN 🍴 **XIX (Nineteen).** Occupying the 19th floor of the historic Hyatt at the Bellevue, XIX is a sophisticated American brasserie with Continental favorites like steak frites, lobster risotto, and crab cakes. Though the menu is not particularly unique, XIX remains a scene for its raw bar, Sunday brunch, and jaw-dropping views. [$] *Average main: $25* ✉ *200 S. Broad St., Center City West* ☎ *215/893–1234* 🌐 *www.hyatt.com* ✍ *Reservations essential.*

$$$$ STEAKHOUSE 🍴 **Palm.** Local movers and shakers broker deals here in the beige space off the lobby of the Hyatt at the Bellevue and beneath their own caricatures hanging on the wall. The steak-house ambience comes complete with bare floors, harried waiters, and huge steaks, chops, and salads whizzing by. The flavorful New York strip steak is fine at dinner, and the stupendous steak sandwich (*no* relation to a cheesesteak) is a lunchtime value. [$] *Average main: $42* ✉ *200 S. Broad St., Center City West* ☎ *215/546–7256* 🌐 *www.thepalm.com* 🕒 *No lunch weekends.*

CHINATOWN

$ CHINESE 🍴 **Lee How Fook.** Literally translated as "good food for the mouth," this unprepossessing spot is now being run by a second generation of restaurateurs. They do an excellent job with the most straightforward fare, like General Tso's chicken, hot-and-sour soup, and steamed dumplings filled with pulled pork, but they are best known for their salt-baked seafood and their hotpots. [$] *Average main: $8* ✉ *219 N. 11th St., Chinatown* ☎ *215/925–7266* 🌐 *www.leehowfookphilly.com* 🕒 *Closed Mon.*

$ CHINESE 🍴 **Ocean City.** It's mostly all locals eating at this smallish banquet space almost on the edge of Chinatown. Things can get a bit hectic with big-

screen TVs hanging from every corner, spangly chandeliers overh
and dim sum carts racing through the aisles. Snag a seat next to
kitchen to flag down the carts as they emerge. You won't often know
what's inside until you take a bite, but the dim sum is excellent and
definitely a bargain. $ *Average main: $11* ⊠ *234 N. 9th St., Chinatown*
☎ *215/829–0688.*

$ ✕ **Penang.** The juxtaposition of bamboo and exposed pipes is indicative
MALAYSIAN   of the surprising mix of flavors in this perennially busy restaurant. A
Fodor'sChoice   taste of India creeps into a scintillating appetizer of handkerchief-thin
★   crepes served with a small dipping dish of spicy chicken curry. Other
preparations are redolent of flavors from several other Asian countries.
Soups with various types of noodles are unusual, tasty, and filling.
$ *Average main: $13* ⊠ *117 N. 10th St., Chinatown* ☎ *215/413–2531*
▭ *No credit cards.*

$ ✕ **Rangoon.** Burmese food is somewhat Chinese and somewhat Indian,
ASIAN   with a touch of other tastes that make the mixture intriguing. The
spring ginger salad and thousand-layer bread served with a potato-
curry dipping sauce are both excellent. Portions are somewhat small,
but because of the fullness of the flavors, diners usually leave satisfied.
$ *Average main: $14* ⊠ *112 N. 9th St., Chinatown* ☎ *215/829–8939*
⊕ *www.rangoonrestaurant.com.*

$ ✕ **Reading Terminal Market.** When the Reading Company opened its train
ECLECTIC   shed in 1892, it was the only one in the country with a market tucked
FAMILY   away in its cellar. The trains are long gone, but the food remains. And
Fodor'sChoice   while disagreeing over the best cheesesteak is a popular pastime in Philly,
★   pretty much everyone can agree on pancakes at the Dutch Eating Place,
the roast pork sandwich at DiNic's, whoopie pies at the Flying Mon-
key, and double chocolate-chip cookies at Famous 4th Street. Recent
years have seen worthy newcomers to the entrenched mix: German deli
Wursthaus Schmitz, Valley Shepherd Creamery's grilled cheese counter,
and La Divisa Meats, for example. Get here early to beat the lunch rush.
Seventy-five-minute tours every Wednesday and Saturday highlight the
market's history and offerings (call *215/545–8007* to make a reservation). $ *Average main: $8* ⊠ *12th and Arch Sts., Chinatown* ☎ *215/922–*
2317 ⊕ *www.readingterminalmarket.org* ⌕ *Reservations not accepted.*

$ ✕ **Sang Kee Peking Duck House.** Although the decor is getting a bit tired,
CHINESE   this Chinatown stalwart continues to dish up delicious noodle soups. Egg
or rice noodles come in different widths and are simmered with duck,
pork, or beef brisket. If you wish, you can have your soup with both
noodles *and* overstuffed, tender wontons. Other traditional foods, besides
the house specialty, duck, are carried from the kitchen with more speed
than style. Beer is available. $ *Average main: $12* ⊠ *238 N. 9th St., Chi-*
natown ☎ *215/925–7532* ⊕ *sangkeechinatown.com* ▭ *No credit cards.*

$ ✕ **Vietnam.** Owner Benny Lai took what started as a noodle shop founded
VIETNAMESE   by his immigrant parents, bought up the building and the surrounding
Fodor'sChoice   property, and turned it into a chic restaurant with an upstairs lounge
★   serving small plates and wacky cocktails like the Flaming Volcano (two
straws included). In the dining room the best bets are the crispy spring
rolls, salted squid, barbecue platter, and soups with rice noodles. Don't
get this excellent restaurant confused with the not-excellent Vietnam

CLOSE UP

Where to Refuel Around Town

For those times when all you want is a quick bite—and you just can't face another cheesesteak or slice of pizza—consider these alternatives.

DiBruno Bros: This uptown outpost of the original Italian Market location is a one-stop gourmet shop where office workers, students, and ladies who lunch rub elbows midday to choose from the eat-in or take-out options. It's well placed for a picnic, with Rittenhouse Square just a few blocks away.

Italian Market: At 9th and Christian are a few lunch spots featuring hot pork and tripe sandwiches in addition to many varieties of hoagies. If you prefer fish, Anastasio's Fish Market at 9th and Washington also serves lunch and dinner.

Market at Comcast Center: The newest, tallest skyscraper in Philadelphia hides its sweet spot underground at the Market at Comcast Center, the best grab-a-bite scenario this side of Reading Terminal Market. Choose from sandwiches and salads from DiBruno Bros., nigiri by Tokyo Sushi, and cannoli by Termini Brothers Bakery.

Street Vendors: A number of lunch carts in Center City offer ethnic food, including Chinese, Japanese, Middle Eastern, and Italian, as well as the more standard hot dogs, hamburgers, and fresh fruit. (The vendor on the northwest corner of 16th and Walnut always has the ripest mango.) In University City the block between 37th and 38th on Sansom Street has various ethnic vendors catering to Penn students.

Palace across the street. [$] *Average main: $10* ✉ *221 N. 11th St., Chinatown* ☎ *215/592–1163* 🌐 *www.eatatvietnam.com* 💳 *No credit cards.*

RITTENHOUSE SQUARE

$ EASTERN EUROPEAN 🍴 **Abe Fisher.** Having successfully turned the country into Israeli food addicts, Michael Solomonov and Steve Cook have now turned their attention to the cuisines of the Ashkenazi Jews in Eastern Europe. Chef Yehuda Sichel is at the helm, creating incognito thrillers like broccoli kugel, black-truffle farfel, and skirt steak finished with Manischewitz steak sauce. Reserve ahead for the famous Montreal-style short rib dinner. [$] *Average main: $14* ✉ *1628 Sansom St., Rittenhouse Square* ☎ *215/867–0088* 🌐 *www.abefisherphilly.com.*

$$$$ MODERN AMERICAN Fodor's Choice ★ 🍴 **a.kitchen.** Smoke, coal, fire, and ash create a through-line for the menu at a.kitchen in the ground floor of the AKA Hotel. Attired in blonde wood and Carrera marble, it looks like a spa in the Italian Alps, and its Rittenhouse address guarantees a scene, but the recent involvement of High Street Hospitality (Fork, High Street on Market) and chef Jon Nodler have transformed it into a "Serious Restaurant" with an ace sommelier and a coals-seared beef tartare that cannot be missed. [$] *Average main: $25* ✉ *135 S. 18th St., Rittenhouse Square* ☎ *215/825–7030* 🌐 *www.akitchenandbar.com.*

$$$ CUBAN 🍴 **Alma de Cuba.** A bit of scrolled ironwork greets diners, followed by a swank bar pulsating with Cuban music that lets everyone know this

is a happening place. Find a seat here because you may wait a while, even with a reservation. The service is a bit chaotic, but the mojitos are refreshing and you won't be easily bored. The decor is evocative of pre-Castro Havana, with dim lighting, mod seating, and larger-than-life images of tobacco fields projected onto the walls. The menu contains a few genuine dishes, such as *lechon asado* (crispy roasted pork) and a wide selection of ceviche, all prepared by star chef Douglas Rodriguez. Although oysters are not generally considered Cuban, they're a knock-out here, served fried over *fufu* (mashed sweet plantains studded with bacon). $ *Average main: $24* ⊠ *1623 Walnut St., Rittenhouse Square* ☎ *215/988–1799* ⊕ *www.almadecubarestaurant.com* ⊙ *No lunch.*

$$ ✕ **Black Sheep.** Converted from a private club with blacked-out windows, this Dublin-style pub has been packing them in for rivers of
IRISH
Irish draft and kitchen specialties. Guinness-battered fish-and-chips could have been produced on the "auld sod," and the malt vinegar to sprinkle over it all does little to dampen the crisp crust. The first-floor bar is noisy and spirited—show up before happy hour to snag a seat—but the mood gets a bit quieter as you climb the steps to the dining room. $ *Average main: $17* ⊠ *247 S. 17th St., Rittenhouse Square* ☎ *215/545–9473* ⊕ *www.theblacksheeppub.com.*

$$$$ ✕ **Butcher & Singer.** One of restaurateur Stephen Starr's many ventures
STEAKHOUSE
is housed in an old wood-paneled and marbled brokerage (from which it borrows its name). Here the dishes are traditional rather than fancy (wedge salad, filet Oscar), portions are hefty, and the sides classic (green beans amandine, creamed spinach). A pair of showstopper chandeliers, a *New Yorker*–style mural depicting tony pooches clad in pencil skirts and smoking robes, and leather banquettes skew closely to the restaurant's avowed 1940s supper club aesthetic. The juicy, dripping burger is the word at lunch. $ *Average main: $34* ⊠ *1500 Walnut St., Rittenhouse Square* ☎ *215/732–4444* ⊕ *www.butcherandsinger.com* ⊙ *No lunch weekends.*

$ ✕ **Continental Mid-town.** You're not sure what decade you're in once
ECLECTIC
you enter the vast, retro playground that shares a name with the Old City martini lounge, also from blockbuster restaurateur Stephen Starr. The cognoscenti have moved on, but others still line up for a spot on the popular rooftop lounge or sit inside, in a swinging wicker basket chair, a sunken banquette, or a baby-blue vinyl booth. The global tapas menu includes Korean tacos, French onion soup dumplings, and lobster mac 'n' cheese. $ *Average main: $13* ⊠ *1801 Chestnut St., Rittenhouse Square* ☎ *215/567–1800* ⊕ *www.continentalmidtown.com.*

$$ ✕ **The Dandelion Pub.** This nonauthentic Stephen Starr–helmed pub is still
BRITISH
as close to an English pub as you'll get—there's a snarling bear head mounted on one wall; an assortment of mismatched divans and armchairs; and toasties, fish-and-chips, and puddings on the menu. The only clue the place just opened in 2010 is the freshness of the wall-to-wall carpeting—it doesn't smell anything like spilled pints. While the entrées are solid, the apps and desserts shine brightest at this sprawling, cozy venue. Anglophiles will rejoice over the afternoon tea service. $ *Average main: $18* ⊠ *124 S. 18th St., Rittenhouse Square* ☎ *215/558–2500* ⊕ *www.thedandelionpub.com.*

$ ✕ **Dizengoff.** Think of Dizengoff as Zahav lite. This graffiti-tagged spin-
ISRAELI   off of the nationally acclaimed Israeli restaurant is modeled after the
hummus stalls of Tel Aviv, specializing in the dreamy chickpea puree
crowned with an array of creative, seasonal toppings. Each bowl is
served on a plastic cafeteria tray with sharp pickles and fluffy, warm-
from-the-oven pita. When the pita runs out, Dizengoff rolls down its
garage door for the day. $ *Average main: $9* ✉ *1625 Sansom St., Rittenhouse Square* ☎ *215/867–8181* ⊕ *www.dizengoffphilly.com.*

$$$$ ✕ **Lacroix at the Rittenhouse.** Jonathan Cichon has proven himself to be
ECLECTIC   a worthy successor to this luxe establishment and one who forges his
Fodor'sChoice   own way with graceful dishes using seasonal, prestige ingredients. He is
★   bigger on elegance and shorter on whimsy than his predecessors, with
dishes like foie gras with mango, scallop terrine, and veal cheeks with
coconut, carrot, and plum. Combined with a 500-plus-label cellar of high-
end bottles and a gorgeous dining room overlooking Rittenhouse Square,
a meal here is guaranteed to be one of your most memorable. There's
also the $75 blowout Sunday brunch—a tremendous value, believe it or
not. $ *Average main: $45* ✉ *210 W. Rittenhouse Sq., Rittenhouse Square*
☎ *215/790–2533* ⊕ *www.lacroixrestaurant.com* ⧑ *Reservations essential.*

$$ ✕ **Monk's Cafe.** Whether steamed in classic style with wine and shallots
BELGIAN   or with cream, mussels are a high point at Monk's. The fries that accom-
pany them draw raves from the regulars who crowd the place. $ *Aver-
age main: $15* ✉ *264 S. 16th St., Rittenhouse Square* ☎ *215/545–7005*
⊕ *www.monkscafe.com.*

$$$ ✕ **PARC.** Restaurateur Stephen Starr's fondness for themes has reached
FRENCH   perfection in this vast but meticulous stage set placed on Philadelphia's
most desirable corner. Brass rails, silvered mirrors, claret-hued ban-
quettes, and oak wainscoting reclaimed from now-shuttered Parisian
restaurants, imbue patina—while small touches like newspapers on
wooden poles, create extra realism. Similarly, standard menu items
(roasted chicken, trout amandine) hold their own, but the little things—
desserts and salads, fresh-baked goods (including house-made maca-
roons), and excellent onion soup—stand out. Ask for an indoor-outdoor
table overlooking the park: you'll get generous views and the pleasant
din of the 150 diners behind you without the deafening buzz that is
the restaurant's one true downside. $ *Average main: $22* ✉ *227 S. 18th
St., Rittenhouse Square* ☎ *215/545–2262* ⊕ *www.parc-restaurant.com.*

$$ ✕ **Pub & Kitchen.** Pub & Kitchen has been a favorite since it opened in
MODERN   2009, but the food has never been better since chef Eli Collins relocated
AMERICAN   here from Daniel Boulud's empire a couple years ago. From house-
Fodor'sChoice   baked whisky-sage bread to gnudi crafted with local ricotta to a kick-
★   ass cheeseburger, Collins can really cook. But even if he couldn't, locals
would flock to this energetic saloon to unwind with friends or catch
the game. In what used to be a dive bar, P&K is an unpretentious,
attractive hangout with hardwood floors, exposed brick walls, tables
fashioned from reclaimed floor joists, and familiar rock music playing
from the speakers. $ *Average main: $17* ✉ *1946 Lombard St., Ritten-
house Square* ☎ *215/545–0350* ⊕ *www.thepubandkitchen.com* ☽ *No
lunch weekdays* ⧑ *Reservations not accepted.*

$$$ MODERN AMERICAN 🍴 **Square 1682.** Stylish young city dwellers visit the bar and lounge at the arty Hotel Palomar (the city's first Kimpton Hotel) because it's a great place for a cocktail and a trendy bar snack. For dinner, you ascend a floating staircase to an upstairs dining room and settle into a plush banquette to sample deviled duck eggs, kale Caesar, and pea-and-carrot gnocchi scented with vanilla. [$] *Average main: $22* ✉ *Palomar Hotel, 121 S. 17th St., Rittenhouse Square* ☎ *215/563–5008* 🌐 *www.square1682.com.*

$$$ MEXICAN 🍴 **Tequila's Restaurant.** David and Annette Suro opened Tequila's way back in 1986, when the local culinary consciousness wasn't quite as familiar with mole poblano and chiles rellenos as it is now. Fortunately, the space was evocative enough (painted Day of the Dead figures, a long hardwood bar, Mexican glassware, colorful ceramics) to get the curious and unfamiliar in the door. The couple has been going strong since, with a deep menu of authentic Mexican plates and, of course, the city's best tequila list. [$] *Average main: $23* ✉ *1602 Locust St., Rittenhouse Square* ☎ *215/546–0181* 🌐 *www.tequilasphilly.com.*

$$$$ SPANISH 🍴 **Tinto Wine Bar.** Chef Jose Garces went to Spain to research food and wine for Amada, his Old City tapas restaurant, and while he was there he fell in love with Basque Country. Tinto is his ode to the bars in San Sebastian that serve up *pinxtos* (small plates), *bocadillos* (sandwiches), charcuterie, and cheeses. Always inventive and never showy, Garces's take on the regional cuisine is defined by surprising combinations—like a morsel of duck confit topped with a black cherry and served on blue cheese–smeared toasted bread. The Basque wine list pairs perfectly. [$] *Average main: $25* ✉ *114 S. 20th St., Rittenhouse Square* ☎ *215/665–9150* 🌐 *www.tintorestaurant.com* 🕑 *No lunch.*

$ AMERICAN 🍴 **Tria.** Tria's brown interior and minimalist signage give off a wallflower vibe, but the tables packed with chic urbanites grazing lightly belie its inner beauty. The knowledgeable staff is serious about the restaurant's focus—the "fermentation trio" of wine, cheese, and beer—but not in a snobby way. They'll casually toss off suggestions for a cheese plate that's a phenomenal medley of textures and flavors. Then they'll recommend a zippy white wine that sets it off perfectly. The café has gotten so popular, it's multiplied several times. [$] *Average main: $10* ✉ *123 S. 18th St., Rittenhouse Square* ☎ *215/972–8742* 🌐 *www.triacafe.com.*

$$ AMERICAN 🍴 **Twenty Manning.** The second venture from local girl made good Audrey Claire Taichman was a hit from the moment it opened in 2000, and is an even bigger one following its 2010 makeover. Large French windows open up onto the sidewalk where tables are always packed in the warmer months with chic young couples and klatches sipping old-fashioneds and Bellinis and supping on plates like oysters on the half, tuna burgers, and beef sirloin noodles scented with lemongrass. [$] *Average main: $18* ✉ *261 S. 20th St., Rittenhouse Square* ☎ *215/731–0900* 🌐 *www.twentymanning.com* 🕑 *No lunch.*

$$$$ MODERN AMERICAN Fodor's Choice ★ 🍴 **Vernick Food & Drink.** South Jersey native Greg Vernick spent the bulk of his career opening restaurants around the world for Jean-Georges Vongerichten. When he and his wife, Julie, wanted to do their own place, they came back to the Delaware Valley and made waves with their bustling (but intimate) bi-level debut a couple of blocks off Rittenhouse. Vernick checks all the boxes of what it means to be a modern American restaurant

in 2016: delicious things on toast, Asian influences, large-format proteins cooked in a wood-burning oven, rosés a-go-go, uni. Expect it all rendered in thoughtful, joyful expressions, and served by a vivacious staff. [$] *Average main: $28* ✉ *2031 Walnut St., Rittenhouse Square* ☎ *267/639–6644* 🌐 *www.vernickphilly.com* 🕓 *Closed Mon.*

THE BENJAMIN FRANKLIN PARKWAY AND FAIRMOUNT

Think of the Benjamin Franklin Parkway as Philadelphia's Museum Row. Around the dignified boulevard are quick-stop cafés and restaurants catering to the fanny pack–wearing crowds, but just north of the Parkway, you'll find lively neighborhood joints and charming BYOBs in residential Fairmount.

FAIRMONT

$$$ MEDITERRANEAN 🍴 **Figs.** A large fig tree sets the tone for this simple restaurant. Some Moroccan specialties are woven through the menu. Otherwise, the flavors of the Mediterranean permeate. The baked Brie in clay pot appetizer with honey, lavender, and almonds is a standout; usually there's a good *tagine* (stew of meat or poultry simmered with vegetables, olives, garlic, and spices) on the menu. [$] *Average main: $21* ✉ *2501 Meredith St., Fairmount* ☎ *215/978–8440* 🌐 *www.figsrestaurant.com* 💳 *No credit cards* 🕓 *Closed Mon.*

$$ MEXICAN FAMILY 🍴 **La Calaca Feliz.** A mural of freewheeling Day of the Dead skeletons gives this neon Fairmount cantina its name, but the polished ceviches, tacos, and enchiladas from Jose Garces veteran, Tim Spinner, are what will really make you happy. A deep tequila library informs the bar and cocktail list; try a flight of añejos or margaritas in flavors like lychee and chili. [$] *Average main: $17* ✉ *2321 Fairmount Ave., Fairmount* ☎ *215/787–9930* 🌐 *www.lacalacafeliz.com* 🕓 *No lunch.*

$$$ AMERICAN 🍴 **London Grill.** Located down the street from Eastern State Pen, London Grill has been around for decades but has never been better than right now. They've annexed an old doctor's office next door and turned it into Paris Wine Bar and continue to reinvent the dinner with on-trend choices like ricotta toast with heirloom tomatoes, Korean fried chicken, and foie mousse on banana bread. Because it's so close to the Art Museum, the restaurant often offers special menus to coincide with blockbuster exhibits, and brunch features a build-your-own Bloody Mary bar. [$] *Average main: $23* ✉ *2301 Fairmount Ave., Fairmount* ☎ *215/978–4545* 🌐 *www.londongrill.com.*

SOUTH PHILADELPHIA

South Philly is a mosaic of many different neighborhoods, from leafy Queen Village to scrappy Newbold. Over the past few years, ascendant East Passyunk Avenue (the main thoroughfare of the neighborhood of the same name) has emerged as the city's eminent dining strip; there are more critically acclaimed restaurants on the avenue's five-block central stretch than anywhere else in town.

SOUTH PHILADELPHIA

$ 🍴**Federal Donuts.** Haters snickered when the crew from Zahav opened a doughnut–and–fried-chicken shop on an obscure corner of residential Pennsport in 2011. They're still eating their words—and hopefully, the fantastic Korean-style bird dusted in Israeli za'atar, hands-down the city's best fried chicken. FedNuts, as locals affectionately call it, has since expanded into other neighborhoods, but the snug South Philly original remains the most charming with its foldout bar stools and hipster-meets-Mummer crowd. On the doughnut front, the made-each-morning "Fancies" entice with flavors like Chocolate Eclair and Grapefruit Brulee, but the "Hot Fresh" ones rolled warm in lavender and cinnamon sugars are almost always more satisfying. [$] *Average main: $10* ✉ *1219 S. 2nd St., South Philadelphia* ☎ *267/687–8258* 🌐 *www.federaldonuts.com.*

CAFÉ
FAMILY

$ 🍴**Jamaican Jerk Hut.** The liquid of choice at this BYOB is rum, to mix with the Hut's selection of house-made mixers like carrot milk and ginger-and-clove spiced sorrel (hibiscus) tea. Jamaican-American owner Lisa Wilson recently took over this mainstay from original owner Nicola Shirley, but the jerk pork and chicken lovingly tenderized over an authentic pit are as good as ever. Cranky neighbors succeeded in getting the charming adjacent garden shut down (developers are building apartments there now) but the festive atmosphere, and spirit, remains [$] *Average main: $14* ✉ *1436 South St., South Philadelphia* ☎ *215/545–8644* 🌐 *jajerkhut.com.*

CARIBBEAN

$ 🍴**John's Roast Pork.** Housed in a cinder-block bunker along a derelict railroad crossing, John's is the quintessential purveyor of roast pork sandwiches. Newbies and lifers line up in a zigzag along the counter and grab seats at the picnic tables outside. The signature pork is juicy, garlicky, and herbaceous; sharp provolone and sautéed spinach (no broccoli rabe here) are de rigueur. John's incidentally makes the city's best cheesesteak, too, and if you're up and exploring early, fantastic breakfast sandwiches lined with fluffy eggs and deep-fried pucks of scrapple. [$] *Average main: $7* ✉ *14 E. Snyder Ave., South Philadelphia* ☎ *215/463–1951* 🌐 *www.johnsroastpork.com* ⏲ *Closed Sun.* ✍ *Reservations not accepted* 💳 *No credit cards.*

DELI
FAMILY
Fodor's Choice ★

$$$$ 🍴**Pumpkin.** Dinner at Pumpkin's produce-driven menu changes daily depending on what has inspired self-taught chef Ian Moroney on that particular day. A $40 five-course tasting menu on Sundays highlights such fresh, eclectic fare as squash blossoms stuffed with sheep's milk cheese, heirloom tomato panzanella, and culotte steak with bacon jus. Calling ahead is essential to snagging a spot in the 28-seat, elbow-to-elbow dining room. [$] *Average main: $25* ✉ *1713 South St., South Philadelphia* ☎ *215/545–4448* 🌐 *www.pumpkinphilly.com* 💳 *No credit cards* ⏲ *Closed Mon. No lunch.*

AMERICAN

$ 🍴**South Philadelphia Tap Room.** Once upon a time, before South Philly was home to the city's hottest zip codes, a little wood-clad tavern named South Philadelphia Tap Room opened with a roster of local, craft beers in the largely Miller-Coors enclave. Twelve years later, the Newbold neighborhood has grown up around this catalyst (SPTR's owner actually coined the name), and the bar has established a reputation for

MODERN AMERICAN
FAMILY
Fodor's Choice ★

Where to Eat in Greater Philadelphia

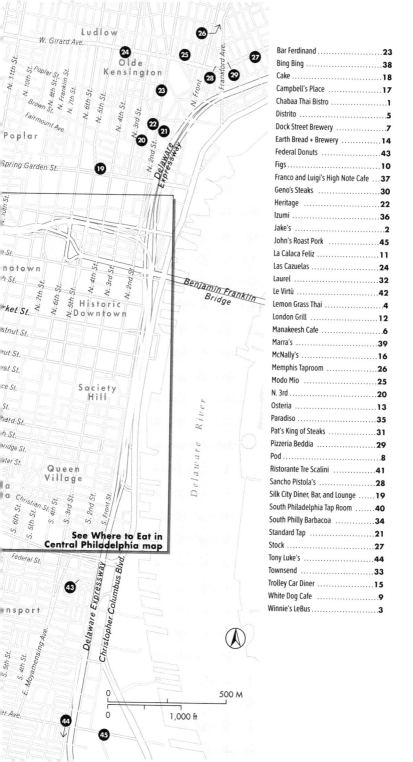

See Where to Eat in
Central Philadelphia map

0   500 M

0   1,000 ft

sourcing some of the best and most exclusive beers around the country. Longtime chef Scott Schroeder is one of the city's most underappreciated; on his menu you can count on grilled halloumi snacks, assertively seasoned salads, and bluefish that will make you love bluefish. Local, organic produce and meats are the focus, served with none of the associated boasting. [$] *Average main: $12* ✉ *1509 Mifflin St., South Philadelphia* ☎ *215/271–7787* 🌐 *www.southphiladelphiataproom.com* ✍ *Reservations not accepted.*

$ AMERICAN 🍴 **Tony Luke's.** The original location—nearly under I–95—earned such a reputation from truckers who stopped for huge beef or pork sandwiches with Italian greens and cheese that locals finally caught on and adopted the dinerlike establishment for their own. The lines are long, though they move quickly, and seating (outside only, under cover) is relatively scarce; still, people flock here from early morning to closing time for generous breakfasts and tasty sandwiches. For large orders, it's possible to call ahead for takeout. [$] *Average main: $6* ✉ *39 E. Oregon Ave., South Philadelphia* ☎ *215/551–5725* 🌐 *www.tonylukes.com* 💳 *No credit cards.*

EAST PASSYUNK

$ ASIAN FUSION 🍴 **Bing Bing.** Funky, unorthodox dim sum gets the graphic artists, indie film producers, and jewelry designers (and all their visiting parents) in the door at Bing Bing. But beyond the high-low appeal of hot dogs swaddled in steamed bao and everything-spice buns with lox and furikake cream cheese, there's real finesse with the doughs and dumplings by chef Ben Puchowitz. For a place that proudly bills itself as inauthentic, Bing Bing gets all the important stuff right. Bonus points for tiger-strength cocktail pitchers and booths fashioned out of Chinese wedding beds. [$] *Average main: $12* ✉ *1648 E. Passyunk Ave., East Passyunk* ☎ *215/279–7702* 🌐 *www.bingbingdimsum.com* 🕒 *No lunch weekdays* 💳 *No credit cards.*

$$ ITALIAN FAMILY 🍴 **Franco and Luigi's High Note Cafe.** Arias from classic operas, sung mostly by fresh-faced young singers who are in training or have done professional stints around Philadelphia and other cities, accompany somewhat unusual, but unquestionably Italian dishes such as veal, shrimp, and scallops sautéed in scampi sauce over a bed of shredded radicchio. Reserve well in advance to ensure seating on weekends. [$] *Average main: $19* ✉ *1547 S. 13th St., East Passyunk* ☎ *215/755–8903* 🌐 *www.francoluigis.com* 🕒 *Closed Mon.*

$ AMERICAN 🍴 **Geno's Steaks.** Geno's is a regular upstart compared to rival Pat's. The latter's been serving sandwiches since 1930; Geno's opened in 1966. That divide manifests itself visually in the contrast between Pat's understated aesthetic and Geno's over-the-top use of neon. The place is lit up so brightly that astronauts can probably see it from space. The other big difference is that Geno's meat is sliced (not chopped). Some aficionados claim that the two serve wildly dissimilar products; others just don't get it, but it's always fun to taste-test, as the buses full of tourists who frequently make their way down Passyunk to Pat's and Geno's can attest. [$] *Average main: $8* ✉ *1219 S. 9th St., East Passyunk* ☎ *215/389–0659* 🌐 *www.genosteaks.com* 💳 *No credit cards* ✍ *Reservations not accepted.*

$$$ JAPANESE Fodor's Choice ★ 🍴 **Izumi.** Facing East Passyunk's nucleus, the Singing Fountain, Izumi (a BYO) is always packed with people toting everything from cult sake to Santa Margherita to drink with creative raw and cooked Japanese dishes. Think scallops and burrata on wasabi crepes, seared pork belly congree, and lots of fresh uni served in their spiky shells. [$] *Average main: $23* ✉ *1601 E. Passyunk Ave., East Passyunk* ☎ *215/271–1222* 🌐 *www.izumiphilly.com* 🕒 *Closed Mon. No lunch.*

$$$$ MODERN AMERICAN Fodor's Choice ★ 🍴 **Laurel.** Reservations were tough to procure at Laurel before Nicholas Elmi won Top Chef's 11th season. Since then, the 26 seats at the intimate, candlelit hideaway book months in advance—but are worth the effort for Elmi's brand of elegant, intelligent American food, presented in a seven-course tasting menu format only five nights a week. Plans are in the works to annex the empty space next door, which will add seating and a liquor license. [$] *Average main: $85* ✉ *1617 E. Passyunk Ave., East Passyunk* ☎ *215/271–8299* 🌐 *www.restaurantlaurel.com* 🕒 *Closed Sun. and Mon. No lunch* ✍ *Reservations essential.*

$$$ ITALIAN 🍴 **Le Virtù.** Sublime charcuterie, ethereal pastas, and interesting wines by the glass are just a few of the details that make Le Virtù one of the best Italian restaurants in town. The sun-washed, terra-cotta–and–buttercup-colored space began with a fierce dedication to the region of Abruzzo, where the owners run culinary tours; that focus has been both broadened *and* more deeply explored under the direction of chef Joe Cicala. Keep an eye out for Le Virtù's events, which range from rare wine tastings to performances by visiting Abruzzese musicians. And don't miss the unique and always delicious desserts from Cicala's wife, Angela Ranalli. [$] *Average main: $24* ✉ *1927 E. Passyunk Ave., East Passyunk* ☎ *215/271–5626* 🌐 *www.levirtu.com* 🕒 *No lunch.*

$$ ITALIAN FAMILY Fodor's Choice ★ 🍴 **Marra's.** One of the longest-tenured restaurants on East Passyunk, this wood-paneled red-gravy hall dates back to the 1920s and oozes South Philly charm. Listen carefully, and you can hear the *thwack* of the chefs pounding veal cutlets for gigantic Parmigianas over the chatter of the been-there-forever waitresses. The cocktail list has changed so little, it doesn't even realize its Rob Roys and Rusty Nails are back in style. [$] *Average main: $16* ✉ *1734 E. Passyunk Ave., East Passyunk* ☎ *215/463–9249* 🌐 *www.marrasone.com* 🕒 *Closed Mon.*

$$$ ITALIAN 🍴 **Paradiso.** When chef Lynne Rinaldi opened Paradiso in 2005 two blocks from where she grew up, she sparked a restaurant renaissance in a section of South Philadelphia formerly known as a source for spaghetti with gravy. By proving that an upscale, sleek eatery can flourish in what was once Rocky country, Rinaldi has developed a reputation as a pioneer and a devoted following. Favorites includes the house-made pastas (especially gnocchi), but Rinaldi is also a talented handler of vegetables, many of them grown on the rooftop garden. [$] *Average main: $21* ✉ *1627 E. Passyunk Ave., East Passyunk* ☎ *215/271–2066* 🌐 *www.paradisophilly.com* 🕒 *Closed Mon. No lunch weekends* ✍ *Reservations not accepted.*

$ AMERICAN 🍴 **Pat's King of Steaks.** New cheesesteak restaurants come and go all the time, but two of the oldest—Pat's and Geno's, at the corner of 9th and Passyunk—have a long-standing feud worth weighing in on. It comes down to a matter of taste. Both serve equally generous portions of rib-eye steak, grilled onions, and melted provolone, American, or Cheez Whiz on freshly baked Italian rolls. The main differences as far as we can tell: Pat's claims to have invented the cheesesteak; Pat's meat is chopped; and Pat's exterior is a bit more understated than Geno's neon extravaganza. [$] *Average main: $8* ✉ *1237 E. Passyunk Ave., East Passyunk* ☎ *215/468–1546* 🌐 *patskingofsteaks.com* 💳 *No credit cards.*

$$ ITALIAN FAMILY 🍴 **Ristorante Tre Scalini.** When this restaurant in South Philadelphia, a locus of down-home Italian, moved from a cozy town house to a generic storefront down the street, patrons worried that the food would suffer. Happily the old favorites, which are more homey than trendy, are intact. Signature dishes like the grilled polenta with broccoli rabe and bruschetta calamari with cannellini beans are carefully prepared and amply plated. Pasta dishes—such as lobster- and cheese-filled ravioli and black pasta with prawns and crabmeat—are best. [$] *Average main: $18* ✉ *1915 E. Passyunk Ave., East Passyunk* ☎ *215/551–3870* 🌐 *www.trescaliniphiladelphia.com* 🕒 *Closed Mon. No lunch.*

$ MEXICAN Fodor's Choice ★ 🍴 **South Philly Barbacoa.** Benjamin Miller and Cristina Martinez have moved their popular weekend taco cart into a permanent no-frills space populated with an industry crowd, Mexican families, food bloggers, and local artists like Isaiah Zagar, whose signature mosaics encrust the restaurant's facade. The weekend-only hours have are now supplemented by weekday lunch hours, too. The couple's namesake specialty remains the same: *barbacoa*, the succulent, slow-cooked lamb of Martinez's homeland. Miller and Martinez chop the meat with a cleaver and pile it on fluffy corn tortillas, which you top at the salsa station with cactus paddle *rajas*, onion-laced jalapeno *escabeche*, chopped cilantro, and fresh lime. Wash 'em down with pastel, tropical fruit aguas frescas in summer and warm, thick, animal-cracker *atoles* in the winter. Go early; though open until 5 on weekends, they often sell out by 3 pm. [$] *Average main: $12* ✉ *1702 S. 11th St., East Passyunk* ☎ *215/694–3797* 🕒 *Closed Mon. No dinner* ✍ *Reservations not accepted* 💳 *No credit cards.*

$$$$ MODERN FRENCH 🍴 **Townsend.** You might expect something majorly molecular from former biochemist Townsend "Tod" Wentz, but the cooking at his eponymous restaurant in East Passyunk is anchored in (but not hamstrung by) French tradition. Think escargots, pot au feu, architectural cheese plates, and sauces that cloak the tongue like silk pajamas. It's all served by a supersmart staff in charcoal-and-cobalt uniforms; the young GM/sommelier trains them in the offbeat wines she curates from producers in Austria, Alicante, and the Sierra Foothills. Late-night, the bar is a magnet for an industry crowd. [$] *Average main: $25* ✉ *1623 E. Passyunk Ave., East Passyunk* ☎ *267/639–3203* 🌐 *www.townsendrestaurant.com* 🕒 *Closed Tues. No lunch.*

BELLA VISTA

$$ FRENCH 🍴 **Beau Monde.** Imported cast-iron griddles are the secret to this crêperie's paper-thin wrappers. In this city, at least, this is the closest you'll find to the crepes of Brittany, where the owners of this casual bistro traveled to study. The menu is split into savory crepes (made with buckwheat flour) and sweet crepes (made with wheat flour). Some tried-and-true combos are ratatouille, goat cheese, and andouille sausage; and ham and Gruyère. The cheese plate is a great value, and there's

Philly's 7 Best Brunch Spots

Just as Philadelphians are famous for their disputes over who makes the best cheesesteak, the best hoagie roll, the best water ice, and the best cannoli, each neighborhood has its own ongoing debate for which weekend morning haunt has the best brunch.

Even still, there's little debate that there are a few exceptional standouts. In no particular order, here are the city's top contenders.

- Beau Monde, Bella Vista
- High Street on Market, Old City
- Lacroix at the Rittenhouse, Rittenhouse Square
- Sam's Morning Glory Diner, Bella Vista
- PARC, Rittenhouse Square
- Sabrina's Café, Bella Vista
- South Philadelphia Tap Room, South Philadelphia

plenty on the menu for vegetarians. When the weather behaves, alfresco dining is an option. $ *Average main: $16* ⊠ *624 S. 6th St., Bella Vista* ☎ *215/592–0656* ⊕ *www.creperie-beaumonde.com.*

$$$$ ✕ **Bibou.** Tiny Bibou is one of the city's best BYOBs, as evidenced by how
FRENCH many tables are occupied by French natives who'd otherwise seem out of place in this tiny restaurant on this residential South Philly block. The other proof is in the intensely flavorful food, from perfectly crisped scallops to pig's feet stuffed with foie gras. The restaurant is a true *maman et père*—Charlotte will charm you, and her husband, chef Pierre Calmel, will emerge from the kitchen to ask how you liked the sweetbreads. The restaurant recently went all-tasting; $100 gets you seven courses, cash-only. $ *Average main: $28* ⊠ *1009 S. 8th St., Bella Vista* ☎ *215/965–8290* ⊕ *www.biboubyob.com* ⊟ *No credit cards* ⌂ *Reservations essential.*

$$$ ✕ **Bistrot La Minette.** The cheery atmosphere inside the long, narrow bis-
FRENCH tro and in the outside courtyard illuminated by candles and twinkling strings of lights exudes warmth and attention to detail, from the flea-market knickknacks picked out by Chef Peter Woolsey and his French wife in Burgundy to the ceramic pitchers of house wine delivered to your table. Woolsey studied at the Cordon Bleu, fell in love with French food, culture, and his wife, a Frenchwoman, and came back to his native Philadelphia to share the bistro experience with his countrymen. The place has quickly become a neighborhood favorite, with regulars swearing by some standouts including the Alsatian-style Flammenkuchen appetizer of caramelized onions, bacon lardoons, and crème fraîche on flatbread; the perfectly simple lemon sole in white-wine butter sauce; and the light and airy beignets that speak to Woolsey's extensive training as a pastry chef. $ *Average main: $23* ⊠ *623 S. 6th St., Bella Vista* ☎ *215/925–8000* ⊕ *bistrotlaminette.com* ⊙ *No lunch weekdays.*

$ ✕ **Paesano's Philly Style.** Philly's cheesesteaks are famous, but hoagie
ITALIAN shops like Paesano's make more artful (and often drippier and more
dor's Choice gluttonous) sandwiches without the long lines. These gut busters just
★ may stop your heart. Favorites are the Bolognese, a fried-lasagna and fried-egg concoction; and the Liveracce, seared chicken livers topped

with sautéed onions, roasted tomato, and Gorgonzola. Sandwiches ar made behind an open counter while regulars (and tourists studying th chalkboard menu in disbelief) wait. Gluten-free bread is always avail able. [$] *Average main: $8* ✉ *1017 S. 9th St., Bella Vista* ☎ *215/440-0371* 🌐 *www.paesanosphillystyle.com* ✍ *Reservations not accepted.*

$$ CAFÉ FAMILY
🍴 **Sabrina's Cafe.** If there's one thing you can count on, it's an hour wai for Sunday brunch at this cozy former bakery around the corner fron the Italian Market. Locals know to phone in their names and wait i out with coffee and the paper at home, and you can, too. Here's wha everyone is waiting for: apple and sharp cheddar omelets, stuffed an caramelized challah French toast with vanilla-bean maple syrup, an the barking Chihuahua breakfast (a burrito filled with scrambled eggs black beans, red peppers, and pepper-jack cheese). [$] *Average main: $1* ✉ *910 Christian St., Bella Vista* ☎ *215/574–1599* 🌐 *www.sabrinascafe com* ⏲ *No dinner* ✍ *Reservations not accepted.*

$$$$ STEAKHOUSE
🍴 **The Saloon.** For many years this classic wood-panel restaurant ha been a favorite among Philadelphia's most discerning diners, wh enjoyed steaks and chops in more-than-generous portions and th always-true-to-their-roots Italian specialties. The superior quality o ingredients still shines, but the menu now has some innovative twist on the preparations (although not so many that they intrude on th sensibilities of the regulars). [$] *Average main: $30* ✉ *750 S. 7th St. Bella Vista* ☎ *215/627–1811* 🌐 *www.saloonrestaurant.net* ⏲ *Close Sun. No lunch Sat. and Mon.*

$ AMERICAN FAMILY
🍴 **Sam's Morning Glory Diner.** The Morning Glory bills itself as a "fine diner," and offers traditional touches such as big mugs of steaming cof fee. But the "finer" comes in the updated, wholesome versions of dine fare such as homemade ketchup on every table, grilled ahi tuna with wasabi mayo on a brioche bun, thick pecan waffles with whipped peacl butter, and enormous, flaky biscuits that accompany breakfast. Unles you're an early weekend riser, weekdays are a better bet. The wait fo weekend brunch can be epic. [$] *Average main: $8* ✉ *735 S. 10th St. Bella Vista* ☎ *215/413–3999* 🌐 *www.themorningglorydiner.com* 💳 *N credit cards* ⏲ *No dinner* ✍ *Reservations not accepted.*

$$$$ MODERN AMERICAN Fodor's Choice ★
🍴 **Serpico.** After earning a James Beard Award for his work at Momo fuku Ko in New York, Peter Serpico teamed up with restaurateur Ste phen Starr and opened this slick, glass-and-onyx box in a rehabbed Foo Locker on South Street. Ingredients like XO sauce and yuzu kosho an dishes like Korean-fried chicken and a stunning dashi suggest an Asiar undercurrent to the menu, but Serpico's flow is just as likely to featur textbook charcuterie, sumptuous vegetable compositions, and confiden riffs on lasagna and ravioli. [$] *Average main: $26* ✉ *604 South St. Bella Vista* ☎ *215/925–3001* 🌐 *www.serpicoonsouth.com* ⏲ *No lunch*

$ GREEK FAMILY
🍴 **South Street Souvlaki.** The first thing you'll see is the large rotisserie trumpeting the ubiquitous gyro—tasty slices of meat are stuffed insid a large fresh pita, with tangy yogurt and some exemplary fresh veggies Other Greek specialties, such as stuffed grape leaves, moussaka, and, o course, souvlaki, round out the menu. No pomp and circumstance here— just casual taverna fare and service that's often indifferent. But they mus be doing something right—Souvlaki has been going strong since 1977

definitely a record on this mercurial street. A new, slightly upscale bistro recently debuted upstairs. [$] *Average main: $12* ✉ *509 South St., Bella Vista* ☎ *215/925–3026* 🌐 *www.southstreetsouvlaki.com* 🕒 *Closed Mon.*

$$$ AMERICAN 🍴 **Supper.** Supper was a pioneer in the city's now-thunderous farm-to-table stampede. Chef Mitch Prensky serves small plates of New American fare sourced from a Bucks County farm. A found-object chandelier made with JELL-O molds and kitchen utensils sets the tone for the menu's clever, whimsical twists on comfort food. Standouts include dayboat scallops with beet-green spanakopita and a confit duck leg on a pecan-sage waffle. The Sunday brunch is especially comforting and delicious. Foodies settle happily into this casual, polished dining room that's all warm woods with pops of orange. [$] *Average main: $24* ✉ *928 South St., Bella Vista* ☎ *215/592–8180* 🌐 *www.supperphilly.com* 🕒 *Closed Mon. No lunch weekdays.*

3

QUEEN VILLAGE

$$ GREEK 🍴 **Dmitri's.** This no-frills eatery has developed a loyal following thanks to its light Mediterranean touch with the freshest of seafood. Locals happily withstand long waits and sitting elbow-to-elbow with their neighbors in order to dip pita wedges into airily whipped hummus and to fork tender chunks of grilled octopus brushed with olive oil and lemon juice. [$] *Average main: $17* ✉ *795 S. 3rd St., Queen Village* ☎ *215/625–0556* 🌐 *www.dmitrisrestaurant.com* 💳 *No credit cards* 🕒 *No lunch* ✍ *Reservations not accepted.*

$ AMERICAN FAMILY 🍴 **Jim's Steaks.** You'll know you're nearing Jim's when the scent of frying onions overwhelms your senses—or when you see people lined up around the corner. Big, juicy, drippy sandwiches of Philly steaks—shaved beef piled high on long crusty rolls—come off the grill with amazing speed when the counter workers hit their stride; but be aware that no matter how hard you beg, they will not toast the rolls. Yell "with wiz" (meaning: "with Cheez Whiz, please") for major *cred* and extra authenticity. Jim's is mostly takeout, but there are some tables and chairs upstairs. [$] *Average main: $6* ✉ *400 South St., Queen Village* ☎ *215/928–1911* 🌐 *www.jimssouthstreet.com* 💳 *No credit cards.*

NIVERSITY CITY AND WEST PHILADELPHIA

In University City you can enjoy the many affordable, funky eateries geared toward Penn and Drexel students. West Philly features some of the city's best ethnic dining, from Ethiopian to Lebanese.

$$ MODERN MEXICAN 🍴 **Distrito.** Star chef Jose Garces's Mexico City–inspired joint is colorful, energetic, and enormous—just like its muse. Distrito's "modern Mexican" menu, made up entirely of small plates, includes cuisine from all over Mexico as well as the capital city's hierarchy of street food to fine food—but always with a Garces twist. The Los Hongos huarache is topped with earthy mushrooms spiked with black truffle and tempered by corn shoots. Slices of buttery yellowtail in hamachi ceviche are plated with a dollop of sangrita sorbet and a dash of mint. Urban (and, on the weekend, suburban) fans of Garces's downtown restaurants rub elbows with packs of Penn and Drexel students who flock here for the delicious food as well as the karaoke room, 60 tequilas, nightly DJ, and a movie

Philly Cheesesteaks

If you feel compelled to have a cheesesteak while in town, here are the must-know details: Philly's best-known culinary creation is simple in theory but complex in the details of its execution. Begin with the basic hoagie roll, which should be slightly crusty with a good amount of chew—Amoroso's is a popular choice. Add to that extremely thin-sliced strips of top round, grilled over a bed of onions until well browned. Then, if you want the full effect, order your sandwich "wiz wit," meaning with a ladle of Cheez Whiz *and* fried onions; if you want only Cheese Whiz, then it's simply "wit wiz." Other cheeses may also be used, including American and provolone, depending on the cultural etiquette of the particular establishment. As befitting a cultural touchstone, there are many other homages on Philly menus, including chicken cheesesteaks, cheesesteak egg rolls, even vegetarian cheesesteaks. In fact, even high-end restaurants pay their respects—including a famous $100 Wagyu rib-eye–and–foie gras version at Stephen Starr's Rittenhouse Square steak house, Barclay Prime.

---

screen flashing scenes from the hit film *Nacho Libre*. The downstairs has been recast as a casual, affordable taqueria $ *Average main: $19* ⊠ *3945 Chestnut St., University City* 🕾 *215/222–1657* ⊕ *grg-mgmt. com/distritorestaurant.com.*

$$ ✕ **Dock Street Brewery.** Housed in a handsome 110-year-old redbrick
PIZZA firehouse, Dock Street is a boho brewpub serving up wood-oven piz-
FAMILY zas, fish-and-chips, vegan burgers, and Greek salads for young families and university staff in West Philly. The six taps spout house-brewed suds that range from approachable (Rye IPA) to . . . experimental; their limited-edition "Walker" (as in *Walking Dead)* American Pale Stout is made with smoked goat brains. $ *Average main: $15* ⊠ *701 S. 50th St., University City* 🕾 *215/726–2337* ⊕ *www.dockstreetbeer.com* ☉ *No lunch weekdays* ⌕ *Reservations not accepted.*

$$ ✕ **Lemon Grass Thai.** With occasional deviations (mostly the lunchtime spe-
THAI cials), the Thai food here is about as authentic as you can get in town. It's conscientious in its presentation, but down-to-earth enough to be a favorite among Penn students. Pad thai with baby shrimp is among the most popular choices, but "Evil Jungle Princess" curry wins for the menu's best name. $ *Average main: $16* ⊠ *3626 Lancaster Ave., University City* 🕾 *215/222–8042* ⊕ *www.lemongrassphila.com* ☉ *No lunch weekends.*

$ ✕ **Manakeesh Cafe.** Housed into a former bank building in the Spruce
LEBANESE Hill area of West Philly, Manakeesh specializes in the Lebanese flatbread
FAMILY of the same name. Served warm from the oven, the puffy, round loaves
Fodor's Choice come with both traditional toppings (za'atar, kafta) and unorthodox ones
★ (B.E.C., cheesesteak), which speak to the diverse crowd of university types and transplants from the Middle East that fill the lounge-y, tapestry-lined space. Encased behind glass along the front counter, pistachio baklava cut in a dozen different shapes glitter like jewelry. A box makes an excellent take-home treat. Note that the bakery closes briefly on Friday afternoons. $ *Average main: $7* ⊠ *4420 Walnut St., University City* 🕾 *215/921–2135* ⊕ *www.manakeeshcafebakery.net* ☉ *Closed 1–2:15 Fri.*

$$$$ ✕ **Pod.** The futuristic atmosphere of this restaurant (all-white tables and
JAPANESE chairs and partially enclosed booths—or pods—whose lighting changes
color with the touch of a button) is a fitting setting for food with strong
Asian overtones that ultimately defies precise description. The sushi
conveyor is an entertaining touch. Dim sum, stir fry, and crab pad thai
share the menu with entrées such as tea-smoked duck breast, whole
branzino with wasabi chimichurri, and takes on fried rice with foie gras
and Wagyu beef. Just be warned: the place can be overrun with Penn
students. $ *Average main: $26* ✉ *3636 Sansom St., University City*
☎ *215/387–1803* ⊕ *www.podrestaurant.com* ☯ *No lunch weekends.*

$$$$ ✕ **White Dog Cafe.** A favorite among University of Pennsylvania stu-
AMERICAN dents and professors, this stalwart specializes in locally sourced,
sustainable foods including free-range chicken with sage-roasted
cheese pumpkin *panzanella* and pasture-raised pork chops stuffed
with apples and pears. At first reading, seasonings and sides can seem
comically complicated, but the combos do work. Reservations are
recommended. White Dog has been doing local/organic before local/
organic was a nationwide movement. Think Tuscan kale-and-melon
salad with shishito vinaigrette, grass-fed steak tartare, and pasture-
raised fried chicken. The small, lively bar has a number of American
beers on tap and in bottles; except for Champagne, the wine list, too,
is all-American. Vegetarians and vegans will find plenty to please
them here. $ *Average main: $27* ✉ *3420 Sansom St., University City*
☎ *215/386–9224* ⊕ *www.whitedog.com.*

ORTHWESTERN PHILADELPHIA

Northwestern Philadelphia includes several interloping neighborhoods
between the banks of the Schuylkill River and the upper forested borders of Fairmount Park. Each has a distinct personality reflected in its
dining scene. With its sharp hills and bustling Main Street, Manayunk
has a collegiate vibe and dining options to match: bro-down bars, barbecue pits, surprisingly excellent Thai. Mount Airy is full of family-
friendly restaurants, but still has more of an urban edge than its tony
neighbor, Chestnut Hill, which is home to chichi brunch spots, bakeries,
and historic pubs.

MANAYUNK

$$ ✕ **Chabaa Thai Bistro.** This Thai bistro is a nice, calming escape from the
THAI noisy restaurant scene of Main Street. Enjoy authentic Thai flavors in
your lime-infused Thai sausage, *po tek* (a spicy seafood hotpot with
basil and lemongrass) portioned for two, or the various face-flushing
curries. They have seven different varieties of pad thai, from crispy
duck to scallop. $ *Average main: $18* ✉ *4371 Main St., Manayunk*
☎ *215/483–1979* ⊕ *www.chabaathai.com* ☯ *Closed Mon. No lunch Fri.*

$$$$ ✕ **Jake's.** The restaurant that started Main Street's transformation into a
AMERICAN place to go follows a pretty simple approach of making good food that
won't leave you hungry. From stuffed quail dressed with bacon-grape
gastrique to shrimp cocktail with jalapeño relish, chef Bruce Cooper
does not shy away from bold, rich flavors. The crab cakes are outstand-
ing, and the signature cookie taco makes a great ending. The dining

room is a little noisy, but it's done up nicely. Next door they've opened the lower-priced, open-to-the-street Cooper's Brick Oven Wine Bar serving brick oven pizza (try the spicy meatball with mozzarella from Claudio's in the Italian Market) in a more casual atmosphere, as well as some tasty small plates like the lobster potato pierogies; you can also order from Jake's menu and vice versa. [$] *Average main: $28* ✉ *4365 Main St., Manayunk* ☎ *215/483–0444* 🌐 *www.jakesrestaurant.com.*

$$ AMERICAN FAMILY

🍴 **Winnie's Le Bus.** It's loud, it's crowded, but something about Le Bus has always kept it upbeat. The longtime Philly bakery and restaurant got its start many years ago selling out of a van at the University of Pennsylvania, and the quality has always remained high. It's mostly comfort food, but with a variety of influences, such as the Thai turkey salad or the mushroom quesadilla glued together with smoked Gouda. Le Bus is a good choice for a Manayunk lunch, as the menu is reasonably priced, and their Cuban sandwiches and Caribbean fish tacos go well with mid-afternoon beers. [$] *Average main: $15* ✉ *4266 Main St., Manayunk* ☎ *215/487–2663* 🌐 *www.lebusmanayunk.com.*

CHESTNUT HILL

$$$ AMERICAN FAMILY

🍴 **Cake.** Located in the former nursery of its next-door neighbor, Robertson's Flowers, Cake has expanded from its bakery roots into a full-fledged restaurant, offering lunch throughout the week, brunch on Sunday, and dinner on Thursday and Friday. The sweets and pastries are still a highlight, although the menu includes creative twists on lunchtime classics: try the Philly cheesesteak marsala or the croque monsieur brushed with apricot mustard. With light streaming in through the greenhouse glass and the florist's fountain still occupying the center of the room, this is a graceful option for starting the day. Dinner is served only on Fridays, reservations required. [$] *Average main: $20* ✉ *8501 Germantown Ave., Chestnut Hill* ☎ *215/247–6887* 🌐 *www.cakeofchestnuthill.com* ⏰ *Closed Mon. No dinner Sat.–Thurs.*

$$ AMERICAN

🍴 **Campbell's Place.** A longtime cozy local tavern, Campbell's now has a legitimate gastropub kitchen to go with the downstairs bar's charm. The difference is in the details—from the house-made General Tso sauce for seared tofu to the Hoegaarten broth for the mussels. There is hefty fare like the large Black Angus burger and meat loaf, but it's nice to dine tapas style on appetizers like the excellent Asian wings, beet-and-goat-cheese salad, and calamari. [$] *Average main: $19* ✉ *8337 Germantown Ave., Chestnut Hill* ☎ *215/242–1818* 🌐 *www.campbellsplace.com.*

$$ AMERICAN FAMILY

🍴 **Earth Bread + Brewery.** Although primarily a restaurant—families are welcome and ever-present—not a bar, this is a beer geek destination. Run by the former owners of Heavyweight Brewery, it always has four specialty brews made on the premise available. The rest of the taps are almost entirely local craft beers (Victory, Stoudts, Sly Fox, etc.) Once a month they dedicate all their taps to one local brewery and pour all their specialty brews. If you want grub to go with your suds, the flatbread pizzas are light and crispy with all natural ingredients (there is an Earth-friendly emphasis) and topped with unique flavors like pumpkin seeds, black beans, and banana-pepper pesto. Meat lovers need not fear—there's also sausage. The salads are excellent, as are snack plates of olives and cheeses. There's also a good and unusual wine list and house-brewed kombucha. [$] *Average main: $16* ✉ *7136 Germantown Ave., Chestnut Hill* ☎ *215/242–6666* 🌐 *www.earthbreadbrewery.com* 🕒 *No lunch weekdays.*

$ AMERICAN FAMILY 🍴 **McNally's.** People come to McNally's more for the food than the beer (families are welcome), and generally order one of the six featured sandwiches. The Schmitter, a cheesesteak on a kaiser roll with fried salami, fried onions, and a special sauce, is insanely delicious. Rivaling the Schmitter is the vegetarian sandwich option, the G.B.S. (George Bernard Shaw), which has mushrooms, peppers, tomato, and lettuce draped in cheese and special sauce. For an even more heavenly taste, ask for fried veggies on the G.B.S. At a close third is the Dickens—hot turkey, stuffing, and cranberry sauce on a kaiser roll. Soups and turkey chili are also worth trying. [$] *Average main: $10* ✉ *8634 Germantown Ave., Chestnut Hill* ☎ *215/247–9736* 🌐 *www.mcnallystavern.com* 🕒 *Closes at 8 pm Sun.* ✍ *Reservations not accepted.*

MOUNT AIRY

$ DINER FAMILY 🍴 **Trolley Car Diner.** Built around a classic 1950s silver diner transported to its current home at the border of Chestnut Hill and Mt. Airy, this family-friendly spot supplements classic diner fare with healthier options and an extensive list of bottled microbrews. Mix-and-match six-packs of those beers can be picked up in the Trolley Car's deli, which also serves sandwiches and baked goods. While it was named for the old trolley tracks that still run along Germantown Avenue outside its doors, an actual trolley car was added to the parking lot in 2003, and now dispenses ice cream during the summer. [$] *Average main: $12* ✉ *7619 Germantown Ave., Mount Airy* ☎ *215/753–1500* 🌐 *www.trolleycardiner.com* ✍ *Reservations not accepted.*

NORTHEASTERN PHILADELPHIA

As Philly has grown as a city in the metaphorical sense, so have the borders of Center City. Nowadays, it's a regular part of daily life for locals (and visitors) to spend time (sometimes most of their time) in outlying neighborhoods like North Philly, Northern Liberites, and Fishtown. Though you probably won't be in North Philly unless you're eating at Marc Vetri's Osteria, Northern Liberites and Fishtown offer a bevy of culinary distractions. The former is more established, with 20-year-old gastropubs and comfort-driven converted diners, while the latter is more ascendant, home to the HQ of local roaster La Colombe and the pizza one glossy food magazine calls the best in America.

NORTH PHILADELPHIA

$$$$ ITALIAN 🍴 **Osteria.** Osteria is more than a consolation prize for the many who are thwarted by the two-month backup in reservations at Marc Vetri's eponymous fine-dining restaurant. His long-awaited second restaurant is a little more affordable and decidedly more casual and versatile with its wide-ranging menu of Italian comfort food under the direction of chef Jeff Michaud. The menu has everything from amazing brick-oven pizzas (try the Lombarda, with cotechino sausage and a soft-cooked egg) to a charred rib-eye for two served over white beans. The neighborhood-making North Broad Street setting with red concrete floors, rustic

CLOSE UP

Philly's Best BYOBs

The scarcity and high cost of liquor licenses available to Pennsylvania restaurateurs combined with the absence of a law prohibiting patrons from bringing liquor into a restaurant has resulted in an active bring-your-own-bottle (BYOB) scene in Philadelphia.

Natives know that BYOBs have the most flavorful food and atmosphere, not to mention a bill that is easier to digest. Bringing your own is penalty-free—there's no extra charge for corkage. Here are some of our favorite BYOBs.

- Dmitri's, Queen Village
- Modo Mio, Fishtown
- Izumi, East Passynk
- Pumpkin, South Philadelphia

wooden tables, and soaring ceilings blends loft and country, industry and art. $ *Average main: $25* ✉ *640 N. Broad St., North Philadelphia* ☎ *215/763–0920* 🌐 *www.osteriaphilly.com* ⏲ *No lunch Sat.–Wed.*

NORTHERN LIBERTIES

$$$ SPANISH 🍴 **Bar Ferdinand.** Owner Owen Kamihira came to this venture with an impressive design pedigree—he put the Buddha in Buddakan. So it's not surprising that Bar Ferdinand has spectacular decor. What is surprising is that a first-time restaurateur got the food so right—the hot and cold tapas, *bocadillos* (sandwiches), and *pinchos* (skewers) are almost good enough to distract you from the dramatic cut-glass mosaic of Ferdinand the Bull. $ *Average main: $24* ✉ *1030 N. 2nd St., Northern Liberties* ☎ *215/923–1313* 🌐 *www.barferdinand.com* ⏲ *No lunch weekdays.*

$$$ MODERN AMERICAN 🍴 **Heritage.** The best restaurant to open in years in once-scrappy, now-uber-developed Northern Liberties is Heritage, an industrial hanger where you'll find live jazz on the dining room stage, live herbs creeping over the reclaimed ceiling beams, and lively cooking from chef Sean Magee. Idiosyncratic seafood towers have quick become the signature order here, though whatever Magee is doing with foie gras is also definitely worth your attention. $ *Average main: $20* ✉ *914 N. 2nd St., Northern Liberties* ☎ *215/627–7500* 🌐 *heritage.life* ⏲ *No lunch weeekdays.*

$$ MEXICAN 🍴 **Las Cazuelas.** This authentically Mexican family-run place is an anomaly in sceney Northern Liberties. The colors, both inside and out, are warm and bright. The food is simple and rather gently spiced, apropos of the family's roots in the town of Puebla. $ *Average main: $18* ✉ *426–28 W. Girard Ave., Northern Liberties* ☎ *215/351–9144* 🌐 *las-cazuelas.net* ⏲ *Closed Mon. No lunch Sun.*

$$ AMERICAN 🍴 **N. 3rd.** North Third is one of the first restaurants to settle in Northern Liberties at the infancy of the neighborhood's transformation. The menu hasn't changed much, mostly because locals love hits like the Moroccan-spiced lamb burger, mushroom flatbread, and house-made pierogies. Weekend brunch here—challah French toast, arugula and beet salad, smoked salmon club sandwich—is one of the best in the area. $ *Average main: $16* ✉ *801 N. 3rd St., Northern Liberties* ☎ *215/413–3666* 🌐 *www.norththird.com* ⏲ *No lunch weekdays.*

$$ ✕ **Silk City Diner, Bar, and Lounge.** Mark Bee, the local restaurateur behind
AMERICAN favorite gastropub N. 3rd, bought the Silk City Diner in 2006, polished off its grease-coated, 1950s-era pink Formica counter, and started serving updated comfort food including a fierce plate of buttermilk fried chicken, cilantro-spiked calamari, the city's best bowl of mac-and-cheese (baked with a garlic bread crust), and some lighter fare (a honey-roasted beet salad) should you want to go next door to the bar and lounge and dance 'til dawn beneath the disco ball. $ *Average main: $16 ⊠ 435 Spring Garden St., Northern Liberties ☎ 215/592–8838 ⊕ www.silkcityphilly.com ⊗ No lunch weekdays.*

$ ✕ **Standard Tap.** This neighborhood gastropub is a Northern Liberties
AMERICAN fixture, popular with the hipsters who populate this particular neighborhood and for good reason. The menu, presented unpretentiously on a chalkboard, is much more ambitious—and much tastier—than you'd expect from average bar food, and since you're in a bar, you can wash down the grilled octopus, duck confit salad, and roasted beets with one of the local microbrews on tap. Sunday brunch (think Bloody Marys and fried oysters) is always busy. $ *Average main: $12 ⊠ 901 N. 2nd St., Northern Liberties ☎ 215/238–0630 ⊕ www.standardtap. com ⊗ No lunch weekdays.*

FISHTOWN

$ ✕ **La Colombe.** When real estate agents want to sell house-hunters
CAFÉ on Fishtown, they take them to the new world headquarters of La
Fodor's Choice Colombe, a combination café, bakery, roaster, distillery, and neighbor-
★ hood clubhouse that would make Noah's Ark look like a canoe. Artsy graffiti covers the crusty brick walls, and communal tables stream down the center of the space. You order at the counter: savory scones, sandwiches on excellent baguettes, kale salad, and coffee, of course. Ask for a Black & Tan (half Pure Black cold-brew, half nitro-draught latte) and no one will know you're not a local. $ *Average main: $8 ⊠ 1335 Frankford Ave., Fishtown ☎ 267/479–1600 ⊕ www.lacolombe.com ⋈ Reservations not accepted.*

$ ✕ **Little Baby's Ice Cream.** Started by a trio of musicians in 2001, Little
CAFÉ Baby's grabbed the city's attention with its anthropomorphic ice cream mascot, playful roving tricycles, and flavors like Earl Grey Sriracha, Balsamic Banana, and Speculoos. True to brand, their Fishtown ice cream parlor (connected to pizzeria/pizza museum, Pizza Brain) is trippy pastel 1980s music video fever dream, and the ice cream, made with local, organic milk and cream, is legit. There are always several nondairy flavors for vegans, too. $ *Average main: $5 ⊠ 2311 Frankford Ave., Fishtown ☎ 267/687–8567 ⊕ www.littlebabysicecream.com ⋈ Reservations not accepted.*

$ ✕ **Memphis Taproom.** Beer aficionado Brendan Hartranft and his wife,
AMERICAN Leigh Maida, are the masterminds behind Fishtown's favorite gastropub. Beef and onion pasties, short ribs, and sweet-onion-filled fried pastry dough are addictively good options for soaking up the many tasty brews available. Vegans swear by the ALT, a version of the BLT with smoked avocado that tastes better than bacon. Expect a rotating list of 30-plus American craft beers in addition to Belgian, German, and English selections by the bottle. Although the space evokes the air of

classic Parisian bistros and Belgian beer cafés, its decor is a nod to th traditional Philadelphia working-class neighborhood corner taprooms [$] *Average main: $14* ✉ *2331 E. Cumberland St., Fishtown* ☎ *212/425-4460* 🌐 *www.memphistaproom.com* ✍ *Reservations not accepted.*

$$ ITALIAN 🍴 **Modo Mio.** Chef and owner Peter McAndrews's narrow, bustlin BYOB on the Northern Liberties/Fishtown divide lures even Main Lin couples into formerly uncharted territory way north of Center City The meal is worth the trek, however, beginning with the homemad bread—a 15-pound Umbrian loaf sliced thick and served with oliv oil and ricotta cheese. The small plates menu is a menagerie of rusti Italian flavors with modern twists, but don't miss the rabbit agnolott with sage brown butter. [$] *Average main: $17* ✉ *161 W. Girard Ave. Fishtown* ☎ *215/203–8707* 💳 *No credit cards* ⏲ *Closed Mon.*

$$$ PIZZA Fodor's Choice ★ 🍴 **Pizzeria Beddia.** When *Bon Appétit* calls your pizza the best in Amer ica, you ramp up production, prepare for the onslaught, and plan a expansion. Right? Not for Joe Beddia, the lanky pizzaiolo statione behind the counter at his eponymous Fishtown shop every night. He' doing the same thing he's done since opening in 2013: craft about 4 pizzas a night from his long-fermented dough and local ingredient like Hidden Hills Dairy's Old Gold aged Gouda and Green Meado Farm bacon. There's no seating, no phone number, no credit cards, an the line starts forming at 4 pm. Yes, they're worth it. [$] *Average main $20* ✉ *115 E. Girard Ave., Fishtown* ☎ *No phone* 🌐 *pizzeriabeddia wordpress.com* ⏲ *Closed Sun.–Tues.* 💳 *No credit cards.*

$ MEXICAN 🍴 **Sancho Pistola's.** An offshoot of Jose Pistola's in Center City, brothe Sancho brought a bigger kitchen for chef Adan Trinidad to showcas his talents. Some of his food is ultra-traditional, like whole-roasted fis Veracruzana and inky black bean soup seasoned with avocado leaf while other plates (oyster po'boy tacos, mole meatballs buns) mas up his Mexican heritage with a global hipster aesthetic. The fresh fruit margaritas flow late into the night. [$] *Average main: $12* ✉ *19 W Girard Ave., Fishtown* ☎ *267/324–3530* 🌐 *www.sanchopistolas.con* ⏲ *No lunch weekdays* ✍ *Reservations not accepted.*

$ VIETNAMESE 🍴 **Stock.** Thanks to a robust Vietnamese population, Philly is practi cally drowning in pho. But pho made with high-quality ingredients You'll have to head to Stock in Fishtown for that. There, in a monasti storefront with a sprinkling of seats and set of induction burners, che Tyler Akin weaves arresting noodle soups, herbaceous salads, and livel crudos with sustainably raised meats, house-grown lime leaves, an chilies from New York's cult spice merchant, La Boîte. [$] *Average main $9* ✉ *308 E. Girard Ave., Fishtown* 🌐 *www.stockphilly.com* ⏲ *Close Tues. and Wed.* ✍ *Reservations not accepted.*

WHERE TO STAY

4

Updated by
Drew Lazor

Philadelphia has lodgings for every style of travel. Thanks to the Pennsylvania Convention Center and a hotel-building boom in the late 1990s, some mid-price chains have moved into town or have spruced up their accommodations. If you have greater expectations, you need look no further than the city's handful of swank hotels, each with its own gracious character.

Budget, moderate, and luxury properties are spread throughout the downtown area. The Historic Area, on the east side of downtown, centers on Independence Hall and extends to the Delaware River, and is a good base for sightseeing. Old City and Society Hill lodgings are also convenient for serious sightseeing; Society Hill is the quietest of the three areas. For business-oriented trips, Center City encompasses the heart of the downtown business district, centered around Broad and Market streets, and Rittenhouse Square hotels are also nearby.

If you prefer to keep your distance from the tourist throngs, check out the Benjamin Franklin Parkway–Museum Area along the parkway from 16th Street to the Philadelphia Museum of Art. There are also a couple of hotels in University City—just across the Schuylkill River in West Philadelphia and close to the University of Pennsylvania and Drexel University—a 5- to 10-minute drive or taxi ride from Center City.

RESERVATIONS

Even with the large number of hotel rooms, sometimes it's difficult to find a place to stay, so advance reservations are advised. Philadelphia has no real off-season, but many hotels offer discount packages when the demand from business travelers and groups subsides. Besides substantially reduced rates, these packages often include an assortment of freebies, such as breakfast, parking, cocktails, and the use of exercise facilities.

PARKING

Most downtown hotels charge an average of $25 a day for parking, but some include it in the rate. You can find street parking if you're willing to put in the effort, but it can be difficult—even for natives. The best time to try is in the early morning or in the early evening, before the nightlife starts up. However, many streets have two-hour time limits until 10 pm, and the two-hour rule goes into effect at 8 am, even on Sunday in many places.

HOTEL PRICES

When pricing accommodations, always ask what's included and what costs extra.

WHAT IT COSTS			
$	$$	$$$	$$$$
Under $150	$150–$225	$226–$300	Over $300

Hotel prices are the lowest cost of a standard double room in high season.

OTEL REVIEWS

Hotel reviews have been shortened. For full information, visit Fodors.com.

IE HISTORIC DOWNTOWN

OLD CITY

$$ **Best Western Plus Independence Park Hotel.** Surrounded by key historic
HOTEL sites as well as many nightlife options, this five-story Best Western hotel
is within walking distance of just about everything you need. **Pros:** free
snacks and wine; intimate boutique hotel near restaurants, nightlife,
and tourist attractions. **Cons:** can be noisy at night; some rooms have
views of brick walls. $ *Rooms from: $189* ⊠ *235 Chestnut St., Old City*
☎ *215/922–4443, 800/624–2988* ⊕ *www.theindependenceparkhotel.*
com ➔ *36 rooms* ⏽⊙⏽ *Breakfast.*

$$$ **The Franklin Hotel at Independence Park.** An ornate fireplace dominates
HOTEL the breathtaking marble lobby of this towering hotel in the historic dis-
FAMILY trict, which recently joined the Marriott family of hotels. **Pros:** excellent location for historic touring and Old City revelry; boutique feel;
good service; nice views; known to offer good sale rates. **Cons:** some
rooms can get noisy at night from proximity to nightlife. $ *Rooms*
from: $229 ⊠ *401 Chestnut St., Old City* ☎ *215/925–0000, 888/236–*
2427 ⊕ *www.marriott.com* ➔ *147 rooms, 3 suites* ⏽⊙⏽ *No meals.*

$$ **Hotel Monaco Philadelphia.** Opened in 2013, Hotel Monaco offers style,
HOTEL sass, and LEED certification in the heart of Philly's historic center, along
dors Choice with the beloved perks of the Kimpton brand: complimentary evening
★ wine hours, free bikes and yoga mats, fitness classes, and pet-friendly
rooms. **Pros:** central location; lots of great perks and freebies; service with
a smile; popular on-site dining and drinking; lovely past-meets-present
design. **Cons:** note that it's pet-friendly, if you have allergies. $ *Rooms*
from: $219 ⊠ *433 Chestnut St., Historic Area* ☎ *215/925–2111* ⊕ *www.*
monaco-philadelphia.com ➔ *251 rooms, 17 suites* ⏽⊙⏽ *No meals.*

$$ **Penn's View Hotel.** This cosmopolitan little hotel in a refurbished 19th-
HOTEL century commercial building on the fringe of Old City has its own brand
of urban charm. **Pros:** good service; generous Continental breakfast
including waffles; romantic atmosphere. **Cons:** gym is tiny; rooms facing
I–95 can be noisy. $ *Rooms from: $162* ⊠ *14 N. Front St., Old City*
☎ *215/922–7600, 800/331–7634* ⊕ *www.pennsviewhotel.com* ➔ *51*
rooms, 2 suites ⏽⊙⏽ *Breakfast.*

$$ **Thomas Bond House.** This bed-and-breakfast in the heart of Old City
B&B/INN is great for travelers who want an authentic taste of historic Philadel-
phia. **Pros:** historic home; good service. **Cons:** some guests complain of
noise when nearby bars let out at 2 am; there are also some complaints

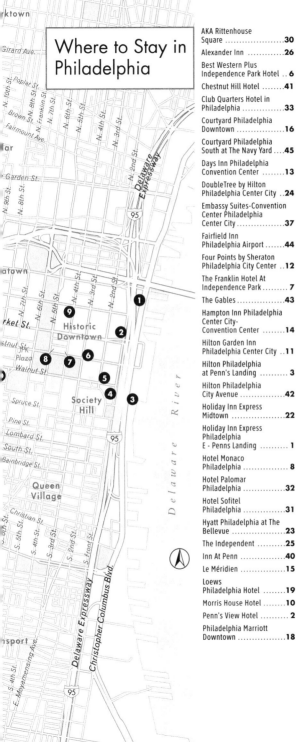

Where to Stay in Philadelphia

about closet space and hot water; no elevator. $ *Rooms from: $170* ✉ *129 S. 2nd St., Old City* ☎ *215/923–8523, 800/845–2663* ⊕ *www. thomasbondhousebandb.com* ⤳ *10 rooms, 2 suites* ❙❍❙ *Breakfast.*

$$$ ⚏ **Wyndham Historic District.** This eight-story hotel sits within what is
HOTEL   billed as the country's "most historic square mile," within a block and a half of the Liberty Bell and Independence Hall. **Pros:** can be a relative bargain located close to major tourist attractions; 24-hour gym. **Cons:** lots of tourists and large groups; rates very high in busy seasons for a Holiday Inn. $ *Rooms from: $295* ✉ *400 Arch St., Old City* ☎ *215/923–8660, 800/843–2355* ⊕ *www.phillydowntownhotel.com* ⤳ *364 rooms, 7 suites* ❙❍❙ *No meals.*

SOCIETY HILL

$$ ⚏ **Morris House Hotel.** This is a lovely bed-and-breakfast option in leafy
HOTEL   Society Hill. **Pros:** great, low-key location; historic; has its own restaurant and bar. **Cons:** no gym; no parking. $ *Rooms from: $189* ✉ *225 S. 8th St., Society Hill* ☎ *215/922–2446* ⊕ *www.morrishousehotel.com* ⤳ *15 rooms* ❙❍❙ *Breakfast.*

$$ ⚏ **Sheraton Society Hill.** Convenient to downtown sights, this Colonial-
HOTEL   style building is two blocks from Penn's Landing, three blocks from Head House Square, and four blocks from Independence Hall. **Pros:** pleasant, airy lobby; choice of two restaurants and a bar on premises; within walking distance of Old City nightlife, but not bothered by its noise at night; $10 shuttle available to airport. **Cons:** can be a bit of a walk to Old City attractions; fee for Wi-Fi. $ *Rooms from: $199* ✉ *1 Dock St., Society Hill* ☎ *215/238–6000, 800/325–3535* ⊕ *www. sheraton.com/societyhill* ⤳ *365 rooms, 13 suites* ❙❍❙ *No meals.*

PENN'S LANDING

$$ ⚏ **Hilton Philadelphia Penn's Landing.** The theme here is "room with a
HOTEL   view." This hotel on the banks of the Delaware River offers dramatic
FAMILY   river views from the 22-story tower; southern-facing rooms have views of both the river and the city. **Pros:** nice indoor pool with option to sit outside; great views. **Cons:** separated from Old City by I–95; it can feel a tad isolated. $ *Rooms from: $199* ✉ *201 S. Columbus Blvd., Penn's Landing* ☎ *215/521–6500,* ⊕ *www.hiltonpennslanding.com* ⤳ *350 rooms, 11 suites* ❙❍❙ *No meals.*

$$$ ⚏ **Holiday Inn Express Penn's Landing.** The reasonable price is the main
HOTEL   attraction at this 10-story hotel. **Pros:** cheaper downtown alternative; nice views of the river and Benjamin Franklin Bridge; free shuttle to Center City. **Cons:** a bit isolated from Center City. $ *Rooms from: $239* ✉ *100 N. Columbus Blvd., Penn's Landing* ☎ *215/627–7900, 800/228– 5150* ⊕ *www.hiepennslanding.com* ⤳ *184 rooms* ❙❍❙ *Breakfast.*

CENTER CITY

CENTER CITY EAST

$ ⚏ **Alexander Inn.** The well-maintained rooms at this small hotel have
HOTEL   an Art Deco feel. **Pros:** great location between Rittenhouse Square and historic district; quiet yet near lively nightlife; away from touristy spots; great service; Web specials on room rate; cheap parking. **Cons:** older

building; no laundry facilities or services; bar downstairs can get noisy; tiny gym. [$] *Rooms from: $119* ✉ *12th and Spruce Sts., Center City East* ☎ *215/923–3535, 877/253–9466* 🌐 *www.alexanderinn.com* 🛏 *48 rooms* 🍴 *Breakfast.*

$$$$ HOTEL 🏨 **Courtyard Philadelphia Downtown.** This hotel is in the historic City Hall Annex, and the original brass, copper, and bronze details on the elevators and staircases have been lovingly refinished. **Pros:** centrally located; architecturally beautiful; good service. **Cons:** central location can make for difficulty in picking up and dropping off car; breakfast is offered but is not complimentary. [$] *Rooms from: $339* ✉ *21 N. Juniper St., Center City East* ☎ *215/496–3200, 800/321–2211* 🌐 *www.marriott.com/hotels/travel/phldc-courtyard-philadelphia-downtown* 🛏 *500 rooms* 🍴 *No meals.*

$$ HOTEL 🏨 **Days Inn Philadelphia Convention Center.** On the edge of Chinatown, this small hotel has a location as good as many other downtown hotels but charges much less. **Pros:** affordable, bare-bones option for Center City. **Cons:** feels congested; neighborhood can seem desolate at night; dominated by convention-goers. [$] *Rooms from: $159* ✉ *1227 Race St., Center City East* ☎ *215/564–2888, 800/578–7878* 🌐 *www.daysinn.com* 🛏 *60 rooms* 🍴 *Breakfast.*

$$ HOTEL 🏨 **Doubletree By Hilton Philadelphia Center City.** The hotel's sawtooth design ensures that each room has a peaked bay window with an eye-popping 180-degree view. **Pros:** great location for the theatergoer; good views; sunny and unique lobby. **Cons:** lots of groups can make for a hectic lobby. [$] *Rooms from: $199* ✉ *237 S. Broad St., Center City East* ☎ *215/893–1600, 800/222–8733* 🌐 *www.philadelphia.doubletree.com* 🛏 *431 rooms, 50 suites* 🍴 *No meals.*

$$ HOTEL 🏨 **Four Points by Sheraton Philadelphia City Center.** With its understated boutique-like charms, this Four Points offers a practical yet homey alternative to some of its larger neighbors in the Pennsylvania Convention Center area. **Pros:** affordable; free Wi-Fi; modern yet intimate; 24-hour gym; cheaper parking compared to some neighbors. **Cons:** no tub for those who like baths; immediate neighborhood can feel forbidding at night. [$] *Rooms from: $169* ✉ *1201 Race St., Center City East* ☎ *215/496–2700* 🌐 *www.fourpointsphiladelphiacitycenter.com* 🛏 *92 rooms* 🍴 *No meals.*

$ HOTEL 🏨 **Hampton Inn Philadelphia Center City-Convention Center.** This hotel bills itself as the "best value hotel in Center City" and backs it up with a gym, business center, and, weather permitting, complimentary breakfast on a patio facing 13th Street. **Pros:** excellent value for convention center events; friendly service. **Cons:** immediate surroundings can be dreary at night; not much nightlife within walking distance. [$] *Rooms from: $139* ✉ *1301 Race St., Center City East* ☎ *215/665–9100, 800/426–7866* 🌐 *www.hamptoninn.com* 🛏 *230 rooms, 20 suites* 🍴 *Breakfast.*

$$ HOTEL 🏨 **Hilton Garden Inn Philadelphia Center City.** This hotel is an affordable alternative to other hotels near the Pennsylvania Convention Center. **Pros:** nice rooms; good value; indoor pool; a central location. **Cons:** convention center neighborhood can be quiet and dark at night. [$] *Rooms from: $159* ✉ *1100 Arch St., Center City East* ☎ *215/923–0100, 800/774–1500* 🌐 *www.hiltongardenphilly.com* 🛏 *161 rooms, 118 suites* 🍴 *No meals.*

$$ RENTAL 🏨 **Holiday Inn Express Midtown.** What this hotel lacks in frills it more than makes up for with its central location, free access to the nearby Optimal Fitness health club, and complimentary breakfast bar. **Pros:** location; big rooms; free Continental breakfast; free Wi-Fi; outdoor seasonal pool. **Cons:** small lobby can get cramped with groups; funky smells in common areas; lots of congested traffic during daylight hours. [$] *Rooms from: $189* ✉ *1305 Walnut St., Center City East* ☎ *215/735–9300, 800/564–3869* 🌐 *www.himidtown.com* 🛏 *168 rooms* 🍴 *Breakfast.*

$$ HOTEL 🏨 **The Independent.** The Independent is among a handful of newer boutique alternatives to Philadelphia's big convention hotels. **Pros:** tasteful, warm decor makes you feel like you're staying with friends; rooms larger than some luxury properties. **Cons:** some complain about noise and inattentive staff. [$] *Rooms from: $169* ✉ *1234 Locust St., Center City East* ☎ *215/772–1440* 🌐 *www.theindependenthotel.com* 🛏 *24 rooms* 🍴 *Breakfast.*

$$ HOTEL FAMILY 🏨 **Loews Philadelphia Hotel.** Topped by the red neon letters PSFS (for the former tenant, Pennsylvania Savings Fund Society), this 1930s building was the country's first skyscraper in the ultramodern international style. **Pros:** architectural gem; cool style throughout; amazing views; nice bathrobes and coffeemakers. **Cons:** some guests have complained about the smell of smoke in rooms; you might need a cab to get to nightlife destinations. [$] *Rooms from: $179* ✉ *1200 Market St., Center City East* ☎ *215/627–1200, 800/235–6397* 🌐 *www.loewshotels.com* 🛏 *581 rooms, 12 suites* 🍴 *No meals.*

$$ HOTEL 🏨 **Philadelphia Marriott Downtown.** This bustling convention hotel fills an entire city block. **Pros:** centrally located; clean rooms; potential for good deals; good for traveling families or businesspeople. **Cons:** crowds, crowds, and more crowds; parking is a whopping $49–$55 a night. [$] *Rooms from: $189* ✉ *1201 Market St., Center City East* ☎ *215/625–2900, 800/228–9290* 🌐 *www.philadelphiamarriott.com* 🛏 *1,408 rooms, 76 suites* 🍴 *No meals.*

$$ HOTEL FAMILY 🏨 **Residence Inn Philadelphia Center City.** Originally the Market Street National Bank, this building from the 1920s has a beautifully restored Art Deco facade. **Pros:** centrally located; novel amenities; nice option for families. **Cons:** pricey parking; central location makes it hard to drop off and pick your car. [$] *Rooms from: $159* ✉ *1 E. Penn Sq., corner of Market and Juniper Sts., Center City East* ☎ *215/557–0005, 800/331–3131* 🌐 *www.residenceinn.com* 🛏 *290 suites* 🍴 *Breakfast.*

CENTER CITY WEST

$$ HOTEL 🏨 **Club Quarters Hotel in Philadelphia.** Hoping to capture the look and feel of an old Scotch-and-cigar parlor, Philadelphia's Club Quarters, sometimes branded as "CQ Hotel," has a little more style than the typical business-minded lodge. **Pros:** excellent location; accommodations for both typical pleasure travelers and extended business travelers; "Sleep Better Kit" available to guests. **Cons:** studio kitchens only have a microwave; no on-site parking. [$] *Rooms from: $179* ✉ *1628 Chestnut St., Center City West* ☎ *215/282–5000* 🌐 *www.clubquartershotels.com/philadelphia* 🛏 *275 rooms* 🍴 *No meals.*

$$$ HOTEL FAMILY
Hyatt Philadelphia at The Bellevue. A Philadelphia institution for almost a century, The Bellevue continually offers elegant lodging at the very heart of the city. **Pros:** centrally located; shopping downstairs; old-school elegance; amazing gym. **Cons:** rooms and hallways could use an upgrade. [$] *Rooms from: $289* ✉ *200 S. Broad St., Center City West* ☎ *215/893–1234, 800/233–1234* 🌐 *philadelphiabellevue.hyatt.com* 🛏 *172 rooms, 13 suites* 🍴 *No meals.*

$$ HOTEL
Le Méridien. Opened in 2010, Le Méridien offers a welcome boutique alternative to the more standard hotels near the convention center. **Pros:** hip boutique alternative near convention center; good service; comfy beds; 24-hour gym; affordable relative to some luxury hotels. **Cons:** rooms could use some extra seating; immediate neighborhood can be a bit empty at night; can take a while to get your car back on busy check-out mornings. [$] *Rooms from: $199* ✉ *1421 Arch St., Center City West* ☎ *215/422–8200, 800/543–4300* 🌐 *www.lemeridien.com* 🛏 *202 rooms* 🍴 *No meals.*

$$$$ HOTEL FAMILY dor's Choice ★
Ritz-Carlton Philadelphia. You'll feel like you're checking into the Pantheon when you enter this neoclassical hotel set in a century-old bank building. **Pros:** stunning architecture (the lobby bar is unparalleled); attentive and friendly service; modern in-room amenities. **Cons:** rooms are smaller than some luxury competitors; street noise can be a problem; fee for Wi-Fi ($9.95 per day); elevators can be slow; gym is spare; pricey parking. [$] *Rooms from: $400* ✉ *10 S. Broad St., Center City West* ☎ *215/523–8000, 800/241–3333* 🌐 *www.ritzcarlton.com* 🛏 *273 rooms, 26 suites* 🍴 *No meals.*

$$ HOTEL
ROOST Apartment Hotel. Nestling thoughtful hypermodern amenities in the bones of the venerable Packard Building, ROOST is an extended-stay establishment designed with the modern traveler in mind. **Pros:** stylish, thoughtfully curated design; excellent location for Center City. **Cons:** not always the best fit for shorter stays. [$] *Rooms from: $155* ✉ *111 S. 15th St., Center City West* ☎ *267/737–9000* 🌐 *www.myroost.com* 🛏 *27 suites* 🍴 *No meals.*

$$ HOTEL
Sonesta Philadelphia Downtown. After a $30-million renovation in 2014, Center City's Sonesta pairs hyperstylized looks with an interesting collection of amenities. **Pros:** great central location; can be a bargain compared to other Center City options; $10 shuttle to airport; outdoor seasonal pool. **Cons:** some guests complain about careless service. [$] *Rooms from: $179* ✉ *1800 Market St., Center City West* ☎ *215/561–7500, 800/227–6963* 🌐 *www.crowneplaza.com* 🛏 *445 rooms, 2 suites* 🍴 *No meals.*

$$$$ HOTEL FAMILY dor's Choice ★
Westin Philadelphia. If luxurious accommodations and plenty of shopping are your top priorities, you're not going to beat the Westin. **Pros:** close to best shopping areas; excellent beds; comfortable furniture; quiet. **Cons:** pricey parking; fee for Internet. [$] *Rooms from: $329* ✉ *99 S. 17th St., at Liberty Pl., Center City West* ☎ *215/563–1600, 800/937–8461* 🌐 *www.westin.com/philadelphia* 🛏 *294 rooms, 19 suites* 🍴 *No meals.*

RITTENHOUSE SQUARE

$$$$ HOTEL
AKA Rittenhouse Square. Though steps away from the popular park and surrounding shopping, the AKA Rittenhouse Square operates in a below-the-radar fashion favored by visiting actors and athletes. **Pros:**

large rooms; homey amenities and atmosphere; nice restaurant and bar. **Cons:** no parking; no room service; some of the lower rooms have views of a brick wall; gym lacks ample equipment. [$] *Rooms from: $30* ✉ *135 S. 18th St., Rittenhouse Square* ☎ *215/825–7000, 888/252–018* 🌐 *www.hotelaka.com* 🛏 *78 rooms* 🍴 *No meals.*

$$ HOTEL FAMILY Fodor's Choice ★ 🏨 **Hotel Palomar Philadelphia.** The Palomar marks the apex of Philadelphia's recent surge of hip hotels; three brightly colored busts of Ben Franklin greet you in this Kimpton property's chic lobby alongside a comfy fireside living room. **Pros:** superhip yet comfortable; eco-friendly and LEED Gold certified; good location near Rittenhouse Square restaurants. **Cons:** allows pets, including barking dogs; standard rooms are cleverly designed but a bit small. [$] *Rooms from: $199* ✉ *117 S. 17th St., Rittenhouse Square* ☎ *215/563–5006, 888/725–1778* 🌐 *www.hotelpalomar-philadelphia.com* 🛏 *247 rooms* 🍴 *No meals.*

$$$$ HOTEL FAMILY 🏨 **Hotel Sofitel Philadelphia.** In the middle of the city's French Quarter this luxury hotel has more of a hip feeling than some of its stuffier Federal-style neighbors. **Pros:** luxury with a hipper feel; excellent location great service. **Cons:** its central location can make driving in and out of the hotel a pain. [$] *Rooms from: $399* ✉ *120 S. 17th St., Rittenhouse Square* ☎ *215/569–8300, 800/763–4835* 🌐 *www.sofitel.com* 🛏 *306 rooms, 67 suites* 🍴 *No meals.*

$ HOTEL 🏨 **Radisson Blu Plaza Warwick Hotel.** This classic hotel, first opened in 1926, has returned to claim its place among the best Philadelphia hotels after extensive renovations in 2013. **Pros:** historic hotel with modern amenities; great location; great service. **Cons:** smallish bathrooms. [$] *Rooms from: $129* ✉ *220 S. 17th St., Rittenhouse Square* ☎ *215/735–6000, 800/333–3333* 🌐 *www.radisson.com/philadelphiapa* 🛏 *301 rooms, 4 suites* 🍴 *No meals.*

$$$ HOTEL FAMILY 🏨 **The Rittenhouse.** The service at Philadelphia's only AAA Five Diamond hotel is unparalleled. **Pros:** great service without the stuffiness, 24-hour room service; complimentary Wi-Fi; among the largest rooms for luxury hotels; quiet. **Cons:** furniture can seem a bit dated; pricey. [$] *Rooms from: $299* ✉ *210 W. Rittenhouse Sq., Rittenhouse Square* ☎ *215/546–9000, 800/635–1042* 🌐 *www.rittenhousehotel.com* 🛏 *87 rooms, 11 suites* 🍴 *No meals.*

$$$ HOTEL Fodor's Choice ★ 🏨 **Rittenhouse 1715.** On a small street near Rittenhouse Square, this refined, European-style mansion offers the luxury of a large hotel in an intimate space. **Pros:** quiet option for downtown; romantic. **Cons:** no parking service; no laundry service. [$] *Rooms from: $249* ✉ *1715 Rittenhouse Sq., Rittenhouse Square* ☎ *215/546–6500, 877/791–6500* 🌐 *www.rittenhouse1715.com* 🛏 *18 rooms, 5 suites* 🍴 *Breakfast.*

BENJAMIN FRANKLIN PARKWAY

$$ HOTEL FAMILY 🏨 **Embassy Suites Philadelphia–Center City.** On Logan Square, this hotel puts you within walking distance of Boathouse Row. **Pros:** large rooms; great views; good bargain compared to neighbors. **Cons:** can get noisy; often a wait for the elevators; short driveway can make for chaotic check-in/out. [$] *Rooms from: $185* ✉ *1776 Benjamin Franklin Pkwy., Benjamin Franklin Parkway* ☎ *215/561–1776, 800/362–2779* 🌐 *www.embassysuites.com* 🛏 *288 suites* 🍴 *Breakfast.*

$$$ **Sheraton Philadelphia Downtown.** Although it's a popular convention
HOTEL   hotel, this hotel also caters to both business and leisure travelers. **Pros:**
good location between art museum and convention center; clean contemporary rooms. **Cons:** large convention crowds; long waits to check in and
out. $ *Rooms from: $239* ✉ *201 N. 17th St., Benjamin Franklin Parkway*
📞 *215/448–2000, 800/822–4200* ⊕ *www.sheratonphiladelphiadowntown.
com* ⇨ *741 rooms, 16 suites* �‖❘ *No meals.*

$$ **The Windsor Suites.** This 24-story all-suites hotel caters to corporate
HOTEL   business travelers as well as to vacationing families. **Pros:** affordable
option on Parkway; balconies offer a good view; rooftop pool during
summer. **Cons:** pool is seasonal. $ *Rooms from: $155* ✉ *1700 Benjamin Franklin Pkwy., Benjamin Franklin Parkway* 📞 *215/981–5678,
877/784–8379* ⊕ *www.windsorhotel.com* ⇨ *148 suites* ❘❙❘ *No meals.*

OUTH PHILADELPHIA

$$ **Courtyard Philadelphia South at The Navy Yard.** A welcome alternative to
HOTEL   cookie-cutter accommodations down by Philadelphia International Airport, this LEED-certified Courtyard takes up residence in the Navy Yard,
a 1,200-acre business campus in deep South Philly that is home to companies like GlaxoSmithKline and Urban Outfitters. **Pros:** close to sports
stadiums, PHL airport. **Cons:** isolated from most of the city. $ *Rooms
from: $199* ✉ *1001 Intrepid Ave., South Philadelphia* 📞 *215/644–9200*
⊕ *www.marriott.com/phlcs* ⇨ *172 rooms* ❘❙❘ *No meals.*

$$ **Fairfield Inn Philadelphia Airport.** As far as airport hotels are concerned,
HOTEL   this South Philadelphia Fairfield Inn is standard, but its staff has a
reputation for being quite accommodating. **Pros:** accommodating staff;
24-hour shuttle service to airport; complimentary guest parking. **Cons:**
not convenient to city. $ *Rooms from: $169* ✉ *8800 Bartram Ave.,
South Philadelphia* 📞 *215/365–2254* ⊕ *www.marriott.com/hotels/
travel/phlfa-fairfield-inn-philadelphia-airport* ⇨ *97 rooms, 12 suites*
❘❙❘ *Breakfast.*

NIVERSITY CITY AND WEST PHILADELPHIA

UNIVERSITY CITY

$ **The Gables.** Built in 1889 by architect Willis Hale and first occupied
B&B/INN   by a prominent doctor and his family, this ornate mansion is a wonderful place for a B&B. **Pros:** off the beaten path; lots of antiques and
Victoriana; free parking. **Cons:** off the beaten path; the abundance
of Victoriana can be a bit much. $ *Rooms from: $110* ✉ *4520 Chester Ave., University City* 📞 *215/662–1918* ⊕ *www.gablesbb.com* ⇨ *9
rooms, 1 suite* ❘❙❘ *Breakfast.*

$$ **Inn at Penn.** Near the University of Pennsylvania, this hotel is a welcome
HOTEL   sight for anyone needing to stay in University City. **Pros:** collegiate feel
near major campuses; neat amenities such as in-room iPads. **Cons:** can get
crazy around graduation; away from Center City. $ *Rooms from: $209*
✉ *3600 Sansom St., University City* 📞 *215/222–0200, 800/445–8667*
⊕ *www.theinnatpenn.com* ⇨ *239 rooms, 4 suites* ❘❙❘ *No meals.*

$$ HOTEL 🏨 **Sheraton Philadelphia University City.** With plush beds and 37-inch flat screen televisions, spacious work areas, and complimentary Interne access, this hotel offers a nice balance of luxury and practicality. **Pros** free Internet access; 24-hour gym. **Cons:** check-in during big weekends such as graduation, can be tiresome; rates can get pricey. [$] *Room from: $209* ✉ *3549 Chestnut St., University City* ☎ *215/387–8000 877/459–1146* 🌐 *www.sheraton.com/universitycity* 🛏 *332 rooms, 2 suites* 🍴 *No meals.*

NORTHWESTERN PHILADELPHIA

CHESTNUT HILL

$ HOTEL 🏨 **Chestnut Hill Hotel.** This is the place to rest if you are looking for a mellow Philadelphia stay, or looking to stay in Northwest Philadelphia. **Pros:** low-key; on the avenue with all the shops, bars, and restaurants. **Cons:** not for those who like all-encompassing hotels. [$] *Room from: $149* ✉ *8229 Germantown Ave., Chestnut Hill* ☎ *215/242–590* 🌐 *www.chestnuthillhotel.com* 🛏 *32 rooms, 4 suites* 🍴 *Breakfast.*

CITY LINE AVENUE

City Line Avenue is a 10-minute ride on the Schuylkill Expressway to Center City.

$$ HOTEL 🏨 **Hilton Philadelphia City Avenue.** Though not in Center City proper, this hotel remains one of the city's most popular spots for weddings, charity events, and bar mitzvahs, greeting guests with an elegant marble lobby and grand chandeliers. **Pros:** beautiful common areas; great steak house; good location if visiting nearby St. Joseph's University. **Cons:** can be dominated by groups for large events; far from Center City. [$] *Rooms from: $159* ✉ *4200 City Ave., City Line Avenue* ☎ *215/879–4000, 800/445–8667* 🌐 *www.philadelphiacityavenue.hilton.com* 🛏 *215 rooms* 🍴 *No meals.*

NIGHTLIFE AND PERFORMING ARTS

Updated by
Drew Lazor

Whether you're a concert addict, a beer lover, or a theater connoisseur, Philadelphia's music, arts, and nightlife scenes have something for you. Local, national, and world-class acts make touring stops in Philadelphia a priority, and there's plenty of homegrown talent waiting to be discovered here, too.

A thriving reputation for live entertainment, coupled with a diversity of large, midsize, and small performance venues, means those seeking a good time can usually find what they're looking for with ease. Philly's music scene is not contained to a single area. During temperate months, there are concerts at Festival Pier and Penn's Landing along the Delaware River, as well as at the Mann Center for the Performing Arts in Fairmount Park. Big-name bands will play at the Wells Fargo Center; the Susquehanna Bank Center in Camden, New Jersey; the Electric Factory; the Keswick Theatre, in suburban Glenside; or the Tower Theater in Upper Darby. Smaller bands fill the bill at venues like the TLA on South Street; the Trocadero in Chinatown; Union Transfer, on Spring Garden Street; Johnny Brenda's and Kung Fu Necktie, in the Fishtown/Kensington area; and World Café Live—home of WXPN's radio broadcast—in University City. There are also a number of bar-restaurants that cater to music lovers, including Time, Heritage, and Chris' Jazz Café.

While a variety of smaller independent venues host cutting-edge stage productions throughout the city, Philly's long-standing reputation for theater is showcased most prominently on Broad Street, particularly along the stretch referred to as The Avenue of the Arts. This world-class cultural strip features a multitude of stops, including the Academy of Music, the Merriam Theater, the Wilma Theater, the Prince Music Theater, and the Kimmel Center for the Performing Arts, the stunning home of the Philadelphia Orchestra.

Depending on the time of year, you might also be able to take part in annual events such as the Roots Picnic, in early summer; Welcome to America!, a July 4 celebration; the Philadelphia Folk Festival and the Made in America Festival, both in late summer; the Philadelphia International Film Festival, held in the fall; or the cutting-edge FringeArts, which attracts experimental theater and performing arts from around the world.

The gay scene in Philadelphia revolves around the "Gayborhood," as it is affectionately referred to, an area in Center City East roughly from Chestnut to Pine and 11th to Broad streets. It is rife with gay-friendly bars, clubs, shops, boutiques, and cafés. For articles and more on the Philly gay scene, including a map of the Gayborhood, check out the *Philadelphia Gay News* (⊕ *epgn.com*).

IGHTLIFE

Generally speaking, you can break down Philly's central nightlife hubs into four distinct areas.

Traditionally, South Street is "where all the hippies meet," according to the 1963 hit by Philly's own The Orlons. The area has become a little less artsy in recent years, with tourist-friendly attraction taking over for some independent businesses, but there's still so much to see and do, particularly along the eastern half of the river-to-river street—packed bars and restaurants, tattoo parlors, sneaker stores, cafés, erotica shops, and more.

Home to the majority of Philadelphia's historical attractions, Old City is equally popular with party people come nightfall. Like South Street, it can get packed on the weekends, with various clubs, bars, and restaurants serving as draws. The crowd is a mix of tourists and locals, with the latter group heavy on "bridge-and-tunnel" types visiting from New Jersey and nearby suburbs. Columbus Boulevard, in particular, features a high concentration of club destinations.

North of Old City lie Northern Liberties and Fishtown. Both neighborhoods have long been associated with Philly's bohemian crowd, a target for edgy artists, chefs, and musicians. More recently, however, both enclaves and the areas surrounding them have come into their own as legitimate cultural contenders citywide with great bars and breweries.

Finally, Rittenhouse Square, in the heart of Center City, is the premier hangout for Philly's moneyed crowd, with a slew of high-profile bars, restaurants, and clubs joining a scattering of under-the-radar gems both old-school and new-school.

Other neighborhoods of interest are University City, with all the standard (and not-so-standard) college-age bars and clubs, plus unique international options in greater West Philly; East Passyunk, a hot strip featuring hip bars and restaurants commingling with South Philly's old-school Italian population; and Manayunk, a nightlife-heavy area to the northwest particularly popular with college kids and recent grads.

Bars and clubs can sometimes close, change hands, or turn over with very short notice, so stay abreast of the latest by following the entertainment pages and respective websites of the *Philadelphia Inquirer* and *Philadelphia Daily News* (⊕ *philly.com*); the *Philadelphia Weekly* (⊕ *phillyweekly.com*); the *Philadelphia Gay News* (⊕ *epgn.com*); and *Philadelphia* magazine (⊕ *phillymag.com*).

In Philadelphia, last call for bars and clubs is 2 am, though there are a handful of places with special licenses that allow for legal after-hours service. Cover charges can range from free to about $12. While Philly tends toward the casual in many of its nightlife venues, there are dress codes enforced in some clubs. Best to check online to make certain if you're venturing into new territory.

People from outside the city might be surprised to see just how popular dancing is here. The persuasive DJ culture has permeated the city, especially in Old City, Northern Liberties/Fishtown, and on South Street.

Philadelphia has a rich jazz and blues heritage that includes such greats as the late, legendary jazz saxophonist John Coltrane and current players like Grover Washington Jr. That legacy continues today in clubs around town.

Though a number of Philly rock/pop venues are owned by Live Nation, a good variety of touring bands is still represented on a nightly basis. And with the advent of the Fishtown live-music scene at venues such as Johnny Brenda's and Kung Fu Necktie, as well as the popular Union Transfer on Spring Garden, there is a greater variety of live music available than ever before.

THE HISTORIC DOWNTOWN

Home to a large proliferation of bars, clubs, and restaurants, the Historic Downtown area of Philadelphia, including Old City and Society Hill, was long thought of as the place South Street revelers eventually headed after they got through adolescence. It remains a major linchpin of out-of-towner socializing, but the area has also accomplished its own kind of maturation.

OLD CITY

BARS AND LOUNGES

Continental Restaurant & Martini Bar. Even restaurant and nightlife mogul Stephen Starr had to start somewhere—the Continental was his very first restaurant, and it continues to be one of his most popular. The retro-fied former diner draws an interesting crowd, a mix of energetic twentysomethings and longtime regulars. The design, featuring lots of stainless steel and campy lighting fixtures, goes well with the martini-driven cocktail list and global small-plates menu. ⊠ *138 Market St., Old City* ☎ *215/923–6069* ⊕ *www.continentalmartinibar.com.*

Fodor's Choice ★ **Eulogy Belgian Tavern.** For those with an insatiable desire to try new and exotic brews, this Old City bar offers an absolutely staggering assortment: 300-plus bottles and 27 rotating taps, with an emphasis on Belgian beers. There's also a full menu to complement the theme, featuring Belgian favorites like *moules frites* (mussels and fries). ⊠ *136 Chestnut St., Old City* ☎ *215/413–1918.*

Il Bar. The wine bar at Ristorante Panorama, a polished northern Italian restaurant in the Penn's View Inn, stands out for its staggering vino selection—more than 150 wines are available by the glass, thanks to a cruvinet preservation system touted as the largest in the world. Other oenophile hooks include "Wine Wednesday" specials and personalized flights. ⊠ *14 N. Front St., Old City* ☎ *215/922–7800* ⊕ *www.pennsviewhotel.com.*

MUSIC CLUBS

Khyber Pass Pub. Historically a loud and fast punk rock club, the Khyber has been reinvented in more recent years as a serious craft beer bar (22 taps) and a restaurant serving authentic New Orleans cuisine. (They still host events and performances upstairs from time to time.) Philly may have lost a regular live-music staple, but it gained a serious beer bar that earns a perennial spot on annual best-of lists. ⊠ *56 S. 2nd St., Old City* ☎ *215/238–5888* ⊕ *www.khyberpasspub.com.*

Tin Angel Acoustic Café. Local and national musicians hold forth at a 115-seat acoustic cabaret above the Serrano restaurant (patrons get preferred seating). You can sit at candlelit tables or at the bar and hear music from blues to folk. ✉ *20 S. 2nd St., Old City* ☎ *215/928–0770* ⊕ *www.tinangel.com.*

PENN'S LANDING
MUSIC FESTIVALS
PECO Multicultural Series. PECO, Philadelphia's primary electric provider, sponsors a series of global celebrations along Penn's Landing over summer weekends. Each installment focuses on a different cultural tradition, a welcome respite from the grueling dog days of the season. ✉ *Columbus Ave. and Chestnut St., Penn's Landing* ☎ *215/922–2386* ⊕ *www.visitphilly. com/events/philadelphia/peco-multicultural-series-at-penns-landing.*

CENTER CITY

5

Including the Washington Square district and Chinatown, Center City offers everything from decadent nightspots to raucous pubs and clandestine holes-in-the-wall.

CENTER CITY EAST
BARS AND LOUNGES
Dirty Frank's. Its outside walls decorated with famous Franks throughout history (Frankenstein's monster, FDR, Sinatra, Zappa, etc.), Dirty Frank's is a Philadelphia classic. An glorious mixture of students, artists, journalists, and resident characters crowds around the horseshoe-shaped bar and engages in friendly, beer-soaked mayhem. ✉ *347 S. 13th St., Center City East* ☎ *215/732–5010.*

Fergie's Pub. Fergus "Fergie" Carey is the jovial proprietor of this casual, cozy, and beloved bar, which has been around longer than most establishments of its ilk in Philly. The taproom, which serves solid craft beer and comfort food, hosts regular entertainment, including music, poetry, Quizzo, and even live theater. There are no televisions on the premises, as Carey believes in the lost art of conversation. ✉ *1214 Sansom St., Center City East* ☎ *215/928–8118* ⊕ *www.fergies.com.*

Franky Bradley's. A former supper club that attracted movers and shakers of yesteryear, the updated Franky's is now under the watch of Mark Bee, architect of N. 3rd and Silk City. A kitschy dining room decorated with Bee's Technicolor flea market finds gives way to an upstairs performance space used by DJs and live acts. They serve food until 1 am nightly. ✉ *1320 Chancellor St., Center City East* ☎ *215/735–0735* ⊕ *www.frankybradleys.com.*

McGillin's Olde Ale House. For longevity alone, McGillin's stands proud. Open since 1860, it's the oldest continually operating pub in the city, as well as one of the oldest in the country. But though there are nostalgic touches, it's a modern watering hole, featuring a bevy of TVs for sports and hugely popular karaoke nights. The beer list, featuring 30 choices on draft, tends toward the local, including a series of signature house ales brewed by Adamstown, Pa.'s Stoudts. ✉ *1310 Drury St., Center City East* ☎ *215/735–5562* ⊕ *www.mcgillins.com.*

MilkBoy. The city outpost of the coffee house and recording studio in Ardmore, MilkBoy Philly features a down-to-earth café and bar on the street level, with a narrow, intimate performance space up top. It attracts mostly indie rock acts, both locals and touring outfits. ✉ *1100 Chestnut St., Center City East* ☎ *215/925–MILK* ⊕ *www.milkboyphilly.com.*

Time. A rocking big-city club from the same owners of the nearby Vintage Wine Bar, Time features three concepts in one—a whiskey-heavy cocktail bar; a dining room with a bar and live music seven nights a week; and an upstairs lounge and music venue. Downstairs acts tend toward the jazz persuasion, while DJs tend to dominate up top. ✉ *1315 Sansom St., Center City East* ☎ *215/985–4800* ⊕ *www.timerestaurant.net.*

Zavino. A small but bustling pizzeria and bar on par with European-style alfresco cafés, Zavino slings creative Neapolitan-style pies and a taut selection of wine and beer. In warmer months, the large open windows and sidewalk seating makes for a humming outdoor scene. ✉ *112 S. 13th St., Center City East* ☎ *215/732–2400.*

GAY AND LESBIAN BARS AND LOUNGES
The Bike Stop. A multifloored space, down a side alley, the Bike Stop caters specifically to those seeking leather-clad adventures. ✉ *206 S. Quince St., Center City East* ☎ *215/627–1662.*

Tavern on Camac. Directly below the popular piano bar and nightclub Tavern on Camac is this late-night haunt, which serves rib-sticking comfort food until 1 am weekdays and 2 am weeknights (closed Tuesdays). Specialties include grilled cheese, a beefy Tavern burger, and cassoulet; they make creative cocktails, too. ✉ *243 S. Camac St., Center City East* ☎ *215/545–1102* ⊕ *www.tavernphilly.com.*

Woody's. Philadelphia's most popular gay nightlife destination is spread over two levels, offering several bars—with monitors playing music videos and campy moments from TV shows and movies—and a large dance floor upstairs. Themed nights include Latin music on Thursdays and country line dancing on Fridays. ✉ *202 S. 13th St., Center City East* ☎ *215/545–1893* ⊕ *www.woodysbar.com.*

DANCE CLUBS
Voyeur. This gay-friendly after-hours joint offers late-night thrills, courtesy of diverse DJ booking and a potent light-and-sound system. Two massive dance floors are filled with gyrating bodies, and a third-level catwalk enables those wanting a rest (or further libations) an excellent vantage point. ✉ *1221 St. James St., Center City East* ☎ *215/735–5772* ⊕ *www.voyeurnightclub.com.*

MUSIC CLUBS
Philadelphia Clef Club of Jazz & Performing Arts. Dedicated solely to jazz, including its history and instruction, the Clef Club boasts a 240-seat theater for live concerts, celebrating both the present and past of Philly jazz. ✉ *738 S. Broad St., Center City East* ☎ *215/893–9912* ⊕ *www.clefclubofjazz.org.*

CENTER CITY WEST
BARS AND LOUNGES

Black Sheep. This handsome pub is just off Rittenhouse Square, in a refurbished town house with a fireplace on the main floor and a quiet dining space on the upper level. Beer lovers can choose from a solid selection of draft, bottled, and canned beers; the food, including U.K.-style entrées like shepherd's pie and bangers and mash, is straightforward and satisfying. ⊠ *247 S. 17th St., Center City West* ☎ *215/545–9473* ⊕ *www.theblacksheeppub.com.*

Continental Mid-Town. A more elaborate offshoot of Stephen Starr's Old City martini lounge, the Mid-Town spreads the cocktail and global small-plate concept across two whimsically appointed floors. The additional room accommodates crowds that swell on weekend evenings. ⊠ *1801 Chestnut St., Center City West* ☎ *215/567–1800* ⊕ *www.continentalmidtown.com.*

XIX (Nineteen). Perched on the 19th floor of the Park Hyatt at the Belle-vue, this high-end lounge bestows beautiful vistas of the city, solid cocktails, a seafood-centric menu, a roaring fireplace, and elegant decorative accents. It's certainly pricey, but the views make up for it. ⊠ *200 S. Broad St., Center City West* ☎ *215/790–1919* ⊕ *www.hyatt.com/ gallery/nineteen/xix.html.*

Fodor's Choice
★ **10 Arts Lounge and Bistro.** Under the soaring, 140-foot-high rotunda of this former bank building, refashioned as the Ritz-Carlton Philadelphia, is an elegant lobby bar with marble floors, dramatic lighting, and plush seating—a gracious spot to have a before- or after-dinner cocktail. Just off the lobby is the handsome restaurant side of 10 Arts, specializing in local and organic farm-to-table cooking. ⊠ *10 S. Broad St., at Chestnut St., Center City West* ☎ *215/523–8000* ⊕ *www.10arts.com.*

Tria. Wine, beer, and cheese is the celebrated trio at this branch of the well-loved collection of tasting-friendly bar/restaurants, which also features a cheffy lineup of clever small plates. The menu is packed with interesting info, as are the well-versed servers and bartenders. ⊠ *2227 Pine St., Center City West* ☎ *215/309–2245* ⊕ *www.triafitlersquare.com.*

COMEDY CLUBS

Helium Comedy Club. Philly's premier comedy club, Helium attracts well-known headliners from television and film, all of whom perform in a straightforward room that serves basic eats and cocktails. ⊠ *2031 Sansom St., Center City West* ☎ *215/496–9001* ⊕ *philadelphia. heliumcomedy.com.*

MUSIC CLUBS

Chris' Jazz Café. This intimate hangout off the Avenue of the Arts (aka Broad Street), Chris' showcases top talent Monday through Saturday. The jazz club stays accessible by doing the simple things right—friendly service, fair prices, great performers. The lunch and dinner menus feature some light New Orleans–style touches. ⊠ *1421 Sansom St., Center City West* ☎ *215/568–3131* ⊕ *www.chrisjazzcafe.com.*

CHINATOWN
BARS AND LOUNGES
Hop Sing Laundromat. Run by mysterious and mononym-using owner Lê, Hop Sing is a drinkers' haven for cocktail fans who take their cocktails clandestine. Hopeful patrons wait in front of a nondescript door in Chinatown, adhering to a dress code and a strict no–cell phones policy; once inside, the high-end spirits and creative cocktails flow in a one-of-a-kind room. ✉ *1029 Race St., Chinatown.*

MUSIC CLUBS
Trocadero. This spacious rock-and-roll club in Chinatown occupies a former vaudeville theater and burlesque house where W. C. Fields and Mae West performed. Much of the old decor remains: mirrors, pillars, and balconies surround the dance floor. Most every up-and-coming band that's passing through Philly plays here to an under-30 crowd. On other nights, local DJs play for dance parties; Monday sees it host a popular film series. ✉ *1003 Arch St., Chinatown* ☎ *215/922–6888* ⊕ *www.thetroc.com.*

RITTENHOUSE SQUARE
BARS AND LOUNGES
a.bar. Attached to the AKA hotel and its restaurant, a.kitchen, a.bar boasts one of the most enviable views in the city, looking right out onto Rittenhouse Square. The food and drink, with its emphases on fresh seafood and cutting-edge cocktails, will encourage return visits. ✉ *AKA Rittenhouse Square, 1737 Walnut St., Rittenhouse Square* ☎ *215/825–7030* ⊕ *www.akitchenandbar.com.*

The Bards. A lively and authentic Irish pub, the Bards has an Irish crowd, Irish food, and a host of full-bodied beers. ✉ *2013 Walnut St., Rittenhouse Square* ☎ *215/569–9585* ⊕ *www.bardsirishbar.com.*

The Franklin Mortgage & Investment Co. One of the city's premier bars for cocktail lovers, the sexy, subterranean Franklin is named after a cover business established by infamous Philly gangster Max "Boo Boo" Hoff. Bartenders whip up potent and elaborate cocktails in a narrow parlor that often requires a wait; upstairs, there's a more casual beer-and-shoot hangout popular with restaurant workers. ✉ *112 S. 18th St., Rittenhouse Square* ☎ *267/467–3277* ⊕ *www.thefranklinbar.com.*

Tria. Wine, beer, and cheese is the celebrated trio at this branch of the well-loved collection of tasting-friendly bar/restaurants, which also features a cheffy lineup of clever small plates. The menu is packed with interesting info, as are the well-versed servers and bartenders. ✉ *123 S. 18th St., Rittenhouse Square* ☎ *215/972–8742* ⊕ *www.triacafe.com* ✉ *1137 Spruce St., Center City East* ☎ *215/629–9200.*

Twenty Manning Grill. The sleek lounge area and bar at this spiffy restaurant-bar is a haven for Rittenhouse regulars, making for some solid people-watching. Though it's largely known in the area as a spot for socializing, it's also an excellent source of creative cocktails and reliable comfort food. ✉ *261 S. 20th St., Rittenhouse Square* ☎ *215/731–0900* ⊕ *www.twentymanning.com.*

Vango Lounge & Skybar. Upstairs from sister joint Byblos, this luxe club and restaurant conjures up a Tokyo vibe, from its Japanese-themed menu to its emphasis on mod design. The real star, however, is the third-floor Skybar, offering panoramic views of the city. ⊠ *116 S. 18th St., Rittenhouse Square* ☎ *215/568–1020* ⊕ *www.vangoloungeandskybar.com.*

GAY AND LESBIAN BARS AND LOUNGES

Stir Lounge. A lesbian-owned bar and club with a dance-loving clientele, Stir prides itself on its inclusive nature and stiff drinks. It's got a primo location in Rittenhouse, though it's tucked out of the way on tiny Chancellor Street. ⊠ *1705 Chancellor St., Rittenhouse Square* ☎ *215/732–2700* ⊕ *www.stirphilly.com.*

COMEDY CLUBS

Comedy Sportz. Anything goes during this once-a-week night of improvisational comedy, formatted as a high-energy competitive sport. The troupe hosts two shows every Saturday at the Adrienne Theater, and audience participation is essential to the experience. ⊠ *2030 Sansom St., Rittenhouse Square* ☎ *877/985–2844* ⊕ *www.comedysportzphilly.com.*

BENJAMIN FRANKLIN PARKWAY AND FAIRMOUNT

BENJAMIN FRANKLIN PARKWAY
MUSIC FESTIVALS
Wawa Welcome America! Festival In the days leading up to Independence Day (July 4), Welcome America! highlights Philly's history with patriotic happenings, from a massive block party on the Benjamin Franklin Parkway to free museum access and historical tours. It all culminates with a concert and fireworks extravaganza held on the Parkway; past performers have included Hall and Oates, John Legend, and Sheryl Crow. ⊠ *26th St. and Ben Franklin Pkwy., Benjamin Franklin Parkway* ☎ *215/683–2200* ⊕ *www.welcomeamerica.com.*

UNIVERSITY CITY AND WEST PHILADELPHIA

UNIVERSITY CITY
MUSIC CLUBS
Fodor's Choice ★ World Cafe Live. A musical flagship in West Philly, WCL's building also houses the radio station WXPN-FM, which emphasizes acoustic, independent, and world-beat contemporary artists. The café also has two theaters—the largest of which, Downstairs Live, seats up to 300 (and can fit more, depending on configurations)—and two restaurants. ⊠ *3025 Walnut St., University City* ☎ *215/222–1400* ⊕ *www.philly. worldcafelive.com.*

NORTHWESTERN PHILADELPHIA

MANAYUNK
BARS AND LOUNGES
The Goat's Beard. A grown-up hangout in college-kid-heavy Manayunk, The Goat's Beard specializes in hearty European bistro-style cooking, local beers, and sharply curated spirits (especially whiskey). The

handsome, high-ceiling space offers a bit more elegance than your average Main Street bar. ⊠ *4201 Main St., Manayunk* ☎ *267/323–2495* ⊕ *www.thegoatsbeardphilly.com.*

Lucky's Last Chance. A down-to-earth pub, Lucky's is well known for its wacky food stylings, including burgers and hot dogs with unexpected toppings. But it's also a solid place to drink, with DJs, dance nights, and special events holding down the entertainment side on occasion. ⊠ *4421 Main St., Manayunk* ☎ *215/509–6005* ⊕ *www.luckyslastchance.com.*

Manayunk Brewery & Restaurant. A long-running destination set right on the banks of the Schuylkill River, this brewpub offers a well-rounded selection of ales and lagers brewed on the premises, as well as some diverse food options, including sushi and pizza. Check out the patio in the spring and summer. ⊠ *4120 Main St., Manayunk* ☎ *215/482–8220* ⊕ *www.manayunkbrewery.com.*

CHESTNUT HILL
BARS AND LOUNGES
McNally's Tavern. This venerable Chestnut Hill tavern is most famous for "The Schmitter," a cheesesteak hybrid sandwich that features unorthodox toppings like grilled salami and "special" sauce. In general, though, it's a broken-in barroom worthy of a visit, as they've been making people happy since 1921. ⊠ *8634 Germantown Ave., Chestnut Hill* ☎ *215/247–9736* ⊕ *www.mcnallystavern.com.*

Tavern on the Hill. Mixed in among Chestnut Hill's quaint shops and boutiques, this friendly hangout, open for lunch, dinner, and drinks, is a popular stop-in with locals. The homey menu features a big selection of sandwiches and hearty, familiar entrées. ⊠ *8636 Germantown Ave., Chestnut Hill* ☎ *215/247–9948.*

MUSIC CLUBS
Mermaid Inn. Head to the Mermaid, as the Northwest Philly locals do, to hear excellent live music (folk, blues, rock, jazz) and drink from an interesting selection of bottled beers. Depending on who is playing, there may be a cover charge of $10. ⊠ *7673 Winston Rd., at Mermaid La., Chestnut Hill* ☎ *215/247–9797* ⊕ *www.themermaidinn.net/home. html* ⊗ *Closed Sun.*

MOUNT AIRY
BARS AND LOUNGES
McMenamins. This Mount Airy favorite has a fantastic choice of craft beer on tap, plus good burgers and fish-and-chips. ⊠ *7170 Germantown Ave., Mount Airy* ☎ *215/247–9920.*

SOUTH PHILADELPHIA

Once known primarily for the Italian Market and cheesesteak icons Pat's and Geno's, South Philly has rapidly developed, adding much welcome diversity in terms of both residents and businesses. In Bella Vista, a plethora of new restaurants have joined existing old-world pasta houses and bars; in Queen Village, new hot spots have sprung up amid familiar staples and BYOs; farther south, there is the burgeoning nightlife draw of the bars, cafés, and restaurants of East Passyunk.

SOUTH PHILADELPHIA
BARS AND LOUNGES

Sidecar Bar & Grille. An anchor establishment in the south–of–Center City neighborhood of Graduate Hospital, the Sidecar delivers with an approachable mix of great beer, creative pub food, interesting people, and positive vibes. (There's *always* good music playing here.) The main bar is accompanied by a second-floor hangout that often plays host to events and get-togethers. ✉ *2201 Christian St., South Philadelphia* ☎ *215/732–3429* ⊕ *www.thesidecarbar.com.*

Triangle Tavern. An old-school South Philly bar converted by the owners of Khyber Pass Pub, Royal Tavern, and Cantina Los Caballitos, the Triangle is at once new and old. While the smart craft beer and spirit selection nods to nouveau drinkers, the bar's old-school menu, featuring pastas, roast pork sandwiches, and other hearty South Philly specialties, is as classic as it gets. ✉ *1338 S 10th St., South Philadelphia* ☎ *215/800–1992* ⊕ *www.triangletavernphilly.com.*

MUSIC CLUBS

Theatre of Living Arts. The TLA, a former independent movie house, is a South Street institution that helped launch the careers of many indie filmmakers, in addition to hosting regular screenings of cult hits like *The Rocky Horror Picture Show.* Today, it presents concerts by a range of rock, blues, hip-hop, and adult alternative acts. ✉ *334 South St., South Philadelphia* ☎ *215/922–1011* ⊕ *venue.tlaphilly.com.*

Warmdaddy's. This rustic, down-home blues club and restaurant right near the Delaware River serves up live blues and soulful Southern cuisine every night of the week. ✉ *1400 Columbus Blvd., at Reed St., South Philadelphia* ☎ *215/462–2000 reservations* ⊕ *www.warmdaddys.com.*

EAST PASSYUNK
BARS AND LOUNGES

The Pub on Passyunk East. Less concerned with the papacy than fine craft beer, the P.O.P.E., as it's called by locals, is a comfy neighborhood joint smack-dab in the middle of the drinking and dining enclave of East Passyunk Avenue. A bona fide neighborhood hangout that gets slammed on the weekends, the bar offers 15 beers on tap and loads more in bottles; the kitchens prepares straightforward fare, including burgers, nachos, and vegetarian options. ✉ *1501 Passyunk Ave., East Passyunk* ☎ *215/755–5125* ⊕ *www.pubonpassyunkeast.com.*

QUEEN VILLAGE
BARS AND LOUNGES

For Pete's Sake. Pete's, in Queen Village, could easily be mistaken for just another neighborhood watering hole, but the menu is eclectic, featuring a regularly changing lineup of creative food alongside the requisite wings and burgers. ✉ *900 S. Front St., Queen Village* ☎ *215/462–2230* ⊕ *www.forpetessakepub.com.*

New Wave Café. To its devoted Queen Village clientele, the New Wave is more than just the place to wait for a table at Dmitri's, the always-crowded seafood restaurant across the street. The regulars come to this long, narrow bar to unwind with a local Yuengling beer (referred

to, simply, as "lager"), play a game of darts, and enjoy the oft-chang
ing gastropub menu. ⊠ 784 S. 3rd St., Queen Village ☎ 215/922–848
⊕ newwavecafe.com.

BELLA VISTA
BARS AND LOUNGES
L'etage. Upstairs from parent restaurant Beau Monde, a fine French crê
perie, this unique spot has a lovely selection of wines and liquors. The
also offer up a slate of unique entertainment that ranges from specialt
cabaret and comedy to DJs and live storytelling. ⊠ 624 S. 6th St., Bell
Vista ☎ 215/592–0656 ⊕ www.creperie-beaumonde.com.

Royal Tavern. In Bella Vista, the stalwart Royal satisfies both aspirin
young barflies and entrenched locals with equal aplomb. Beer, whethe
poured from one of the eight taps or sipped from a bottle, is abundan
as is the crazy-hearty comfort-food menu, featuring one of the city's bes
burgers. If your late-night snacking requires a sound track, they've go
a great jukebox, rocking the likes of Iggy Pop and The Kinks. ⊠ 937 E
Passyunk Ave., Bella Vista ☎ 215/389–6694 ⊕ www.royaltavern.com

NORTHEASTERN PHILADELPHIA

An influx of new residents and businesses has brought Northern Liber
ties and the nearby neighborhoods of Fishtown, Kensington, and Por
Richmond into the zeitgeist. The neighborhoods, still largely residential
have a working-class feel, though much of the area's old industry—
including printing, textiles, and metalworking—is long gone.

NORTHEAST PHILADELPHIA
BARS AND LOUNGES
Memphis Taproom. A pioneering beer bar in this part of town, Memphi
offers more than 18 diverse beers on tap, plus 2 in casks; they're equall
liked for their food, inventive gastropub grub with plenty of vegetaria
and vegan options. Their adjacent beer garden, featuring a stationar
food truck and a projection screen for games and movies, is a favorite i
the warmer months. ⊠ 2331 E. Cumberland St., Northeast Philadelphi
☎ 215/425–4460 ⊕ www.memphistaproom.com.

NORTHERN LIBERTIES
BARS AND LOUNGES
The Abbaye. NoLibs' reliable corner bar takes a Belgian approach, serv
ing the appropriate beers (Chimay, Duvel) along with local crafts, i
bottle and on draft. The hearty pub menu skews Euro, too, with som
twists (vegan versions of wings, meatballs, and cheesesteaks). ⊠ 637 N
3rd St., Northern Liberties ☎ 215/627–6711.

Bar Ferdinand. One of Philly's steadiest spots for authentic Iberian sabor
the inviting Ferdinand slings a wide variety of both traditional and mod
ern Spanish tapas, along with an impressive wine list. ⊠ 1030 N. 2n
St., Northern Liberties ☎ 215/923–1313 ⊕ www.barferdinand.com.

North Bowl. Cleverly located in the thick of Northern Liberties' Secon
Street scene, this boozing-friendly bowling alley delivers in the tenpi
department. The large, colorful space serves a snacky menu, featurin

CLOSE UP

Philly's Music History

Philly holds a special place in pop music history. *American Bandstand*, hosted by Dick Clark, began here as a local dance show. When it went national in 1957, it gave a boost to many hometown boys, including teen heartthrob Fabian, Bobby Rydell, Frankie Avalon, and Chubby Checker, of "Twist" fame. Sun Ra, the legendary jazz pianist, was from Philly, in keeping with the city's rich tradition of jazz luminaries such as saxophonists Grover Washington Jr., Stan Getz, and John Coltrane, drummer Philly Joe Jones, and vocalist Billie Holiday.

In the 1970s, the Philadelphia Sound—a polished blend of disco, pop, and R&B—came alive through producers Kenny Gamble and Leon Huff at the famed Philadelphia International Records studios for

artists like The Ojays, Lou Rawls, Teddy Pendergrass, and Three Degrees, whose megahit "Love Train" helped to define the '70s era. That lush sound was kept alive by chart toppers such as Hall and Oates, Patti LaBelle, Boyz II Men, Will Smith, Jill Scott, The Roots (now the house band for *Late Night With Jimmy Fallon*, among other accomplishments), neo-soul stylist Musiq Soulchild, pop queen Pink, and R&B sensation Jazmine Sullivan.

Contemporary rock acts from Philly that have gained national renown include Dr. Dog, Kurt Vile, Man Man, Hop Along, Circa Survive, and The War on Drugs. The local DJ scene is also potent, with stalwart spinners like King Britt, Rich Medina, and The Roots' Questlove paving the way for a new generation of party starters.

a big selection of wackily topped tater tots. ⊠ *909 N. 2nd St., Northern Liberties* ☎ *215/238–2695* ⊕ *www.northbowlphilly.com.*

N. 3rd. One of the first places of its kind in NoLibs, owner Mark Bee's N. 3rd (North Third) is a bar and restaurant with a kitschy kitchen perspective. The worldly but accessible menu is right for this well-rounded neighborhood; outdoor seating along the titular street is a hot commodity in spring and summer. ⊠ *801 N. 3rd St., Northern Liberties* ☎ *215/413–3666* ⊕ *www.norththird.com.*

Fodor's Choice ★ **Standard Tap.** A pioneering establishment in Philadelphia's pub culture, Standard Tap has been pairing local beer with thoughtful seasonal food since 1999. (The owners also have Johnny Brenda's close by.) The dimly light, multilevel interior, all beautiful dark wood and tucked-away nooks, endear it to locals as a gathering space, as does the consistent food and drink. ⊠ *901 N. 2nd St., Northern Liberties* ☎ *215/238–0630* ⊕ *www.standardtap.com.*

DANCE CLUBS

The Barbary. Owned by Philly DJ John Redden (aka JHN RDN), the Barbary is a go-to for live shows and DJs. Between the dance-y, disco ball–adorned downstairs and the smaller "Barbarella" subconcept upstairs, the space draws diverse crowds tuned in to all sorts of different musical genres. ⊠ *951 Frankford Ave., Northern Liberties* ☎ *215/634–7400* ⊕ *www.instagram.com/the_barbary.*

The 700. Plenty has changed in Northern Liberties over the years, but the 700 remains an approachable, no-frills neighborhood joint. The ground-floor bar, a popular gathering place for soccer fans and boasting a beer selection of 90+, gives way to a living room-like upstairs where DJs spin three nights a week. ⊠ *700 N. 2nd St., Northern Liberties* ☎ *215/413–3181* ⊕ *www.the700.com.*

Fodor'sChoice ★ **Silk City Diner Bar & Lounge.** A consistent player in Philly's club scene, Silk City combines a quirky club and live performance venue with a diner side specializing in creative comfort food. The lively crowds feature all sorts but the vibe especially caters to those of the hip-hop, R&B, and soul persuasions. ⊠ *435 Spring Garden St., Northern Liberties* ☎ *215/592–8838* ⊕ *www.silkcityphilly.com.*

MUSIC CLUBS

Electric Factory. Named in honor of the original Electric Factory, which opened in 1968 and hosted acts ranging from Jimi Hendrix to the Grateful Dead, this current incarnation occupies a cavernous former warehouse just north of Center City and presents mainly alternative rock bands. It has a capacity of about 2,500, but that number mostly refers to standing room; the main concert area doesn't have seats, although you can sit down at a balcony bar and watch the proceedings from there. ⊠ *421 N. 7th St., Northern Liberties* ☎ *215/568–3222* ⊕ *www.electricfactory.info.*

Ortlieb's Lounge. Back open and humming after a series of ownership changes, this out-of-the-way venue in NoLibs has expanded its musical scope well beyond the traditional jazz. The vintage barroom, named after a defunct Philly brewery, now books indie rock, hip-hop, funk, and more. Hit up the bar for the cheap tacos, pretty close to the perfect drinking snacks. ⊠ *847 N. 3rd St., Northern Liberties* ☎ *267/324–3348* ⊕ *ortliebslounge.ticketfly.com.*

Union Transfer. A former train station and restaurant converted into a haven for live music, Union Transfer might be Philly's best pound-for-pound place to catch a show. The spacious layout, impressive booking, and incredible sound make for an easygoing, one-of-a-kind concert experience. ⊠ *1026 Spring Garden St., Northern Liberties* ☎ *215/232–2100* ⊕ *www.utphilly.com.*

FISHTOWN
BARS AND LOUNGES

Frankford Hall. Stephen Starr's big, loud, and lively beer garden brings a bit of Bavaria to Fishtown's nightlife scene. You and your crew can sit outside at one of the largest picnic tables, or hang indoors when it's frigid. Draft beers, many of them German, come in half or full liters, accompanied by rib-sticking pretzels, wurst, and schnitzel. ⊠ *1210 Frankford Ave., Fishtown* ☎ *215/634–3338* ⊕ *www.frankfordhall.com.*

Johnny Brenda's. A funky, welcoming bar, restaurant, and music venue, JB's epitomizes the bridging of old and new frequently found in Fishtown. A local beer-heavy tavern, complete with billiards, blends seamlessly into a solid casual restaurant downstairs. Upstairs hosts an edgily booked lineup of performers in a diversity of genres. ⊠ *1201 N. Frankford Ave., Fishtown* ☎ *215/739–9684* ⊕ *www.johnnybrendas.com.*

MUSIC CLUBS

The Fillmore Philadelphia. One of Philadelphia's newest venues for live music, the 25,000-square-foot Fillmore capitalizes on the rising relevance of the Fishtown neighborhood, introducing a rock club experience for the 21st century. Three raised balconies providing solid sight lines for as many as 2,500 concertgoers, with a secondary club, the Foundary, holding about 450. ✉ *29 E. Allen St., Fishtown* ☎ *215/309–0150* ⊕ *www.thefillmorephilly.com.*

Kung Fu Necktie. A block removed from the major intersection of Frankford and Girard, KFN hosts indie music acts in a small, moody barroom hidden underneath the elevated tracks of SEPTA's Market-Frankford line. They book both local and national bands. ✉ *1250 N. Front St., Fishtown* ☎ *215/291–4919* ⊕ *kungfunecktie.com.*

PERFORMING ARTS

5

Of all the performing arts, it's music for which Philadelphia is most renowned and the Philadelphia Orchestra of which its residents are most proud. Though the Orchestra has undergone some financial hardships in recent years, the hope is it can rebound and regain its place among the world's elite. The city also serves as a major stop for touring productions of shows from *A Chorus Line* to *Spring Awakening,* and the local theater scene, which supports more than two dozen regional and local companies, is thriving.

Since the opening of the Kimmel Center in 2001, Philadelphia has enjoyed an embarrassment of riches when it comes to performance space. The Academy of Music, the Philadelphia Orchestra's previous home, remains open in all its finery; the Annenberg and Painted Bride house everything from theater to performance art; and both the Mann Center and the Susquehanna Bank Center remain premier outdoor amphitheaters.

Classical music in Philadelphia begins with the world-renowned Philadelphia Orchestra, which, under music director Yannick Nézet-Séguin, has kept its remarkable pedigree. But there is also the Chamber Orchestra, which is also housed in the glorious Kimmel Center; the venerable Philly Pops; and the very talented students of the Curtis Institute, to round out the bill.

INFORMATION AND TICKETS

For current performances and listings, the best guides to Philly's performing arts are the "Guide to the Lively Arts" in the daily *Philadelphia Inquirer,* the "Weekend" section of the Friday *Inquirer,* and the "Friday" section of the *Philadelphia Daily News.*

Independence Visitor Center. The Independence Visitor Center is open daily 8:30 to 7, and has information about performances. ✉ *6th St. between Market and Arch Sts., Historic Area* ☎ *800/537–7676* ⊕ *www. independencevisitorcenter.com.*

THE HISTORIC DOWNTOWN

OLD CITY

CONCERT HALLS

Painted Bride Art Center. By day it's a contemporary art gallery showing bold, challenging works. By night it's a multidisciplinary, multicultural performance center, with performance art, prose and poetry readings, folk and new music, jazz, dance, and avant-garde theater. The gallery is open Tuesday–Saturday noon–6. ⊠ *230 Vine St., Old City* ☎ *215/925–9914* ⊕ *www.paintedbride.org.*

THEATER

Arden Theatre Company. The Arden, formed in 1988, is known for premiering new works and offering a mix of classic drama, comedy, and musicals, with a special affinity for the works of Stephen Sondheim; the company has won many local Barrymore Awards. Its home is in Old City. ⊠ *40 N. 2nd St., Old City* ☎ *215/922–1122* ⊕ *www.ardentheatre.org.*

SOCIETY HILL

THEATER

Society Hill Playhouse. For more than 50 years, this small off-Broadway–style theater, just off South Street, has mounted original plays. The main stage is for contemporary works; the smaller Red Room features cabaret and musical comedies. ⊠ *507 S. 8th St., Society Hill* ☎ *215/923–0210* ⊕ *www.societyhillplayhouse.org.*

CENTER CITY

CENTER CITY EAST

FILM FESTIVALS

Philadelphia Film Festival. This two-week extravaganza in late October organized by the Philadelphia Film Society is filled with screenings, seminars, and events attended by critics, scholars, filmmakers, and cinema buffs. It's held at various venues around the city. ⊠ *Philadelphia* ⊕ *filmadelphia.org.*

qFLIX Philadelphia. This summer festival of contemporary Queer cinema takes place in a variety of venues around the city. The organization hosts other film-related events throughout the year. ⊠ *Philadelphia* ⊕ *www.qflixphilly.com.*

THEATER

Forrest Theatre. The Forrest is the place to catch Broadway blockbusters in Philadelphia. About eight high-profile shows are presented each season—think hits like *The Book of Mormon, Bullets Over Broadway, Pippin,* and *The Sound of Music.* ⊠ *1114 Walnut St., Center City East* ☎ *215/923–1515* ⊕ *www.forrest-theatre.com.*

Walnut Street Theatre. Founded in 1809, this is the oldest English-language theater in continuous use in the United States. The schedule includes musicals, comedies, and dramas in a lovely 1,052-seat auditorium where almost every seat is a good one. Smaller stages showcase workshop productions of new plays, and are rented by other theater companies. ⊠ *825 Walnut St., Center City East* ☎ *215/574–3550* ⊕ *www.walnutstreettheatre.org.*

Wilma Theater. Under founding artistic directors Blanka and Jiri Zizka, the Wilma has gained favorable critical notices for innovative presentations of American and European drama. Its season runs from September to June. ⊠ *265 S. Broad, at Spruce St., Center City East* ☎ *215/546–7824* ⊕ *www.wilmatheater.org.*

CENTER CITY WEST

CLASSICAL MUSIC

Chamber Orchestra of Philadelphia. Directed by Dirk Brossé, this prestigious group performs chamber music from September to May at the Perelman Theater at the Kimmel Center for the Performing Arts. ⊠ *Broad and Spruce Sts., Center City West* ☎ *215/790–5800, 215/545–5451 concert information* ⊕ *www.chamberorchestra.org.*

Philadelphia Chamber Music Society. From October to May, the society presents 60 concerts featuring nationally and internationally known musicians. The schedule is packed with a piano, vocal, and chamber music series, a special-events and jazz series, and string recitals. Performances are held in the Perelman Theater at the Kimmel Center for the Performing Arts, at the Philadelphia Museum of Art, and at other locations in the city. ⊠ *Philadelphia* ☎ *215/569–8587 information, 215/569–8080 box office* ⊕ *www.pcmsconcerts.org.*

Philadelphia Orchestra. Considered one of the world's best symphony orchestras, the Philadelphia Orchestra is overseen by the effervescent Yannick Nézet-Séguin. The orchestra's present home is the cello-shaped Verizon Hall at the Kimmel Center for the Performing Arts. The 2,500-seat hall is the centerpiece of the performing-arts center at Broad and Spruce streets—a dynamic complex housed under a glass-vaulted roof. Orchestra concerts during the September–May season are still among the city's premier social events. In summer the orchestra performs at the Mann Center for the Performing Arts. ⊠ *Broad and Spruce Sts., Center City West* ☎ *215/893–1999 box office, 215/893–1900 info* ⊕ *www.philorch.org.*

The Philly Pops. Music director Michael Krajewski leads an orchestra of local musicians in programs that swing from Broadway to big band, or from ragtime to rock and roll, with ease. They perform at the Kimmel Center, as well as at other local venues, from October to May. ⊠ *Broad and Spruce Sts., Center City West* ☎ *215/893–1900* ⊕ *www.phillypops.com.*

CONCERT HALLS

Academy of Music. Inspired by Milan's La Scala opera house and completed in 1857, the Academy of Music is the oldest grand opera house in the country still used for its intended purpose. An architectural marvel as well as a center for culture, the Academy features a lavish, neobaroque interior, with red velvet seats, gilt, carvings, ceiling murals, and a huge crystal chandelier. Home to the Opera Company of Philadelphia and the Pennsylvania Ballet, the landmark also plays host to performances by major orchestras, theatrical and dance touring companies, and solo artists. ⊠ *Broad and Locust Sts., Center City West* ☎ *215/893–1999* ⊕ *www.academyofmusic.org.*

Fodor'sChoice   **Kimmel Center for the Performing Arts.** This striking complex evokes Phila
★   delphia's traditional redbrick structures, while making a contempo
rary design statement. The 450,000-square-foot facility by architec
Rafael Viñoly includes the 2,500-seat cello-shaped Verizon Hall, the
more intimate 650-seat Perelman Theater, a restaurant run by che
Jose Garces, a rooftop terrace, and public plaza—all topped by a dra
matic glass-vaulted roof. Along with its resident companies, such as
the Philadelphia Orchestra, the Chamber Orchestra, and the America
Theater Arts for Youth, the center presents touring orchestral, jazz
and dance performances. ⊠ *Broad and Spruce Sts., Center City Wes*
☎ *215/893–1999* ⊕ *www.kimmelcenter.org.*

DANCE

Nextmove. The NextMove series, which presents work from both
national and internationally known companies, began calling the Prince
Theater home during its 2015–2016 season. ⊠ *Prince Theater, 1412
Chestnut St., Center City West* ☎ *215/422–4580* ⊕ *www.princetheater
org/next-move.*

Pennsylvania Ballet. Artistic director Angel Corella leads the company
through a season of classic favorites and new works; they dance on
the stage of the Academy of Music and at the Merriam Theater at the
University of the Arts. Their annual production of George Balanchine's
The Nutcracker is a holiday favorite. ⊠ *Broad and Locust Sts., Center
City West* ☎ *215/551–7000* ⊕ *www.paballet.org.*

Philadelphia Dance Company. This modern troupe, also known as
PHILADANCO, is recognized for its innovative performances that
weld contemporary and classical forms and the traditions of other
cultures, with a particular emphasis on African-American dance heritage. ⊠ *Broad and Spruce Sts., Center City West* ☎ *215/387–8200*
⊕ *www.philadanco.org.*

OPERA

Opera Company of Philadelphia. The company stages five or six productions a year between October and May at the Academy of Music; some
operas have international stars. All performances are in the original
language, with English supertitles above the stage. ⊠ *Broad and Locust
Sts., 420 Locust St., Suite 210, Center City West* ☎ *215/893–3600*
⊕ *www.operaphilly.com.*

THEATER

Merriam Theater. Built in 1918 as the Shubert, the ornate 1,688-seat
theater has had many stage greats, including Al Jolson, Helen Hayes,
Katharine Hepburn, Sammy Davis Jr., Angela Lansbury, and Sir Lau-
rence Olivier. Now owned by the University of the Arts and named after
a local benefactor, the lavishly decorated Merriam hosts a full schedule
of national tours of Broadway shows, modern dance companies, and
solo performers, from the magicians Penn & Teller to tap dancer Savion
Glover. ⊠ *250 S. Broad St., Center City West* ☎ *215/710–5800* ⊕ *www.
merriam-theater.com.*

Philadelphia Theatre Company. Philadelphia and world premieres of
works by contemporary American playwrights are performed here. In
2007 they moved to their new permanent home, the 365-seat Suzanne

Roberts theater on the Avenue of the Arts. ✉ *480 S. Broad St., between Lombard and Pine Sts., Center City West* ☎*215/985–0420* ⊕*www.philadelphiatheatrecompany.org.*

Prince Music Theater. Owned and operated by the Philadelphia Film Society, the Prince has evolved into a regular venue for movie screenings, though it also hosts concerts, cabaret, opera, comedy, and more. ✉ *1412 Chestnut St., Center City West* ☎*215/569–9700* ⊕*www.princemusictheater.org.*

RITTENHOUSE SQUARE

CLASSICAL MUSIC

Curtis Institute of Music. The gifted students at this world-renowned music conservatory give free recitals several times a week from October through May at 8 pm. All of its students are on full scholarships; its alumni include such luminaries as Leonard Bernstein, Samuel Barber, and Anna Moffo. The school also has an opera and symphony orchestra series. ✉ *1726 Locust St., Rittenhouse Square* ☎*215/893–5252 hotline, 215/893–7902 ticket office* ⊕ *www.curtis.edu.*

OPERA

AVA Opera Theatre. The resident artists at the Academy of Vocal Arts, a four-year, tuition-free vocal training program, present four or five fully staged opera productions during their September to May season. They are accompanied by the Chamber Orchestra of Philadelphia and perform at various venues in and around the city. ✉ *1920 Spruce St., Rittenhouse Square* ☎*215/735–1685* ⊕ *www.avaopera.org.*

THEATER

The Adrienne. The main stage has been home to a number of established theatrical groups over the years, many of which have gone on to establish their own permanent spaces. It hosts improv comedy nights, productions from visiting theater companies, rehearsals, and private events on a rental basis. ✉ *2030 Sansom St., Rittenhouse Square* ☎*267/240–4887* ⊕ *www.adriennelive.org.*

N FRANKLIN PARKWAY AND FAIRMOUNT

FAIRMOUNT

CONCERT HALLS

Mann Center for the Performing Arts. Pop, jazz, contemporary music, Broadway theater, opera, dance, and Shakespeare are presented in this open-air amphitheater in Fairmount Park from May through September. In the summer months, the Philadelphia Orchestra is in residence, along with noted soloists and guest conductors. International food booths and a tented buffet restaurant offer dinner before the show. ✉ *5201 Parkside Ave., in W. Fairmount Park, Fairmount* ☎*215/898–0400* ⊕ *www.manncenter.org.*

SOUTH PHILADELPHIA

SOUTH PHILADELPHIA

CONCERT HALLS

Wells Fargo Center. Philly's primary arena for big rock concerts on par with Bruce Springsteen and Beyoncé, the Wells Fargo is also home to the city's 76ers (NBA) and Flyers (NHL). Regular calendar event also include monster truck shows, professional wrestling, and circus shows. ⊠ *S. Broad St. and Pattison Ave., off I–95, South Philadelphi.* ☎ *800/298–4200* ⊕ *www.wellsfargocenterphilly.com.*

UNIVERSITY CITY AND WEST PHILADELPHIA

UNIVERSITY CITY

CONCERT HALLS

Annenberg Center. The performing-arts complex on University of Penn sylvania's campus features multiple stages, from the 115-seat Bruc Montgomery Theatre to the 936-seat Zellerbach. Something's alway going on—including productions of musical comedy, drama, dance, an children's theater. ⊠ *3680 Walnut St., University City* ☎ *215/898–390(* ⊕ *www.pennpresents.org.*

MUSIC FESTIVALS

Clark Park Summer Solstice Festival. The vivacious Clark Park Summer Sol stice Festival has a full lineup of live bands, performers, vendors, and the fabulous, multicultural energy of all West Philly has to offer. ⊠ *Baltimor Ave. and 43rd St., University City* ☎ *215/552–8186* ⊕ *clarkparkfest wordpress.com.*

NORTHEASTERN PHILADELPHIA

NORTH PHILADELPHIA

THEATER

Freedom Theatre. The oldest and most active African-American the ater in Pennsylvania is nationally renowned. Performances are sched uled throughout the year, primarily from September through June ⊠ *1346 N. Broad St., North Philadelphia* ☎ *215/765–2793* ⊕ *www. freedomtheatre.org.*

NORTHERN LIBERTIES

MUSIC FESTIVALS

Roots Picnic. A one-day free-for-all on the Festival Pier of the Delawar waterfront in early June, the Roots Picnic is hosted by Philly's own hip-hop legends, The Roots, and includes a slew of hip-hop, indie and DJ performances, including previous performers TV on the Radio Public Enemy, and Nas. ⊠ *Columbus Blvd. and Spring Garden St. Northern Liberties* ☎ *215/569–9400 box office* ⊕ *www.okayplayer com/rootspicnic.*

THEATER

Philadelphia Live Arts Festival & Philly Fringe. The Philadelphia Live Art Festival and Philly Fringe, known collectively as FringeArts, is a per forming arts festival that takes over the city for approximately two weeks each September. Live Arts offers cutting-edge dance and theater from international and local groups, while the Fringe is a free-for-all of longtime established companies to fly-by-night operations that produce their own shows. Productions, once spread far across the city, are now concentrated at the org's headquarters at Columbus and Race streets. ⊠ *Box office at the Hub:, 919 North 5th St., SW corner of 5th and Fairmount Sts., Northern Liberties* ☎ *215/413–1318* ⊕ *fringearts.com.*

UTSIDE PHILADELPHIA

CONCERT HALLS

Keswick Theatre. This 1,300-seat hall is a former vaudeville house and cinema that's on the National Register of Historic Places. Known for its fine acoustics, it hosts rock, jazz, country, comedy, and other entertainment. ⊠ *291 N. Keswick Ave., Glenside* ☎ *215/572–7650* ⊕ *www.keswicktheatre.com.*

Susquehanna Bank Center. Across the Delaware River in Camden, New Jersey, the Susquehanna Bank Center programs everything from classical to rock and roll in an adaptable space. Between the outdoor and indoor areas, it can host crowds as large as 25,000, with the indoor facility able to accommodate 7,000. ⊠ *1 Harbor Blvd., Camden* ☎ *856/365–1300 ticket information and directions* ⊕ *www.livenation.com/susquehanna-bank-center-tickets-camden/venue/16465.*

MUSIC FESTIVALS

dor's Choice ★ **Philadelphia Folk Festival.** First held in 1961, the oldest continuously running folk festival in the country takes place each year in late August. Arlo Guthrie, Levon Helm, Trombone Shorty, Doc Watson, Taj Mahal, Joan Baez, and Judy Collins are just a few of the artists who have performed here. ⊠ *Old Pool Farm, near Schwenksville* ☎ *215/247–1300, 800/556–3655* ⊕ *www.pfs.org/folk-festival.*

SHOPPING

Updated by
Adam Erace

Shopaholics love the City of Brotherly Love for its style—funky artwork and highbrow housewares, fine jewels, and haute couture.

Indeed, Philadelphia has spawned some influential fashion retailers. The Urban Outfitters chain was born in a storefront in West Philadelphia. Its sophisticated sister, Anthropologie, also has its roots in Philadelphia. Lagos, the popular high-end jewelry line, was founded here, and all items are still produced locally. High-fashion boutiques Joan Shepp, Knit Wit, and Elle Lauri, all in the Rittenhouse Square area, are well regarded by locals for designer clothing and accessories.

Some of the most spirited shopping in town is also pleasing to the palate. The indoor Reading Terminal Market and the outdoor Italian Market are bustling with urban dwellers buying groceries and visitors searching for the perfect Philadelphia cheesesteak. Equally welcoming is the city's quaint, cobblestone Antiques Row, the three-block stretch of Pine Street crammed with shops selling everything from estate jewelry to stained glass and vintage furniture. Also worth a trip is the Third Street Corridor in Old City, home to scads of independent, funky boutiques. In Northern Liberties, the Piazza at Schmidt's is a giant mixed-use development inspired by Rome's Piazza Navona, which houses 100,000 square feet of retail space bursting with creative entrepreneurs.

Neighborhoods are presented clockwise starting from the Old City, a commercial waterfront turned arts enclave on the Delaware River, moving south to South Philadelphia, then west to Center City and Rittenhouse Square, across the Schuylkill River to University City around the University of Pennsylvania campus, and ending in the north with Northern Liberties.

THE HISTORIC DOWNTOWN

Lofts, art galleries, furniture stores, and unique home-decor shops line the streets of the Old City in the Historic Downtown; there are also wonderful clothing stores with work by local up-and-coming designers. After dark, young professionals and students—many live in converted warehouses in the area—flock to the neighborhood's bars and clubs. Some great restaurants can also be found here. One of the best times to explore Old City's gallery scene is during First Friday. As the name implies, on the first Friday of each month, Old City galleries are open to the public from 5 to 9 at night. Many offer refreshments, and the street scene becomes quite festive.

OLD CITY

ANTIQUES

Moderne Gallery. Gallerist Bob Aibel is the world's foremost authority on furniture designer George Nakashima, who made his most famous work just north of Philadelphia, in New Hope. Aibel always has some

Nakashima for sale as well as other pieces of furniture from the American Craft movement and Art Deco furniture, accessories, and lighting. ⊠ *111 N. 3rd St., Old City* ☎ *215/923–8536* ⊕ *www.modernegallery. com* ⊗ *Tues.–Sat. noon–5.*

ART GALLERIES

The Center for Art in Wood. This hub for the international wood-art community recently moved to a more visible new home and changed its name from the Wood Turning Center. Housed here is a store with gorgeous work—some by the accomplished artists whose work has been displayed in the adjacent gallery, including those who come every year as part of the organization's annual Windgate ITE International Residency program. There is also a free museum on the premises. ⊠ *141 N. 3rd St., Old City* ☎ *215/923–8000* ⊕ *www.woodturningcenter.org* ⊗ *Tues.–Sat. 10–5.*

Clay Studio. A nonprofit organization runs the gallery and conducts classes as well as an outreach program to inner-city schools. There are clay works and pottery by well-known artists; the gallery has juried shows and group exhibits. ⊠ *137–139 N. 2nd St., Old City* ☎ *215/925–3453* ⊕ *www.theclaystudio.org* ⊗ *Mon.–Sat. 11–7, Sun. noon–6.*

Larry Becker Contemporary Art. Gallerist Becker and his wife, Heidi Nivling, display the kind of austere, abstract art that prompts people who don't know any better to say, "Hey, my kid could do that." Look more closely at the conceptual paintings featured in this small gallery and you'll notice the great skill required to make minimalist art with maximal effect. ⊠ *43 N. 2nd St., Old City* ☎ *215/925–5389* ⊗ *Fri. and Sat. 11–5; other times by chance or appointment.*

Locks Gallery. This gallery shows works by an impressive assortment of contemporary regional, national, and international painters, sculptors, and mixed-media artists, including Frank Stella and Enda Andrade. ⊠ *600 S. Washington Sq., Old City* ☎ *215/629–1000* ⊕ *www. locksgallery.com* ⊗ *Tues.–Sat. 10–6.*

Muse Gallery. Established in 1978 by the Muse Foundation for the Visual Arts, Muse Gallery is an artists' cooperative committed to increasing the visibility of local artwork and presenting experimental work in a variety of mediums. ⊠ *52 N. 2nd St., Old City* ☎ *215/627–5310* ⊗ *Wed.–Sun. noon–5.*

Snyderman-Works Galleries. One-of-a-kind handmade furniture pieces, glass objects, and craft-oriented fine art are displayed on the first floor of this venerable Old City gallery, with an emphasis on ceramics and fiber arts. ⊠ *303 Cherry St., Old City* ☎ *215/238–9576* ⊕ *www. snyderman-works.com* ⊗ *Tues.–Sat. 10–6.*

Wexler Gallery. This gallery is known for specializing in historic and contemporary glass, but it always has an interesting mix of 20th- and 21st-century handcrafted furnishings and art. ⊠ *201 N. 3rd St., Old City* ☎ *215/923–7030* ⊕ *www.wexlergallery.com/index.php* ⊗ *Tues.–Sat. 10–6, Mon. by appointment.*

6

CLOTHING AND ACCESSORIES

Lost & Found. This laid-back shop has something for everyone (women and men both) with its well-curated mix of young, contemporary designers from Asia, Europe, and the United States. It also has a range of delightful accessories including vintage belt buckles, printed canvas totes, and unique jewelry. Prices here are lower than at many of the neighboring boutiques. ✉ *133 N. 3rd St., Old City* ☎ *215/928–1311* ⊕ *lostandfoundshop.com* ⊙ *Weekdays 11:30–7, Sat. 11–7, Sun. noon–6.*

Sugarcube. Some know Sugarcube as a vintage boutique; others go for its stock of hard-to-find designers like A.P.C., Dunderdon, Lavender Brown, and Penumbra. The stylish, friendly owner is usually on hand to advise how to match your Williamsburg Garment Company jeans with your Rag and Bone shawl-collar cardi. ✉ *124 N. 3rd St., Old City* ☎ *215/238–0825* ⊕ *www.sugarcube.us* ⊙ *Mon. 11–7, Tues.–Sat. noon–7, Sun. noon–5.*

The Third Street Habit. With designers like Isabel Marant, Zadig & Voltaire, Oliveve, and Burning Torch, this stylish, trendy, Old City mainstay services feminine fashionistas who favor a low-key look (more neutrals than colors) and who don't blink an eye at dresses with prices in the triple digits. Beautifully made bags, jewelry, and shoes complement the studiously slouchy looks. ✉ *153 N. 3rd St., Old City* ☎ *215/925–5455* ⊕ *thirdstreethabit.com* ⊙ *Mon.–Sat. 11–7, Sun. noon–6.*

Vagabond. The two designing women/co-owners of Vagabond pioneered a formula—selling vintage wares alongside new, edgy labels and featuring under-the-radar brands like their own (Stellapop and City of Brotherly Love). It's been imitated plenty ever since, but this boutique still does it best. ✉ *37 N. 3rd St., Old City* ☎ *267/671–0737* ⊕ *www.vagabondboutique.com* ⊙ *Mon.–Sat. 11–7, Sun. 11–5.*

GIFTS AND SOUVENIRS

Art in the Age of Mechanical Reproduction. This flagship store for a brand launched in 2008 by a local ad man set the stage for an idiosyncratic mix of wares made using pre–Industrial Age methods. On sale are handcrafted blanket rolls, bar tools and accessories, hand-dyed T-shirts, and bottles of spirits inspired by the original recipes for gingersnaps and root beer. ✉ *116 N. 3rd St., Old City* ☎ *215/922–2600* ⊙ *Mon.–Sat. 11–7, Sun. noon–6.*

Scarlett Alley. Founded by Mary Kay Scarlett and her daughter Liz, and now owned by Liz alone, this delightful shop at the corner of 3rd and Race near the Betsy Ross House features an ever-changing assortment of unique jewelry, housewares, and stationery, as well as toys, soaps, and teas. Items are displayed on furniture designed and handcrafted by Richard Scarlett, Liz's father; it's also for sale or custom order. ✉ *241 Race St., Old City* ☎ *215/592–7898* ⊕ *scarlettalley.com* ⊙ *Weekdays 11–7, Sat. 10–6, Sun. noon–5* Ⓜ *2nd and Market.*

Xenos Candy and Gifts. Asher chocolates and Philly souvenirs from key chains to T-shirts are stocked here, near the sights of the historic district. ✉ *231 Chestnut St., Old City* ☎ *215/922–1445* ⊕ *www.xenosgifts.com* ⊙ *Weekdays 10–6, Sat. 10:30–7, Sun. 11–6.*

MALLS

Bourse. Across the street from the Liberty Bell is the Bourse, an elegantly restored 1895 commodities exchange building. The six-story skylighted atrium contains a few fun shops catering to tourists, such as Destination Philadelphia, as well as a festive international food court. ⊠ *111 S. Independence Mall E, between Market and Chestnut Sts., Old City* ☎ *215/625–0300* ⊗ *Mon.–Sat. 10–6; Mar.–Nov., also Sun. 11–5.*

ENTER CITY

Center City, especially Center City East (meaning the blocks east of Broad Street) has a lot of great shopping up Pine Street (Antique Row) near Washington Square and also a few blocks west, along the fun, colorful, bustling 13th Street corridor, also called Midtown Village. Antique Row has some holdovers that are traditional antiques shops, but some quirky housewares and gift shops make their home there, too. Street parking is possible by Antique Row but is harder to find near 13th Street. Nearby Macy's has a parking garage, but your best bet is to cab it, walk, or take the bus. You'll also find many upscale chains in Center City West, especially along Walnut Street between Broad and 18th streets, including Cole Haan, Banana Republic, Madewell, and Barneys Co-Op. There is more local flavor off the beaten path, down numbered streets and smaller streets around Rittenhouse Square. Parking is tough in this area, and you'll pay a pretty penny for a meter or a lot. You'll have more fun and see much more if you walk these lively streets and let yourself get a little lost.

ENTER CITY EAST

ANTIQUES

Antique Row. Pine Street from 9th Street to 12th Street has long been Philadelphia's Antique Row. The three-block area has a good number of antiques stores and curio shops, many specializing in expensive period furniture and Colonial heirlooms. ⊠ *Center City East.*

Arader Galleries. This is the flagship store of a highly respected chain that stocks the world's largest selection of 16th- to 19th-century prints and maps, specializing in botanicals, birds, and the American West. ⊠ *1308 Walnut St., Center City East* ☎ *215/735–8811* ⊕ *www.aradergalleries. com* ⊗ *Weekdays 10–6, Sat. 10–5.*

Blendo, Past and Present. More like a favorite flea market than an antiques shop, the truckload of finds at Blendo is so plentiful they overflow onto the sidewalk. There are new, retro-flavored items and plenty of vintage goodies including clothing, lamps and small furniture, jewelry, prints, and linens. It has the magical, memorable effect of grandma's attic, assuming grandma had cultured and eclectic tastes. ⊠ *1002 Pine St., Center City East* ☎ *215/351–9260* ⊗ *Tues.–Sat. 11–6, Sun. 11–5:30; also open some Mon., call ahead to verify* Ⓜ *Bus 40.*

Fleisher/Ollman Gallery. You can find fine works by 20th-century self-taught American artists here, such as Martin Ramirez, Joan Nelson, and Joseph Yoakum. ⊠ *1216 Arch St., 5A, Center City East* ☎ *215/545–7562* ⊕ *www.fleisher-ollmangallery.com* ⊙ *Tues.–Fri. 10:30–5:30; Sept.–June, also Sat. noon–5.*

M. Finkel & Daughter. Late-18th- and early-19th-century American furniture, needlework, samplers, and folk art make this an important outpost for lovers of Americana. They also publish the antiques journal *Samplings.* ⊠ *936 Pine St., Center City East* ☎ *215/627–7797* ⊕ *samplings. com* ⊙ *Weekdays 9:30–5:30, weekends by appointment only.*

ART GALLERIES

Fabric Workshop and Museum. A nonprofit arts organization runs this center and store dedicated to creating new work in fabric and other materials, working with emerging and nationally and internationally recognized artists. ⊠ *1214 Arch St., Center City East* ☎ *215/561–8888* ⊕ *www.fabricworkshopandmuseum.org* 🖂 *$3 adults; children under 12 free* ⊙ *Weekdays 10–6, weekends noon–5.*

Show of Hands. You'll find one-of-a-kind artisan crafts—exquisite jewelry, colorful vases, textiles, Murano glass, and unique lamps—in a wide range of price points here. The friendly owner is on hand to answer questions and encourages you to handle the fragile objects. ⊠ *1006 Pine St., Center City East* ☎ *215/592–4010* ⊙ *Wed.–Sun. noon–6; also some Mon. by appt.*

BOOKSTORES

AIA Bookstore & Design Center. Run by the Philadelphia chapter of the American Institute of Architects (AIA), this shop specializes in books on architectural theory, building construction, interior design, and furnishings. It also sells architectural drawings and watercolors, blueprint posters, international magazines, home furnishings, unusual gifts, and a great selection of unique cards. ⊠ *1218 Arch St., Center City East* ☎ *215/569–3188* ⊕ *www.aiabookstore.com* ⊙ *Mon.–Sat. 10–6, Sun. noon–5.*

Philly AIDS Thrift @Giovanni's Room. Although longtime owner Ed Hermance retired and sold the building, closing this historic bookstore in the spring of 2014, new tenants Philly AIDS Thrift have revived it for a new generation interested in LGBTQ fiction and nonfiction. Focusing on books dealing with gay, lesbian, and feminist topics, this well-regarded store stocks an extensive inventory and sponsors many author appearances. ⊠ *345 S. 12th St., Center City East* ☎ *215/923–2960* ⊕ *www.queerbooks.com* ⊙ *Mon.–Thurs. 11–8, Fri. and Sat. 11–9, Sun. 11–7* Ⓜ *Walnut–Locust on the Broad St. Line.*

CLOTHING

I. Goldberg Army and Navy. This store is hip and practical, with an emphasis on sporting apparel and camping gear. Goldberg's is crammed with government-surplus, military-style clothing; jeans and work clothes; unusual footwear; and exclusive foreign imports. Rummaging here is a sport in itself. ⊠ *1300 Chestnut St., Center City East* ☎ *215/925–9393* ⊕ *igoco.com* ⊙ *Mon.–Thurs. and Sat. 9:30–6, Fri. 9:30–7.*

CLOTHING FOR CHILDREN

FAMILY **Lolli Lolli.** Everything you'll find at this shop for babies and kids is non-licensed (i.e., no T-shirts or toys advertising Disney, TV, or movie characters). The boutique-label brands (Tea Collection, Petit Bateau) are adorable if pricey, and toys such as wooden puzzles by Melissa & Doug and latex-free hopper horses please parents and children alike. The back of the store has bookshelves crammed with new titles and classics. ⊠ *713 Walnut St., Center City East* ☎ *215/625–2655* ⊕ *www.lollilolli. net* ⊗ *Mon., Tues., Thurs., and Fri. 10–6; Wed. and Sat. 10–7; Sun. 11–5.*

COSMETICS

Duross & Langell. The two co-owners for whom this shop is named make most of the colorful wedges of soap and the organic scrubs, shampoos, and other skin- and hair-care products locally and infuse them with scents like ginger and mojito. The shop recently expanded to offer a full-service hair salon and a yoga studio on-site. ⊠ *117 S. 13th St., Center City East* ☎ *215/592–7627* ⊕ *www.durossandlangel.com* ⊗ *Mon. 11–7, Tues.–Thurs. 10–8, Fri. and Sat. 10–7, Sun. noon–5. Salon: Tues.–Thurs. 10–8, Fri. 10–6, Sat. 10–5* ☞ *Yoga studio open for classes only, see website for class schedule.*

DEPARTMENT STORES

Macy's. Macy's displays the chain's classic merchandise in the spacious former John Wanamaker department store, a Philadelphia landmark. Its focal point is the nine-story grand court with its 30,000-pipe organ—the largest ever built—and a 2,500-pound statue of an eagle, both remnants of the 1904 Louisiana Purchase Exposition in St. Louis. During Christmastime, the space is filled with families and office workers gazing (and listening) in awe at the store's legendary holiday sound-and-light show and organ performances. ⊠ *Surrounded by 13th, Juniper, Market, and Chestnut Sts., 1300 Market St., Center City East* ☎ *215/241–9000* ⊕ *l.macys.com/philadelphia-pa* ⊗ *Mon.–Wed. 9–8, Thurs. and Fri. 9–9, Sat. 10–9, Sun. 11–7.*

GIFTS AND SOUVENIRS

Verde. If you're hunting for a gift that makes you look thoughtful, this is the place to go—here you'll find gorgeous, fresh bouquets of flowers; sparkly jewelry, scarves, and stylish handbags with a handcrafted look; and a smattering of easy, pretty clothing. This is also the home of Marcie Blaine Artisanal Chocolates with delicious, exotic flavors like blood orange, spiked eggnog, and elderflower and champagne. ⊠ *108 S. 13th St., Center City East* ☎ *215/546–8700* ⊕ *www.verdephiladelphia. com* ⊗ *Mon.–Sat. 11–8, Sun. noon–6.*

HOME DECOR

Open House. This modern, hip, urban home boutique strikes the balance between edgy hipster and hip hostess. The furniture, baby clothes, jewelry, candles, and soaps all manage to be clever and quirky. It's as fun to browse as it is to buy, as there's no pressure from the friendly sales staff. ⊠ *107 S. 13th St., Center City East* ☎ *215/922–1415* ⊕ *www. openhouseliving.com* ⊗ *Mon.–Sat. 11–8, Sun. noon–6.*

Ten Thousand Villages. Woven rugs, pottery, carvings, and other handcrafted gifts made by skilled artisans in 32 countries such as Kenya,

6

Thailand, and India make this fair-trade store a favorite for innova
tive gifts with a social conscience. ⊠ *1122 Walnut St., Center Cit
East* ☎ *215/574–2008* ⊕ *www.tenthousandvillages.com/philadelphi.*
☺ *Mon.–Sat. 10–7, Sun. noon–5.*

JEWELRY

Halloween. If the sheer quantity of baubles crammed into this tiny sho
doesn't take your breath away, the gorgeous, one-of-a-kind designs wil
The shelves, drawers, displays, and even the second-floor balcony over
flow with rings, necklaces, earrings, bracelets, pins, and much more
The jewelry ranges from classic pearls to mystical amber. Owner Henr
David (who designs some pieces) is well known for his lavish and outra
geous Halloween fetes. He can do custom work, such as creating mate
for single earrings. ⊠ *1329 Pine St., Center City East* ☎ *215/732–771.*
☺ *Tues.–Fri. noon–6, Sat. 11–4.*

Jewelers' Row. Centered on Sansom Street between 7th and 8th streets
and on 8th between Chestnut and Walnut, Jewlers' Row is one of th
world's oldest and largest markets of precious stones: more than 35(
retailers, wholesalers, and craftspeople operate here. The 700 block o
Sansom Street is a brick-paved enclave occupied almost exclusively b
jewelers. ⊠ *Center City East.*

MARKETS

Market Place East. In a historic building saved from the wrecker's ball a
the 11th hour, this century-old former Lit Brothers department store wen
through a $75 million renovation to emerge as an office building wit
a five-level atrium full of moderately priced stores and restaurants. It'
more interesting for its historic facade—it's the only complete block o
Victorian architecture in the city—than for the chain stores inside. ⊠ *70*
Market St., between 7th and 8th Sts., Center City East ☎ *215/592–890.*
☺ *Management offices weekdays 7–5; retailers set own hrs, but most are*
open Mon.–Thurs. 9:30–7, Fri. 9:30–8, Sat. 10–7, Sun. noon–6.

Fodor'sChoice **Reading Terminal Market.** The roots of the Reading Terminal Market dat
★ to 1892, when the Reading Railroad commissioned a food bazaar to b
built in the train shed's cellar as part of its grand expansion plans. Stro
amid the bustling stalls and you can see and smell old and new culi
nary delights. Amish merchants sell baked goods and produce straigh
from the farm alongside vendors offering the latest gourmet vegetariar
dishes, artisanal breads, and sushi. Vendors also sell exotic spices, flow
ers, crafts, jewelry, clothing, and cookbooks. Eighty-six merchants are
represented here, but try not to miss Amish-owned Miller's Twist fo
piping hot, freshly rolled soft pretzels; Bassetts Ice Cream, America'
oldest ice-cream makers; Metropolitan Bakery, for hearty breads anc
light pastries; and the Down Home Diner for affordable Southern-styl
fare. The market is open Monday through Saturday 8–6, and Sunday
9–5. The Amish vendors are open Wednesday through Saturday. ⊠ *51*
N. 12th St., at Arch St., Center City East ☎ *215/922–2317* ⊕ *www*
readingterminalmarket.org ☺ *Mon.–Sat. 8–6, Sun. 9–5.*

‌NTER CITY WEST

CLOTHING

Nicole Miller. You can find loads of this successful designer's quirky scarves, boxer shorts, and ties at eponymous boutiques in Center City and Manayunk. Women's collections include simple and elegant sportswear, evening wear, and handbags in beautiful colors. ⊠ *Shops at the Bellevue, 200 S. Broad St., at Walnut St., Center City West* ☎ *215/546–5007* ⊕ *www.nicolemillerphiladelphia.com* ⊘ *Mon., Tues., and Thurs.–Sat. 10–6; Wed. 10–8; Sun. noon–5* Ⓜ *Broad and Walnut; or stop 16 on the Trolley Works Philadelphia Tours.*

CLOTHING FOR CHILDREN

FAMILY **Children's Boutique.** The store carries a look between conservative and classic in infant to preteen clothes and shoes. You can buy complete wardrobes, specialty gifts, and handmade items. An extensive toy department carries the latest in kiddie crazes. ⊠ *The Shops at Liberty Place, 1625 Chestnut St., Center City West* ☎ *215/732–2661* ⊕ *www. echildrensboutique.com* ⊘ *Mon.–Sat. 10–6, Sun. noon–5.*

GIFTS AND SOUVENIRS

Holt's Cigar Company. Stogie aficionados make a point of stopping by this cigar emporium, whose Philadelphia roots date back more than 100 years. The shop features a comfortable smoking lounge and one of the nation's largest walk-in humidors. Find private-label Ashton cigars, a wide array of smoking accessories and humidors, and writing instruments from Mont Blanc, Waterman, and Cross. Upstairs is the Ashton Cigar Bar, which pairs cigars with rare whiskeys and also specialty cocktails. ⊠ *1522 Walnut St., Center City West* ☎ *215/732–8500* ⊕ *www. ashtoncigarbar.com* ⊘ *Weekdays 9–8, weekends 10–6.*

Loop Yarn. Loop is a knitting store stocked with supplies including natural fiber, luxury, and hand-dyed yarn in a rainbow of hues artfully arranged in stark-white ceiling-high cubbies, softened by the addition of comfy couches where crafty types can (and do) bond. ⊠ *1914 South St., Center City West* ☎ *215/893–9939* ⊕ *www.loopyarn.com* ⊘ *Weekdays 11–6, weekends 10–5.*

HOME DECOR

Kitchen Kapers. From one store in South Jersey, this family business has grown to be one of the largest independent kitchenware stores in the United States. This is a good source for fine cookware, French copper, cutlery, coffees, and teas. ⊠ *213 S. 17th St., Center City West* ☎ *215/546–8059* ⊕ *www.kitchenkapers.com/ba2.html* ⊘ *Mon., Tues., Thurs., and Fri. 10–7; Wed. 10–8; Sat. 10–6; Sun. 11–5.*

Usona. Furniture and accessories are what the owner calls "global modern," reflecting a fusion of different styles, periods, and materials. Accent pieces, like picture frames and mirrors, are interesting and affordable. ⊠ *113 S. 16th St., Center City West* ☎ *215/496–0440* ⊕ *www. usonahome.com* ⊘ *Weekdays 10–4, Sat. 11–4 by appointment only.*

6

JEWELRY

Tiffany & Co. This is the local branch of the store, famous for its exqui site gems, fine crystal, and china, and, of course, its signature blue gift box. ⊠ *Shops at the Bellevue, 1414 Walnut St., Center City West* ☎ *215/735–1919* ⊕ *www.tiffany.com* ☉ *Mon.–Sat. 10–7, Sun. noon–6.*

MALLS

Fodor'sChoice **Rittenhouse Row.** Shop-'til-you-droppers make a beeline for Rittenhouse
★   Row, the area between Broad and 21st streets and Spruce and Market streets. Lately the chains have been taking over Walnut Street between Rittenhouse Square and Broad Street, but this is still the greatest concentration of swanky stores and tony boutiques, art galleries, and jewelers you'll find in the city. ⊠ *Center City West* ⊕ *www.rittenhouserow.org*

Shops at the Bellevue. The elegant Shops at the Bellevue include Polo-Ralph Lauren, with the designer's classic styles; the chic clothes of Nicole Miller; Tiffany & Co.; and a Williams-Sonoma cookware store. A downstairs food court is bustling at lunchtime; several upscale restaurants in the historic building, which also houses an elegant hotel, are popular in the evening. ⊠ *Broad and Walnut Sts., Center City West* ⊕ *www.bellevuephiladelphia.net/shop.php* ☉ *Mon., Tues., and Thurs.- Sat. 10–6; Wed. 10–8; Sun. shops open at own discretion.*

Shops at Liberty Place. At 16th and Chestnut streets is the upscale Shops at Liberty Place. The complex features a food court and popular stores including Loft, Aveda, Victoria's Secret, Express, J. Crew, and the Body Shop. More than 40 stores and restaurants are arranged in two circular levels within a strikingly handsome 90-foot glass-roof atrium. ⊠ *162.5 Chestnut St., Center City West* ☎ *215/851–9055* ⊕ *www.shopsatliberty. com* ☉ *Mon.–Sat. 9:30–7, Sun. noon–6.*

SHOES

Sherman Brothers Shoes. This discount retailer of men's shoes has name-brand merchandise and excellent service. The store stocks extra-wide and extra-narrow widths, as well as sizes up to 16. Look for classic comfort shoes by Cole Haan, Clarks, and Rockport. ⊠ *1520 Sansom St., Center City West* ☎ *215/561–4550* ⊕ *www.shermanbrothers.com* ☉ *Mon., Tues., Thurs., and Fri. 9:30–6; Wed. 9:30–7; Sat. 9:30–5:30; Sun. 11:30–4:30.*

RITTENHOUSE SQUARE

ANTIQUES

Calderwood Gallery, 20th Century Design. French Art Deco, Modernist and post-war furniture and objects from the '40s and '50s tempt discerning collectors at this fine establishment housed in a beautifully renovated historic town house. ⊠ *631 N. Broad St., Rittenhouse Square* ☎ *215/546–5357* ⊕ *www.calderwoodgallery.com* ☉ *Weekdays 11–5, weekends by chance or appointment* Ⓜ *Broad and Locust Sts.*

Freeman's. Founded in 1805, this is the city's most prominent auction house and America's oldest. Specialty departments include fine paintings, American and European furniture and decorative arts, 20th-century design, and rare books and prints. It's known for Pennsylvania impressionists, Colonial-period Pennsylvania furniture, and lately for a growing presence in modern and contemporary furniture and art. Freeman's auctioned one of the original fliers on which the Declaration of Independence was printed and posted throughout the city. It sold for $404,000 in 1968. Check out its website for info on upcoming auctions. ⊠ *1808 Chestnut St., Rittenhouse Square* ☎ *215/563–9275* ⊕ *www. freemansauction.com* ⊙ *Mon.–Thurs. 9–5, Fri. 9–3.*

Niederkorn Silver. A fine selection of silver items, including jewelry, pieces for the desk and dresser, and a nice selection of baby silver, makes this a worthwhile stop. ⊠ *2005 Locust St., Rittenhouse Square* ☎ *215/567–2606* ⊕ *www.niederkornsilver.com* ⊙ *Tues.–Thurs. 11:30–7, Fri. and Sat. 11:30–5.*

ART GALLERIES

David David Gallery. American and European paintings, drawings, and watercolors from the 16th to the 20th century are on display. ⊠ *260 S. 18th St., Rittenhouse Square* ☎ *215/735–4244* ⊕ *www. daviddavidgallery.com* ⊙ *Weekdays 9–5:30, weekends by appointment.*

Gross McCleaf Gallery. This gallery is a good place to see works by both prominent and emerging artists, with an emphasis on Philadelphia painters. ⊠ *127 S. 16th St., between Walnut and Chestnut Sts., Rittenhouse Square* ☎ *215/665–8138* ⊕ *www.grossmccleaf.com* ⊙ *Tues.–Sat. 10–5 and by appointment.*

Newman Galleries. The city's oldest gallery dates back to 1865, and displays works that range from 19th-century paintings to contemporary lithographs and sculpture. Many of the most notable 20th-century painters from the Bucks County area are shown here. ⊠ *1625 Walnut St., Rittenhouse Square* ☎ *215/563–1779* ⊕ *www.newmangalleries.com* ⊙ *Tues.–Sat. 10–4 or by appointment.*

The Print Center. The frequent exhibitions at this two-story gallery down a charming side street attract fans of contemporary printmaking and photography. ⊠ *1614 Latimer St., Rittenhouse Square* ☎ *215/735–6090* ⊕ *www.printcenter.org/100* ⊙ *Tues.–Sat. 11–6.*

Schmidt/Dean Gallery. Between 16th and 18th streets you can find some wonderful galleries specializing in contemporary art, such as Schmidt/Dean Gallery, which presents paintings by local artists. ⊠ *1719 Chestnut St., Rittenhouse Square* ☎ *215/569–9433* ⊕ *schmidtdean.com* ⊙ *Tues.–Sat. 10:30–6, Mon. by appointment only.*

Schwarz Gallery. American and European paintings of the 18th to 20th century are the focus, with an emphasis on Philadelphia artists. ⊠ *1806 Chestnut St., Rittenhouse Square* ☎ *215/563–4887* ⊕ *www. schwarzgallery.com* ⊙ *Tues.–Fri. 10–6, Sat. by appointment only.*

Works on Paper. The contemporary prints here by American masters like Chuck Close and Robert Rauschenberg and by artists represented by the gallery have won Works on Paper a reputation as one of the city's best. ⊠ *1611 Walnut St., Suite B (mezzanine), Rittenhouse Square* ☎ *215/988–9999* ⊕ *www.worksonpaper.biz* ⊙ *Tues.–Sat. 11–5.*

BOOKSTORES

Fat Jack's Comicrypt. For more than 30 years, Fat Jack's has been a mecca for local comic devotees with fresh-off-the-presses copies from major and independent publishers, including Japanese mangas plus 3-D posters, action figures, and the obligatory Dungeons & Dragons supplies. ⊠ *2006 Sansom St., Rittenhouse Square* ☎ *215/963–0788* ⊕ *www.comicrypt.com* ⊙ *Mon.,Tues., Thurs., and Sat. 10–6; Wed. and Fri. 10–7:30; Sun. 1–6.*

Joseph Fox. Quaint and cozy, this small bookstore specializes in art, architecture, and design—all well organized in diminutive quarters. ⊠ *1724 Sansom St., Rittenhouse Square* ✛ *Between 17th and 18th Sts.* ☎ *215/563–4184* ⊕ *www.foxbookshop.com* ⊙ *Mon., Tues., and Thurs.–Sat. 9:30–6; Wed. 9:30–7.*

CLOTHING

Anthropologie. The flagship shop of the locally based national chain takes up three floors of an elegant Rittenhouse Square building (once someone's mansion, of course). The sales floors that encircle the grand stone staircase are brimming with lush colors, floral patterns, and vintage and ethnic-inspired styles that offer a departure from the ordinary. Pretty jewelry, stylish shoes and handbags, and other accessories add an enchanting femininity to fashion. Head downstairs for an array of home decor, including glassware, pottery, pillows, and mirrors. Be sure to check out the lower level for racks of bargain-priced sale items, and don't forget to look up at the towering first-floor ceiling of the onetime front parlor. ⊠ *1801 Walnut St., Rittenhouse Square* ☎ *215/568–2114* ⊕ *www.anthropologie.com/anthro/index.jsp* ⊙ *Mon.–Sat. 10–8, Sun. 11–6.*

Boyds. Beneath the royal-blue canopy and white-marble entrance, you can find the largest single-store men's clothier in the country, with nine shops that present the traditional English look, avant-garde Italian imports, and dozens of other styles and designers, from Armani to Zegna. The store has departments for extra tall, large, and short men; formal wear; and shoes; and there's free valet parking, and 60 tailors on the premises. Women can find a small selection of high-quality designer clothes, too. ⊠ *1818 Chestnut St., Rittenhouse Square* ☎ *215/564–9000* ⊕ *www.boydsphila.com* ⊙ *Mon., Tues., and Thurs.–Sat. 9:30–6; Wed. 9:30–8* ☞ *Free valet parking.*

Duke & Winston. Scuffed antiques, preppy flags, tufted sofas, and woodwork create an Ivy League vibe at Duke & Winston in Rittenhouse. The boutique definitely looks heritage-male, but sells its own lines of both mens- and womenswear. Think lived-in T-shirts, hoodies and ball caps, plus beer cozies, canvas totes, and more, much of it emblazoned with the store's bulldog mascot (who can often be found lounging about). ⊠ *1822 Chestnut St., Rittenhouse Square* ☎ *267/639–5594* ⊕ *www. duke-winston.com.*

Jacques Ferber. Since 1879, this famed furrier has been offering high-style furs in sable, mink, and more, as well as shearlings, outerwear, and accessories that make a fashion statement. ⊠ *1708 Walnut St., Rittenhouse Square* ☎ *215/735–4173* ⊕ *www.jacquesferber.com* ⊙ *Mon.–Sat. 10–5.*

Joan Shepp. Cutting-edge fashion is displayed in a setting reminiscent of a New York loft. Notable designers include Phillip Lim, Ivan Grundahl, Rich Owens, Etro, Marni, Moschino, and shoes by Robert Clergerie ⊠ *1811 Chestnut St., Rittenhouse Square* ☎ *215/735–2666* ⊕ *www.joanshepp.com* ⊙ *Mon.,Tues., and Thurs.–Sat. 10–6; Wed. 10–8; Sun. noon–5.*

Kiki Hughes. This funky, luxe boutique on the corner of a residential street stocks unusual garments that stand out for their unexpected twists—a wide-leg pant in black velvet, a white oxford embroidered with flowers—as well as outright showstoppers like Asian tunics with mandarin collars and shimmering silk taffeta skirts. The owner designed the store interior herself, down to the hand-carved vines in the woodwork and the draped-fabric ceiling. ⊠ *259 S. 21st St., Rittenhouse Square* ☎ *215/546–1534* ⊕ *www.kikihughes.com* ⊙ *Tues.–Sat. 11–7 or by appointment.*

Knit Wit. High-fashion clothes and accessories from sportswear to cocktail dresses are the focus here. Blumarine, Vera Wang, Norma Kamali, Stella McCartney, and Paul Smith are among the designers you can find here, along with a few unique vintage shoes. ⊠ *1718 Walnut St., Rittenhouse Square* ☎ *215/564–4760* ⊙ *Mon., Tues., and Sat. 10–6; Wed.–Fri. 10–7; Sun. noon–5.*

Skirt. Personal stylists help you peruse the racks of labels like Vince, DVF, and J Brand at Skirt, whose clean-cut Rittenhouse location recently joined sister stores in Bryn Mawr and Stone Harbor. ⊠ *212 S. 17th St., Rittenhouse Square* ☎ *215/309–8419* ⊕ *www.shop-skirt.com.*

Sophy Curson. In this shop that dates back to 1929, women's fashions from top American and European designers, such as Blumarine and Krizia, are presented in a salon setting, with experienced sales staff selecting the latest styles that are totally you. ⊠ *19th St. and Sansom St., Rittenhouse Square* ☎ *215/567–4662* ⊕ *www.sophycurson.com* ⊙ *Weekdays 9:30–5:30, Sat. 9:30–5.*

Urban Outfitters. What started out as a storefront selling used jeans to students in West Philadelphia is now a trendsetting chain on campuses across the country. Three floors showcase an eclectic array of hip clothing, unusual books, and funky housewares that can go from the dorm room to the family room. ⊠ *1627 Walnut St., Rittenhouse Square* ☎ *215/569–3131* ⊕ *www.urbanoutfitters.com/urban/stores/en/ urban-outfitters-walnut-street* ⊙ *Mon.–Thurs. 10–9:30, Fri. and Sat. 10–10, Sun. 11–8.*

CLOTHING FOR CHILDREN

FAMILY **Born Yesterday.** This shop is filled with unique clothing and toys for haute tots. Specialties include handmade goods, imported fashions, and styles not available elsewhere. ⊠ *1901 Walnut St., Rittenhouse Square* ☎ *215/568–6556* ⊕ *www.bornyesterdaykids.com* ⊙ *Mon.–Sat. 10–6, Sun. 11–5.*

COSMETICS

Bluemercury. Makeup and skin-care junkies can get their fix at this sleek shop featuring products from Aqua di Parma, Bliss, Bumble & Bumble, Fresh, Trish McEvoy, Nars, Laura Mercier, and many others. Sweetly

scented candles and fragrances in intoxicating blends of fruits and spice
fill the shop. In the back of the store, spa services are offered in a
serene setting. ⊠ *1707 Walnut St., Rittenhouse Square* ☎ *215/569–3100*
⊕ *www.bluemercury.com* ☉ *Mon.–Sat. 10–7, Sun. 11–6.*

Kiehl's Since 1851. Step inside this store and you can feel like you're in an
old-world apothecary—with a sleek, modern twist. The staff is friendly
and helpful and knows everything about the extensive line of natural
lotions, balms, and cosmetics. This chain is known for giving away
generous samples. ⊠ *The Shops at Liberty Place, 1625 Chestnut St.,
Rittenhouse Square* ☎ *215/636–9936* ☉ *Mon.–Sat. 10–7, Sun. noon–6.*

Lush. The soaps, lotions, and other unguents made by this Canadian
based chain are so boldly fragrant you can smell the place when you're
still half a block away. This pioneer in the organic-cosmetics industry
is loved for its ethical sourcing and anti-animal-testing policy as much
as it is for its fizzy bath bombs and aromatic (in a good way) lotions
and potions. ⊠ *1525 Walnut St., Rittenhouse Square* ☎ *215/546–5874*
⊕ *www.lushusa.com* ☉ *Mon.–Sat. 10–8, Sun. 11–7.*

Sephora. Locals rejoiced when the national cosmetic chain finally landed
in Center City. It stocks lots of must-have makeup, skin-care, hair
care, and perfume brands, including Bare Minerals, Nars, Benefit
Laura Mercier, and Stila. ⊠ *1714 Chestnut St., Rittenhouse Square*
☎ *215/563–6112* ☉ *Mon.–Sat. 10–7, Sun. 11–5.*

FOOD

Di Bruno Bros. There are three locations to tempt the palate—the original
one in the Italian Market and the hipper ones in Rittenhouse Square and
Washington West. Di Bruno's is a mecca for cheese lovers—the store
carries more than 300 different varieties from around the world, as well
as some house-made kinds. You can also find barrels of olives, imported
olive oils, Abbruzze sausage, and balsamic vinegar that's been aged for
75 years. The staff is very knowledgeable and will provide friendly
advice on storage, preparation, and serving ideas. Ask for recipes and
samples. ⊠ *1730 Chestnut St., Rittenhouse Square* ☎ *215/665–9220*
⊕ *www.dibruno.com* ☉ *Weekdays 9–8:30, Sat. 9–8, Sun. 9–7.*

Metropolitan Bakery. This Philadelphia institution was founded on the
principle of artisanal baking, which explains why its loaves have such an
intense flavor and crackly crust. Stop here for a round of cracked wheat
or multigrain or for a small treat such as a sour cherry–chocolate chip–
sea salt cookie. The store also sells its signature granola, plus cheese,
honey, and preserves by other artisans. ⊠ *262 S. 19th St., Rittenhouse
Square* ☎ *215/545–6655* ⊕ *www.metropolitanbakery.com* ☉ *Weekdays
7:30–7, weekends 8–6.*

Premium Steap. This tiny tea-lover's paradise stocks a bevy of rare
loose-leaf teas (Papaya Pineapple Green Tea; Earl Gray Lavender) in
brass canisters that line the walls. Try a variety or two at the little
bar in the back, where the intense yet extremely knowledgeable owner
is often brewing a cuppa. There's a great, if limited, selection of tea
ware. ⊠ *111 S. 18th St., Rittenhouse Square* ☎ *215/568–2920* ⊕ *www.
premiumsteap.com* ☉ *Weekdays 10–7, Sat. 10–6, Sun. noon–6.*

GIFTS AND SOUVENIRS

Omoi Zakka. Owner Elizabeth Seiber studied in Japan as a teenager and came back with a taste for "zakka" shops—small stores carrying compelling, everyday things. She resolved to create one with Omoi, a cozy space on a residential block that carries cute, kitschy, and charming tchotchkes, jewelry, housewares, and stationery from Japan, France, and other places far and near. ☒ *1608 Pine St., Rittenhouse Square* ☎ *215/545–0963* ⊕ *www.omoionline.com* ☉ *Mon. noon–7, Tues.–Sat. 11–7, Sun. noon–6.*

HOME DECOR

Manor Home & Gifts. This popular spot for local bridal registries is also a wonderful place for anyone pre- or postnuptials to peruse beautiful china by Bernaudad, Hermès of Paris, Royal Limoges, and other prestigious brands; to find elusive English-made Cornishware and handblown glass and pottery by Simon Pearce; and to be transported to the Italian countryside by a collection of vibrant, hand-painted Italian bowls and platters. ☒ *210 S. 17th St., Rittenhouse Square* ☎ *215/732–1030, 866/406–2667* ⊕ *www.manorhg.com* ☉ *Mon.,Tues., and Thurs.–Sat. 9:30–6:30; Wed. 9:30–8; Sun. noon–6.*

JEWELRY

Egan Day. This low-key, stripped-down boutique set in a beautiful town house specializes in fine jewelry by contemporary designers like Jonathan Wahl and Maria Beaulieu, who craft refined, restrained pieces that highlight the materials and the wearer. ☒ *260 S. 16th St., Rittenhouse Square* ☎ *267/773–8833* ⊕ *www.eganday.com* ☉ *Mon.–Sat. 11–6.*

LAGOS–The Store. Lagos jewelry, sold in upscale department stores, gets top billing here. All pieces are handcrafted and designed in Philadelphia by Steven Lagos. Aficionados are thrilled by the selection, including the Diamonds & Caviar, and Signature designs. ☒ *1735 Walnut St., Rittenhouse Square* ☎ *215/567–0770* ⊕ *www.lagos.com* ☉ *Mon.–Sat. 10–7; call for extended seasonal hrs* Ⓜ *15th and Market.*

Richard Kenneth. Jewelry from the late-Georgian, Victorian, Art Nouveau, Art Deco, and '40s-retro periods are what you can find at this shop near Rittenhouse Square. Kenneth specializes in repairs and appraisals. ☒ *202 S. 17th St., Rittenhouse Square* ☎ *215/545–3355* ⊕ *www. richardkennethjewelers.com* ☉ *Mon.–Sat. 10–6, Sun. noon–6, or by appointment* ☞ *Appraisals and estate evaluations by appointment only.*

SHOES

Head Start Shoes. Floor-to-ceiling windows showcasing a huge selection of Italian shoes and boots beckon to shoppers passing by this hip shop. Inside you can find women's, men's, and children's footwear in the trendiest styles. ☒ *126 S. 17th St., Rittenhouse Square* ☎ *215/567–3247* ⊕ *www. headstartshoes.com* ☉ *Mon. and Tues. 10–6, Wed.–Sat. 10–7, Sun. 11–6.*

SPORTING GOODS

City Sports. Besides sports equipment from in-line skates to bike helmets, the store carries plenty of brand-name active wear and its own line of clothing. ☒ *1608 Walnut St., Rittenhouse Square* ☎ *215/985–5860* ⊕ *www.citysports.com/center-city-city-sports-store.aspx* ☉ *Mon.–Sat. 8–9:30, Sun. 10–8:30.*

6

Rittenhouse Sports. Its focus is on gear for triathlon sports—running, swimming, and cycling—but the store also stocks shoes for aerobics and other activities. ⊠ *1717 Chestnut St., Rittenhouse Square* ☎ *215/569-9957* ⊕ *www.rittenhousesportsspecialties.wordpress.com* ⊙ *Mon.–Sat. 10–6; closed Sun.*

BENJAMIN FRANKLIN PARKWAY AND FAIRMOUNT

Museum gift shops anchor the shopping scene around the Parkway. Along Fairmount Avenue and nestled in the residential streets behind it, you'll find independent shops and galleries.

FAIRMOUNT

ART GALLERIES

I. Brewster. The specialty here is contemporary paintings and prints by such artists as Salvador Dalí, Peter Max, Marc Chagall, Louis Icart, Erté, Andy Warhol, Pablo Picasso, and Roy Lichtenstein. ⊠ *210 N. 21st St., Fairmount* ☎ *215/731–9200* ⊕ *www.ibrewster.com/main.php*

SOUTH PHILADELPHIA

South Philadelphia is made up of a few smaller neighborhoods, including Society Hill, South Street, Queen Village (home to Fabric Row), and the Italian Market, and the shopping here is as varied as these nabes. South Street's street-wear shops and hippie holdovers give way to indie boutiques and thrift shops in the satellite streets. The quirky Italian Market's specialty stores are a home cook's dream. A few excellent independent bookshops survive throughout South Philly.

SOUTH PHILADELPHIA

BOOKSTORES

Brickbat Books. The charming, worn-in feel of this store lined with wooden shelves befits the merchandise for sale: the focus is on rare, small-press used and new books, although it's not unheard-of to find a $4 Hardy Boys paperback next to a first-edition Edward Gorey. The store also acts as a venue for fringe musicians from near and far. ⊠ *709 S. 4th St., South Philadelphia* ☎ *215/592–1207* ⊕ *www.brickbatbooks. com* ⊙ *Tues.–Sat. 11–7, Sun. 11–6; closed Mon.*

Garland of Letters. This is the original New Age bookstore that hails from the days when hippies arrived on South Street in 1972 and turned it into an arts enclave. Follow the smell of incense and step inside to find books on astrology, tarot, shamanism, and world religions and cultures, plus a large selection of jewelry, crystals, and candles. ⊠ *527 South St., South Philadelphia* ☎ *215/923–5946* ⊙ *Weekdays noon–9, Sat. 11–9:30, Sun. noon–8.*

Headhouse Books. Sunlight streams into the front windows of this well-curated indie bookshop. It's the kind of place that attracts regulars who sit sipping tea and reading for hours with a dog curled at their feet. This inviting shop has become a meeting place for the local literary community—both the readers and the writers. ⊠ *619 S. 2nd St., South Philadelphia* ☎ *215/923–9525* ⊕ *www.headhousebooks.com* ☾ *Mon.– Thurs. 10–7, Fri. and Sat. 10–8, Sun. 11–5.*

CLOTHING

Fabric Row. In the early 1900s, 4th Street, today's Fabric Row, was teeming with pushcarts selling calico, notions, and trimming, and was known as "der Ferder" or "the Fourth" in Yiddish. Today several century-old fabric stores still stand, like stalwarts Maxie's Daughter and Fleishman Fabrics and Supplies, but many of the storefronts are home to locals selling wares from European-label shoes to fair-trade coffee. There's also a resurgent restaurant scene. ⊠ *South Philadelphia.*

Passional Boutique. Only the adventurous dare enter this shop where a blue-haired saleswoman will fit you for your very own luxurious hand-crafted corset. The work on these custom steel-boned pieces is beautiful and unique. The high-end wares sold here are the real deal as compared to the many of its neighbors on South Street that specialize in fishnets and Sexy Nurse costumes. You'll also find leather and bondage gear here. ⊠ *317 South St., South Philadelphia* ☎ *215/829–4986* ⊕ *www. passionalboutique.com* ☾ *Sun.–Tues. noon–9, Wed.–Sat. noon–10.*

FOOD

Cardenas Oil & Vinegar Taproom. You've seen shops like Cardenas Oil & Vinegar Taproom in small-town downtowns all across the country. At this Italian Market shop, they've got the requisite refillable oils and vinegars (in flavors that include blood orange and coconut), but distinguish themselves with a serious lineup of rare, unadulterated elixirs sourced from Italy, Spain, even South Africa. The team is generous with samples. ⊠ *942 S. 9th St., South Philadelphia* ☎ *267/928–3690* ⊕ *www.cardenastaproom.com.*

Di Bruno Bros. This is the original location of the famed cheese shop; the other, larger stores are in Rittenhouse Square and Washington Square West. The major difference among them really is size. Its uptown siblings are enormous and can be overwhelming. This shop is tiny—long, narrow, and cave-like, with salamis hanging from the ceiling like stalactites. Still, it's jam-packed with all the specialties you expect from the Di Brunos—cheeses, olive oils, prepared foods—plus a sandwich counter and the usual über-knowledgeable staffers. ⊠ *930 S. 9th St., South Philadelphia* ☎ *215/922–2876* ⊕ *www.dibruno.com* ☾ *Mon. 9–5, Tues.–Sat. 8–6, Sun. 8–4.*

House of Tea. This small shop feels timeless with its wood floors, wood counter, and built-in wood cubbies holding large brass tins of loose-leaf teas from around the world. It also stocks a good number of beautiful tea sets. ⊠ *720 S. 4th St., South Philadelphia* ☎ *215/923–8327* ⊕ *www.houseoftea.com* ☾ *Thurs.–Sat. 10–5; hrs may vary seasonally, please call ahead.*

Italian Market. If you want local color, nothing compares with South Philadelphia's Italian Market. On both sides of 9th Street from Christian Street to Washington Avenue and spilling out onto the surrounding blocks, hundreds of outdoor stalls and indoor stores sell spices, cheeses, pastas, fruits, vegetables, and freshly slaughtered poultry and beef, not to mention household items, clothing, shoes, and other goods. It's crowded and filled with the aromas of everything from fresh garlic to imported salami. The vendors can be less than hospitable, but the food is fresh and the prices are reasonable. Food shops include Grassia's Spice Company, Di Bruno Brothers House of Cheese, Claudio's, and Talluto's Authentic Italian Foods. Fante's is well known for cookware. The market's hours are Tuesday–Saturday 9–5:30; some vendors open earlier and others close around 3:30. Some shops are open Sundays and even Mondays as new vendors expand the markets. It's best to call ahead to specific shops and check. ✉ *9th St., between Washington Ave. and Christian St., and the surrounding neighborhood, South Philadelphia.*

GIFTS AND SOUVENIRS

Eyes Gallery. The three floors of this unique store feel like a folk-art museum with Peruvian alpaca sweaters, Day of the Dead art, and instruments, jewelry, and decorative items from all over Mexico and South America for sale. From basement to skylight, the store's interior is filled with mosaics by famed local artist Isaiah Zagar, who owns the shop with his wife. ✉ *402 South St., South Philadelphia* ☎ *215/925–0193* ⊕ *www.eyesgallery.com* ☽ *Mon.–Thurs. 11–7, Fri. and Sat. 11–8, Sun. noon–7.*

HOME DECOR

Fante's Kitchen Shop. One of the nation's oldest gourmet supply stores has the largest selection of coffeemakers and cooking equipment in the United States. Family owned since 1906, Fante's is famous for oddball kitchen gadgets such as truffle shavers and pineapple peelers; restaurants and bakeries all over the country and overseas order from the store. It's in the Italian Market, so you can combine a visit here with other food shopping. ✉ *1006 S. 9th St., South Philadelphia* ☎ *215/922–5557, 800/443–2683* ⊕ *www.fantes.com* ☽ *Tues.–Sat. 9–5, Sun. 9–1* Ⓜ *Broad and Ellsworth.*

JEWELRY

Bario-Neal Jewelry. Stunningly simple earrings, bracelets, and necklaces are designed and handcrafted locally at this store-workshop by two women (Anna Bario and Page Neal) who create environmentally friendly jewelry. All materials are reclaimed, ethically sourced, or retrieved using low-impact practices. Even the packaging—reclaimed glass bottles with cork stoppers—is green. ✉ *700 S. 6th St., 19147, South Philadelphia* ☎ *215/454–2164* ☽ *Wed. and Thurs. noon–6:30, Fri.–Sun. 11–6* ☞ *Appointments preferred.*

MALLS

South Street. For some of the most entertaining people-watching in the city, head to South Street, just south of Society Hill. Pierced and tattooed teens vie for space with moms wheeling strollers on this bustling strip from Front Street near the Delaware River to 9th Street. More than 300 unusual stores—high-fashion clothing, New Age books, music and health food, avant-garde art galleries, and 100 restaurants—line the area. Most shops are open in the evening. You can find a few of the national chains, but 95% of the stores are locally owned, selling things you won't find in the mall back home. ⊠ *South Philadelphia.*

SHOES

Benjamin Lovell. This small, locally based chain specializes in stylish comfort, including brands like Dansko, Naot, Clarks, La Canadienne, Uggs, and Birkenstocks. The prices are high, but this South Street location (there's another by Rittenhouse Square) takes the sting out with its large sale section in the back. ⊠ *318 South St., South Philadelphia* ☎ *215/238–1969* ⊕ *www.blshoes.com* ⊗ *Mon.–Thurs. 11–8, Fri. and Sat. 11–9, Sun. 11–6.*

Bus Stop Boutique. Owned by a British expat, this shop sells fashion-forward, cutting-edge shoes by European labels like Fluevog, Coclico, United Nude and Fly London that are hard to find on this side of the pond. ⊠ *727 S. 4th St., South Philadelphia* ☎ *215/627–2357* ⊕ *www.busstopboutique. com* ⊗ *Mon.–Thurs., and Sat. 11–6; Fri. 11–7; Sun. noon–5.*

∎ST PASSYUNK

CLOTHING

Metro. Well-dressed gents populate this handsome menswear boutique on a high-profile East Passyunk corner. Shopkeeper Tom Longo stocks Scotch & Soda denim, Penguin polos, Parke & Ronen swimsuits, and more. The window displays are epic. ⊠ *1600 E. Passyunk Ave., East Passyunk* ☎ *267/324–5172* ⊕ *metromensclothing.com.*

FOOD

Green Aisle Grocery. Food writer Adam Erace and his brother Andrew curate a selection of local, organic, and gourmet foods in their tiny 260-square-foot market on East Passyunk, the original of three Philly locations. Grab a tub of Dizengoff hummus, puck of Pennsylvania Camembert, and box of fancy crackers and have an impromptu picnic at the Singing Fountain up the street. Don't overlook the brothers' seasonal house-made pickles and preserves in flavors like Blueberry Cardamom and Salty Strawberry; they make excellent souvenirs. ⊠ *1618 E. Passyunk Ave., East Passyunk* ☎ *215/465–1411* ⊕ *www. greenaislegrocery.com.*

GIFTS AND SOUVENIRS

Analog Watch Co. Chic unisex watches composed of natural materials like marble and bamboo (and featured the New York's MoMA!) are the get at Analog, a combo boutique-workshop tucked on a side street off East Passyunk. The friendly craftsmen there can help find you find the watch that fits your style. ⊠ *1214 Moore St., East Passyunk* ☎ *484/808–5831* ⊕ *www.analogwatchco.com.*

Fabric Horse. It's impossible to spend any time wandering around East Passyunk without spotting locals with Fabric Horse's stylish, cycling-inspired messenger bags, bike lock holsters, and utility belts slung about their bodies. The designers use landfill-destined materials like seat belts and yoga mats in many of the products. ⊠ *1737 E. Passyunk Ave., Eas. Passyunk* ☎ *215/480–1934* ⊕ *www.fabrichorse.com.*

Occasionette. Shopkeeper–cum–crafting maven Sara Villari got her star screen-printing tea towels and totes under her line, Girls Can Tell. Bu her wholesale and online business eventually grew enough to open a bricks-and-mortar shop, Occasionette, on East Passyunk. The store is a cheerful menagerie of thoughtful gifts and trinkets: indie greeting cards eco-friendly water bottles, alluring candles, cocktail mixers, as well as the full breadth of Villari's original line. Check her website for multiple special events and deals. ⊠ *1825 E. Passyunk Ave., East Passyunk* ☎ *215/465–1704* ⊕ *www.occasionette.com.*

UNIVERSITY CITY AND WEST PHILADELPHIA

Most of the action in University City revolves around the universities, specifically the University of Pennsylvania and Drexel University. An active retail scene has sprouted around the U. of Penn campus to serve that huge population of students. A pocket of interesting, eclectic shops and restaurants has also sprung up farther west, in a residential area that's home to mostly grad students and professors on the other side of Clark Park.

UNIVERSITY CITY

ART GALLERIES

VIX Emporium. Local artists and designers consign their works—from ceramics to handmade hats—in this former millinery with the original built-in cabinetry and beveled-glass windowpanes. The owners, a couple, both have a background in retail and are artisans themselves—she makes jewelry and he's a graphic designer. That's typical of the creative entrepreneurs popping up in West Philadelphia. ⊠ *5009 Baltimore Ave., University City* ☎ *215/471–7700* ⊕ *www.vixemporium.com* ⊙ *Tues.– Fri. 11–7, Sat. 10–6.*

BOOKSTORES

House of Our Own. Despite its location in a brownstone flanked by University of Pennsylvania fraternity houses, there's nothing fratty about this erudite bookstore. Its two floors of rambling rooms with shelves reaching up to the soaring ceilings boast an enormous amount of literature mixed in with course books for Penn students and used books. Spend a frivolous hour perusing books in a place that makes you feel like you're back in college. ⊠ *3920 Spruce St., University City* ☎ *215/222–1576* ⊕ *www.biblio.com/bookstore/house_of_our_own_ philadelphia* ⊙ *Mon.–Sat. 10:30–5:30.*

Penn Bookstore. The 60,000-square-foot store, operated by Barnes & Noble, is one of the largest academic bookstores in the United States. Highlights include tomes from the University of Pennsylvania faculty, loads of Penn-insignia clothing and memorabilia, a multimedia section, and a children's reading room. You can also find a Starbucks and the requisite best sellers. ⊠ *3601 Walnut St., University City*

📠215/898–7595 ⊕*www.upenn.bncollege.com* ⊙ *Weekdays 8:30 am–9:30 pm, Sat. 10–9:30, Sun. 10–8.*

GIFTS AND SOUVENIRS

Avril 50. This narrow shop fulfills several functions: as an international newsstand—if you're looking for a particularly obscure foreign periodical, you'll find it here; and as purveyor of excellent coffee and espresso shot, unusual postcards, high-end chocolate, and specialty cigarettes and tobacco. The patio seating is an added bonus—enjoy your newspaper and coffee while people-watching. ✉ *3406 Sansom St., University City* 📠*215/222–6108* ⊕ *www.avril50.com* ⊙ *Weekdays 7:30–6, weekends 10–5.*

HOME DECOR

Hello World. In late 2014 the Rittenhouse Square outposts of Hello World, which focused on gifts and accessories, and Hello Home, which focused on the home and struck a mid-century modern note with furniture and accessories, closed their Center City locations and joined forces in one large lifestyle store that offers a bit of everything from artisan children's toys to whimsical kitchen accessories to, yes, mid-century modern furniture, for the discerning shopper. ✉ *3610 Sansom St., University City* 📠*215/382–5207* ⊕ *www.shophelloworld.com* ⊙ *Weekdays 11–6, weekends 11–5.*

SPORTING GOODS

Eastern Mountain Sports. Outdoorsmen and -women will find a large selection of clothing and equipment for activities like running, skiing, camping, and boating. On the University of Pennsylvania campus, the shop features an in-store rock-climbing wall. Equipment rentals are available. ✉ *3401 Chestnut St., University City* 📠*215/382–0930* ⊕ *www.ems.com/store-details?StoreID=155* ⊙ *Daily 11–7.*

NORTHWESTERN PHILADELPHIA

Make sure to visit Northwestern Philadelphia's historic and hip neighborhood of Manayunk. This former mill town along the Schuylkill River is crammed with art galleries and clothing boutiques, and with one-of-a-kind stores selling everything from clocks and crystals to board games and Balinese artifacts. Alfresco dining, lively bars, and stay-open-late shops make this a great evening destination.

MANAYUNK

GIFTS AND SOUVENIRS

FAMILY **Spectrum Scientifics.** Catering to proud science geeks young and old, this shop specializes in toys for the brainy set, from telescopes and magnifying glasses to hologram illusions and chemistry sets. ✉ *4403 Main St., Manayunk* 📠*215/667–8309* ⊕ *www.spectrum-scientifics.com* ⊙ *Tues.– Sat. 10–6, Sun. and Mon. 11–5.*

HOME DECOR

Dwelling. Modern, exciting furniture that will make you want to redecorate your pad into the coolest, most comfortable apartment in town. A must, even if you're not planning to buy. ⊠ *4050 Main St., Manayunk* ☎ *215/487–7400* ⊕ *www.dwellinghome.com* ☺ *Mon.–Sat. 10–6, Sun. noon–5.*

JEWELRY

Gary P. Mann Design. Noted local goldsmith Gary Mann creates elegant custom jewelry. The store is also known for its estate jewelry, carved jade and emerald pieces, stack rings, and Judaica. ⊠ *4349 Main St., Manayunk* ☎ *215/482–7051* ⊕ *www.garymannjewelry.com* ☺ *Tues.– Sat. 11–6.*

CHESTNUT HILL

ANTIQUES

The Philadelphia Print Shop, Ltd. It's easy to get lost amid the arcana at this charmingly cluttered shop, which has been dealing in historic prints, antique maps, and related reference books for more than 35 years. ⊠ *8441 Germantown Ave., Chestnut Hill* ☎ *215/242–4750* ⊕ *www. philaprintshop.com* ☺ *Mon.–Sat. 10–5.*

FOOD

Baker Street Bread. Cross the street if you don't want to get lured inside by the enticing aromas of fresh-baked artisanal breads and pastries at this small bakery at the base of Chestnut Hill. There's also a small selection of sandwiches and pizzas if you need to refuel before trekking up Germantown Avenue. ⊠ *8009 Germantown Ave., Chestnut Hill* ☎ *215/248–3296* ⊕ *www.bakerstreetbread.com* ☺ *Weekdays 7–6:30, Sat. 7–6, Sun. 7–5.*

Bredenbeck's Ice Cream Parlor. The bakery half of the store is nothing to write home about, but on the ice-cream side they scoop Bassetts ice cream. If you've tried Bassetts—there's also a counter in Reading Terminal Market—you'll know why this is important information. ⊠ *8126 Germantown Ave., Chestnut Hill* ☎ *215/247–7374* ⊕ *www.bredenbecks. com* ☺ *Mon.–Sat. 6:30 am–7 pm, Sun. 8–6; June–Sept., hrs may vary.*

JEWELRY

Caleb Meyer's. You'll find elegant and distinctive jewelry in gold and platinum at this well-known shop. They also have a curated collection of crafts in wood, glass, pottery, and silver. ⊠ *8520 Germantown Ave., Chestnut Hill* ☎ *215/248–9250* ⊕ *www.calebmeyer.com* ☺ *Tues.–Fri. 10–5:30, Sat. 10–5.*

MARKETS

Market at the Fareway. Not your traditional market, this collection of stands is short on fresh produce, focusing more on meats and small eateries. Even if you can't take advantage of the local butchers, you can still grab fresh takeout from the good Mexican, hoagie, seafood, Persian, and Caribbean stalls (there are also a few tables for those wanting to grab a quick bite). While permanently housed behind the Chestnut Hill Hotel, the bulk of the market is only open three days a week—Thursday through Saturday. For more traditional fruits and vegetables, the Chestnut Hill Farmers' Market sets up shop outdoors on Winston Road between Germantown Avenue and Mermaid Lane on Saturday mornings from 9:30 to 1. ⊠ *8229 Germantown Ave., Chestnut Hill* 🕾 *215/242–5905* ⊕ *www.marketatthefareway.com* ⊗ *Thurs. and Fri. 9–6, Sat. 8–5.*

ORTHEASTERN PHILADELPHIA

North Philadelphia's Northern Liberties neighborhood is a taxi or bus ride from Old City, but it's worth checking out, especially since the Piazza at Schmidt's, a retail space on the former site of Schmidt's Brewery, opened in 2009. Its more than 100,000 square feet of independent shops, galleries, and restaurants have strengthened the pulse of this already lively neighborhood with an industrial heritage and an artsy vibe.

ORTHERN LIBERTIES

ANTIQUES

Architectural Antiques Exchange. Victorian embellishments from saloons and apothecary shops, stained and beveled glass, gargoyles, and advertising memorabilia entice shoppers here. ⊠ *715 N. 2nd St., Northern Liberties* 🕾 *215/922–3669* ⊕ *www.architecturalantiques.com* ⊗ *Mon.– Sat. 10–5* Ⓜ *Spring Garden stop on the Market–Frankford Line.*

ART GALLERIES

Art Star. Two grads of the local Tyler School of Art run this retail shop and gallery that carries independent designers and artists with a crafty bent. You'll find everything from necklaces made with recycled bottle caps and silk-screened T-shirts to original art. ⊠ *623 N. 2nd St., Northern Liberties* 🕾 *215/238–1557* ⊕ *www.artstarphilly.com* ⊗ *Tues.–Sat. 11–7, Sun. noon–6.*

FOOD

Brown Betty Dessert Boutique. One of the many women-owned businesses in the nabe, Brown Betty is revered for its pineapple pound cake and for its long menu of cupcakes. The overall favorite might be Jean's Road Trip (a cupcake with red-velvet cake and cream-cheese buttercream icing), but it's a toss-up. Enjoy a treat on the cozy bakery's curvaceous antique couch. ⊠ *722 N. 2nd St., Northern Liberties* 🕾 *215/629– 0999, 215/988–1888 mini-shop at The Shops at Liberty Place* ⊕ *www. brownbettydesserts.com* ⊗ *Mon.–Sat. noon–7, Sun. 11–4.*

JEWELRY

Millésimé. This high-design concept store sells a mix of items curated by a Paris-centric store owner, including gold-link chain necklaces embellished with bears' heads and paws by Lille native Lena Klax; silk scarves by French brand milleneufcentquatrevingtquatre; charmingly offbeat kitchenware by Invotis Orange; and kitchen linens by Moutet. ⊠ *41 S. 3rd St., Northern Liberties* 🕾 *267/455–0374* ⊕ *www.millesime.us* ⊗ *Tues.–Sat. 11–6, Sun. and Mon. by appointment only.*

6

SHOPPING DISTRICTS AND MALLS

Piazza at Schmidt's. This local developer's mixed-use interpretation of Rome's Piazza Navona was a long time coming, and was the cause of so much controversy over the years that locals were almost shocked to see it finally open in summer 2009. A "curator" handpicks the independent retailers and gallerists who fill nearly 40 ground-floor commercial spaces. (Condos occupy the floors above.) They ring a giant plaza with pavement scalloped in the same pattern as in Rome and featuring a giant stage and screen. Especially during warm-weather months, there's usually some kind of event or live entertainment going on at the piazza. ⊠ *2nd and Hancock Sts., Northern Liberties* ⊕ *atthepiazza.com.*

FISHTOWN

ART GALLERIES

Nexus Foundation for Today's Art. A group of artists started this nonprofit organization in 1975. The emphasis is on experimental art as well as new directions in traditional mediums. ⊠ *Crane Arts LLC, 1400 N. American St., Fishtown* ☎ *215/684–1946* ⊗ *Wed.–Sun. noon–6.*

SIDE TRIPS FROM
PHILADELPHIA

Updated by
Adam Erace

It's easy to expand your view of the Philadelphia area by taking one or more day trips to destinations that are within an hour's drive of the city. Whether you head north or south, in 30 minutes you can be immersed in a whole new world—or make that "worlds."

First you can see the verdant hills and ancient barns of the Brandywine Valley, home to three generations of Wyeths and other artists inspired by the rural landscapes outside their windows. Then you can visit the extravagant realm of du Pont country, including Pierre S. du Pont's resplendent Longwood Gardens, whose summer fountain displays are world-renowned, and Winterthur, an important repository of American decorative furnishings, over the border in Delaware. Or you can explore the Revolutionary War battlefield of Brandywine at Chadds Ford. These attractions are year-round favorites of Philadelphians, and area bed-and-breakfasts and inns make the Brandywine appealing as an overnight or weekend trip and as a day excursion.

The historical park at Valley Forge adds another dimension to the revolutionary story that began in Independence Hall. Not far away, the town called King of Prussia dates to that period, but is now primarily synonymous with shopping, thanks to its huge upscale mall. It's a half hour from Philadelphia and also accessible by public transportation.

To the north, Bucks County is known for art colonies and antiques, summer theater, and country inns.

ORIENTATION AND PLANNING

GETTING ORIENTED

The Brandywine Valley's major attractions are less than an hour's drive from each other, so you can cover a fair amount of ground. In just a few days' time you can explore quiet country roads, admire the art collections and gardens of some of the region's best-known families, visit key sites from the Revolutionary War, taste a little wine, and hike, walk, or bike along some of the area's most lovely byways.

The Brandywine Valley. Ruled by two families, the Wyeths and the du Ponts, there are many reasons to stay awhile here, whether it's to take in the quintessential Brandywine vistas or explore other top attractions like Winterthur and Longwood Gardens.

Valley Forge. The two main draws of Valley Forge are at odds with one another—George Washington's Revolutionary War encampment at Valley Forge National Historical Park on the one hand and the King of Prussia mall on the other.

Bucks County. The main draws here are Washington Crossing, an area rich in American Revolutionary history, and New Hope, a cosmopolitan village known for its antiques stores and day-trippers.

LANNING

WHEN TO GO

Each season provides plenty of reasons to visit the Brandywine, which is about 45 minutes' to an hour's drive from Center City Philadelphia; Bucks County is about an hour north. Spring and summer bring a Technicolor display of flowers at Longwood and verdant green to the Brandywine Valley countryside, Valley Forge National Park, and Bucks County. The chance to witness some spectacular fall foliage and crisper weather is a compelling case for an autumnal visit, although the spectacular holiday light show at Longwood and the chance to relax by a cozy fire at a charming inn are reason enough to come during the cold-weather months. Christmas brings holiday festivals to Bucks County as well, including the annual reenactment of Washington Crossing the Delaware. You can easily make day trips to any of these regions from the city, but be sure to avoid traveling west on I–76, and to a lesser extent, north or south on I–95, during rush hour. Weekends, spring through fall, tend to be the busiest season for visitors.

GETTING HERE AND AROUND

While some of these attractions can be reached by public transportation, the only practical way to tour Bucks County is by car.

BUS TRAVEL

To get to Valley Forge, you can take SEPTA Bus 124 from 13th and Market streets (it leaves twice an hour starting at 4:30 am) for King of Prussia (including the Plaza and the Court) and continue on to Valley Forge National Historical Park.

Contacts **SEPTA.** ☏ *215/580–7800* ⊕ *www.septa.com.*

CAR TRAVEL

For the Brandywine Valley, take U.S. 1 south from Philadelphia; it is about 25 miles away, and many attractions are on U.S. 1. To reach Wilmington, pick up U.S. 202 south just past Concordville or take I–95 south from Philadelphia.

For Valley Forge, take the Schuylkill Expressway (I–76) west from Philadelphia to Exit 327 (Mall Boulevard). Make a right onto Mall Boulevard and a right onto North Gulph Road. Follow the road 1½ miles to Valley Forge National Historical Park. Mall Boulevard also provides easy access to the Plaza and the Court shopping complex.

The most direct route to Bucks Country is I–95 north, which takes you near sights in the southern part of the county. Before you cross into New Jersey, take the exit and continue on Route 32, which runs along the Delaware past Washington Crossing Historic Park. New Hope is about 40 miles northwest of Philadelphia.

7

TRAIN TRAVEL

Amtrak has frequent service from Philadelphia's 30th Street Station to Wilmington's station at 100 South French Street on the edge of downtown. It's a 25-minute ride.

SEPTA's Wilmington/Newark commuter train has hourly departures to Wilmington from Philadelphia's Suburban, 30th Street, and Market East train stations. The trip takes one hour.

Contacts Amtrak. ☎ *800/872-7245* ⊕ *www.amtrak.com.* **SEPTA.** ☎ *215/580-7800* ⊕ *www.septa.org.*

TOURS

Brandywine Outfitters rents out canoes and kayaks and offers a range of scenic trips on the Brandywine River April through September.

Contacts Brandywine Outfitters. ⊠ *2096 Strasburg Rd., Coatesville* ☎ *610/486-6141, 610/772-6207 ask for Rick* ⊕ *www.canoepa.com.*

HOTELS

Many of the region's accommodations may be considered bed-and-breakfasts because of their intimate atmosphere, but they're far from the typical B&B—which is usually a room in a private home—and are more accurately characterized as inns or small hotels.

Hotel reviews have been shortened. For full information, visit Fodors.com.

RESTAURANTS

It seems that most restaurants in both the Brandywine Valley and Bucks County serve American cuisine, with creative contemporary touches at the better establishments. You'll find both sophisticated restaurants and casual country spots. Most also present local specialties—fresh seafood from Chesapeake Bay and dishes made with Kennett Square mushrooms. As an added pleasure, some of the region's best restaurants are in restored Colonial and Victorian homes.

WHAT IT COSTS				
	$	$$	$$$	$$$$
RESTAURANTS	Under $15	$15–$19	$20–$24	Over $24
HOTELS	Under $150	$150–$200	$201–$250	Over $250

Restaurant prices are the average cost of a main course at dinner or, if dinner is not served, at lunch. Hotel prices are the lowest cost of a standard double room in high season.

VISITOR INFORMATION

The visitor center at the entrance to Longwood Gardens is operated by the Chester Country Conference and Visitors Bureau. It's open daily 10–6.

Bucks County maintains a visitor center in Bensalem, but the county website has information on all the region's sights, restaurants, and B&Bs.

Contacts **Bucks County Conference and Visitors Bureau.** ⊠ *3207 Street Rd., Bensalem* ☎ *215/639–0300 Bucks County Visitor Center* ⊕ *www. visitbuckscounty.com.* **Chester County Conference and Visitors Bureau.** ⊠ *300 Greenwood Rd., Kennett Square* ☎ *484/770–8550* ⊕ *www.brandywinevalley.com.*

HE BRANDYWINE VALLEY

You'll probably experience a strong sense of déjà vu during a journey to the Brandywine Valley. While creating some of the most beloved works in 20th-century American art, Andrew Wyeth made the valley's vistas instantly recognizable. Using colors quintessentially Brandywine—the earthen brown of its hills, the slate gray of its stone farmhouses, and the dark green of its spruce trees—the famous American realist captured its unostentatiously beautiful personality. He also inspired many people to flock to this valley and fall in love with its peaceful byways. The Philadelphia suburbs are encroaching: new housing developments continuously crop up, and the main highways, U.S. 1 and Route 202, bring with them traffic snarls. Yet, traveling down country roads, particularly those that intersect Route 52, makes you feel you have discovered a remote treasure.

The Brandywine Valley actually incorporates parts of three counties in two states: Chester and Delaware counties in Pennsylvania and New Castle County in Delaware. Winding through this scenic region (about 25 miles southwest of Philadelphia), the Brandywine River flows lazily from West Chester, Pennsylvania, to Wilmington, Delaware. Although in spots it's more a creek than a river, it has nourished many of the valley's economic and artistic endeavors.

The valley is also the site of one of the more dramatic turns in the American Revolution, the Battle of Brandywine, and a fascinating museum dedicated to helicopters. Antiques shops, fine restaurants, and cozy country inns dot the region. Your best bet is to rent a car and explore on your own.

If you start early enough, and limit your time at each stop, you can tour the valley's top three attractions—the Brandywine River Museum, Longwood Gardens, and Winterthur—in one day. If you have more time to spend in the valley, you can visit additional sites in Pennsylvania and then move on to Wilmington.

EST CHESTER

30 miles west of Philadelphia via I–95.

The county seat since 1786, this historic mile-square city holds distinctive 18th- and 19th-century architecture, with fine examples of Greek Revival and Victorian styles. A small but vital downtown has shopping possibilities as well as restaurants and bars serving everything from classic American fare to the latest microbrews. Fine examples of classical architecture, including the Chester County Courthouse and Market Street Station, can be found near the intersection of High and Gay

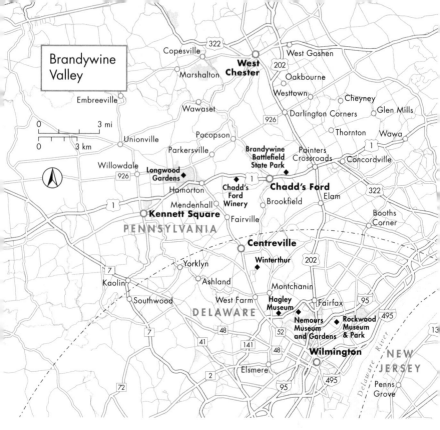

Brandywine Valley

0   3 mi

0   3 km

PENNSYLVANIA

DELAWARE

NEW JERSEY

streets. The town is also home to one of the area's most visited attractions, the QVC Studios, in an industrial park off U.S. 202.

GETTING HERE AND AROUND

From Philadelphia, West Chester is a 45-minute drive via I–95 and U.S. Route 322 West and U.S. Route 202 South. The town itself is highly walkable, but you will need a car to access QVC Studios and other nearby attractions.

ESSENTIALS

Visitor Information Chester County Conference and Visitors Bureau.
✉ *300 Greenwood Ave., Kennett Square* ☎ *484/770–8550, 800/228–9933*
⊕ *www.brandywinevalley.com.*

EXPLORING

FAMILY   **American Helicopter Museum & Education Center.** Ever since Philadelphian Harold Pitcairn made the first rotorcraft flight in 1928, the Southeastern Pennsylvania area has been considered the birthplace of the helicopter industry. In fact, two of the three major U.S. helicopter manufacturers trace their roots to this region. This heritage is represented here, and you can learn about and climb aboard nearly three dozen vintage and modern aircraft that reflect the copter's historic roles in war and rescue missions, in agriculture, and in police surveillance.

✉ *1220 American Blvd.* ☎ *610/436–9600* ⊕ *www.americanhelicopter. museum* 🎫 *$10* 🕙 *Wed.–Sat. 10–5, Sun. noon–5.*

Chester County Historical Society. The society's architectural complex, known as the History Center, includes a former opera house where Buffalo Bill once performed. Galleries tell about the region's settlers and the decorative furniture they crafted. A hands-on history lab lets you churn butter and dress up in a hoop skirt. The society's collection of American cross-stitch samplers is extensive; in the museum shop you can get everything you need to start stitching yourself. ✉ *225 N. High St.* ☎ *610/692–4800* ⊕ *www.chestercohistorical.org* 🎫 *$6* 🕙 *Tues.–Sat. 9:30–4:30.*

QVC Studio Park. This is the world's largest electronic retailer, which in one year alone answered more than 180 million phone calls, shipped more than 165 million packages, and recorded nearly $8 billion in sales. On a one-hour guided tour of the company headquarters you can catch a glimpse of its round-the-clock live broadcast from five studio views and see how QVC products make the route from testing to television. The tour is designed for ages seven and up. If you want free tickets to be part of a studio audience for a live broadcast, call ahead or visit the website to reserve a seat. The studio is wheelchair accessible. ✉ *1200 Wilson Dr.* ☎ *800/600–9900* ⊕ *www.qvc.com* 🎫 *Tours $10* 🕙 *Daily tours offered at 10:30, noon, and 2:30.*

WHERE TO EAT

$$$$ ✕**Dilworthtown Inn.** Fresh, locally sourced seafood, mushroom ragout
AMERICAN vol-au-vent, and chateaubriand are among the entrées at this longtime
dor's Choice favorite for romantic dining. The 15 dining rooms of the elegant 1754
★ country inn are carefully restored and decorated with antiques and Oriental rugs. The wine cellar, one of the region's best, stocks more than 800 vintages, including a merlot and a chardonnay bottled exclusively for the inn. Jackets are suggested for men. The restaurant also offers cooking and wine classes at its Inn Keeper's Kitchen. $ *Average main: $33* ✉ *1390 Old Wilmington Pike* ✢ *5 miles south of downtown West Chester* ☎ *610/399–1390* ⊕ *www.dilworthtown.com* 🕙 *No lunch.*

$$$ ✕**High Street Caffe.** Massive mirrors and silver beaded lighting fixtures
SOUTHERN create a fun and sexy vibe at this small café. Everything here is done up in the color purple—walls, tablecloths, and even the coffee mugs. The staff in the kitchen and dining room is attentive to details. Louisiana smoked alligator sausage and crawfish tails in a spicy barbecue sauce are popular starters. Jambalaya, étouffée, and other favorites from the French Quarter predominate, but you can also find seared ahi tuna and mesquite-grilled hangar steak on the menu. There's live music on the third Friday of each month. $ *Average main: $21* ✉ *322 S. High St.* ☎ *610/696–7435* ⊕ *www.highstreetcaffe.com* 🕙 *No lunch Sat.–Mon.*

$$$ ✕**Iron Hill Brewery.** An old Woolworth's building with tin ceilings and
AMERICAN maple floors has been converted into this bustling restaurant and pub. Jaegerschnitzeland Hawaiian-spiced ahi tuna are two of the creatively prepared entrées. Smaller plates include a house-smoked barbecue pork sandwich, honey sriracha popcorn chicken, and pizzas baked in a wood oven. True to the name, the eatery also brews a large variety of beers and

ales, many of which have won local awards. In warm weather the outdoor tables provide a nice spot for people-watching. [$] *Average main: $20* ✉ *3 W. Gay St.* ☎ *610/738–9600* 🌐 *www.ironhillbrewery.com/westchester.*

SHOPPING

Baldwin's Book Barn. Baldwin's Book Barn is a book lover's dream. This off-the-beaten-path bookstore in a converted barn has nooks and crannies filled with more than 300,000 used and rare books on almost every subject, along with historic maps and prints. ✉ *865 Lenape Rd.* ☎ *610/696–0816* 🌐 *www.bookbarn.com* 🕒 *Daily 10–6.*

CHADDS FORD

11 miles south of West Chester, 30 miles southwest of Philadelphia via I–95 and U.S. 322.

Immortalized in Andrew Wyeth's serene landscapes, Chadds Ford was less bucolic in the 18th century, when one of the bloodiest battles of the Revolutionary War was fought here along Brandywine Creek. A battlefield park and a fine art museum celebrating American masters, including Brandywine Valley natives, make this historic town appealing. There are some pretty side roads to explore as well.

GETTING HERE AND AROUND

From Philadelphia, take I–95 South to U.S. Route 322 toward West Chester and follow signs to U.S. Route 1. The latter is the major thoroughfare to visit the various attractions in Chadds Ford, and can get congested on weekends, so be prepared for lots of stop-and-go traffic.

ESSENTIALS

Visitor Information **Delaware County's Brandywine Conference and Visitors Bureau.** ✉ *1501 N. Providence Rd.* ☎ *800/343–3983,* 🌐 *www.brandywinecvb.org.*

EXPLORING

Brandywine Battlefield State Park. Brandywine Battlefield State Park is near the site of the Battle of Brandywine, where British general William Howe and his troops defeated George Washington on September 11, 1777. The Continental Army then fled to Chester, leaving Philadelphia vulnerable to British troops. The visitor center has displays about the battle that are a good introduction to the area's history. On the site are two restored Quaker farmhouses that once sheltered Washington and General Lafayette. The 50-acre park is a fine place for a picnic. ✉ *1491 Baltimore Pike* ☎ *610/459–3342* 🌐 *www.brandywinebattlefield.org* 🎟 *Park and grounds free; house tours, museum, and film $8; museum admission and film only $3* 🕒 *Mar., Fri. and Sat. 9–4, Sun. noon–4; Apr., Thurs.–Sat. 9–4, Sun. noon–4; May–mid-June and Sept.–Dec., Wed.–Sat. 9–4, Sun. noon–4; mid-June–Aug., Tues.–Sat. 9–4, Sun. noon–4* ☞ *Tours offered at 10, 11, 1, 2, and 3 when the park is open. Tickets may be stamped for readmission the next day.*

Fodor's Choice ★ **Brandywine River Museum.** In a converted Civil War–era gristmill, the Brandywine River Museum contains the art of Chadds Ford native Andrew Wyeth, a major American realist painter, as well as his father, N. C. Wyeth, illustrator of many children's classics; and his son, Jamie. The collection also emphasizes still lifes, landscape paintings, and

American illustration, with works by such artists as Howard Pyle and Maxfield Parrish. The glass-wall lobby overlooks the river and countryside that inspired artists from the area. The museum uses a system of filters, baffles, and blinds to direct natural light. Outside the museum, you can visit its wildflower and native plant gardens and follow a 1-mile nature trail along the river.

The N. C. Wyeth House and Studio, where N. C. painted and raised his children, is open part of the year. The 1911 home, set on a hill, holds many of the props N. C. used in creating his illustrations. His daughter, Carolyn, lived and painted here until 1994. You can also tour the Kuerner Farm, a mile away. Andrew discovered it on a walk when he was 15; he used the farm's landscape, buildings, and animals as the subjects of many of his best-known paintings. A shuttle takes you from the museum to the house and studio or to the farm for an hour-long guided tour. ✉ *1 Hoffman's Mill Rd.* ✣ *At U.S. 1 and Rte. 100* ☎ *610/388–2700* 🌐 *www.brandywinemuseum.org* 🎫 *$15 museum, free until noon on Sun. from mid-Jan.–mid.-Nov.; $8 house, $8 studio, $8 farm; combination admission packages are available* ⏲ *Museum daily 9:30–4:30; house Apr.–Nov., daily 10–12:45; studio, Apr.–Nov., daily 10–3:15; farm Apr.–Nov., daily 10–3:15* ☞ *No children under 6 permitted on tours of outbuildings. Tours hrs for each building may vary from day to day.*

Chaddsford Winery. In a restored barn, the Chaddsford Winery offers tastings and tours of its wine-making facilities. Bring a picnic and enjoy music under the stars during regularly scheduled summer concerts and festival weekends. ✉ *632 Baltimore Pike, U.S. 1* ☎ *610/388–6221* 🌐 *www.chaddsford.com* 🎫 *Free. Weekday wine tastings $7, weekend wine tastings $10–$20 depending on tasting options* ⏲ *Mid-Sept.–mid-May, Tues.–Fri. and Sun. 11–6 (tastings 11:30–5:30), Sat. 11–8 (tastings 11:30–7:30), closed Mon.; mid-May–mid-Sept., Sun.–Fri. 11–6 (tastings 11:30–5:30), Sat. 11–8 (tastings 11:30–7:30)* ☞ *Complimentary guided tours at 2 and 4 on weekends; no reservations required.*

WHERE TO EAT

$ AMERICAN 🍴 **Hank's Place.** Locals flock to this wood-panel outpost for hearty breakfast specials, such as omelets with Kennett Square shiitake and portobello mushrooms and eggs Benedict topped with chipped beef. Hank's is also open for home-style lunches and dinners (come early, as it closes at 7 pm). Old-fashioned favorites like calves liver, fresh fish, and "Steerburger" with fresh sautéed local mushrooms beckon. The strawberry pie and apple dumplings are specialties. [$] *Average main: $9* ✉ *1625 Creek Rd.* ✣ *U.S. 1 and Rte. 100* ☎ *610/388–7061* 🌐 *www.hanks-place.net* 💳 *No credit cards* ⏲ *No dinner Sun. and Mon.*

WHERE TO STAY

$ B&B/INN 🏨 **Brandywine River Hotel.** Near the Brandywine River Museum, this two-story hotel has tasteful Queen Anne–style furnishings, classic English chintz, and floral fabrics that create a homey B&B feel. **Pros:** convenient to attractions; good value for money; friendly staff. **Cons:** decor is uninspired; some rooms could use updating; not as charming as a B&B. [$] *Rooms from: $139* ✉ *1609 Baltimore Pike*

☎ 610/388–1200 ⊕ www.brandywinehotelpa.com ⇨ 29 rooms, 1(suites 🍴 Breakfast ☞ Pet-friendly rooms available.

$$ B&B/INN **Fairville Inn.** This B&B, halfway between Longwood Gardens anc Winterthur, has bright, airy rooms furnished with Queen Anne anc Hepplewhite reproductions and dramatic white-draped canopy beds **Pros:** gracious hosts; central location; spacious rooms. **Cons:** some stree noise; some bathrooms need updating; some rooms have small TVs *[$] Rooms from: $175 ✉ 506 Kennett Pike, Rte. 52 ☎ 610/388–590(⊕ www.fairvilleinn.com ⇨ 13 rooms, 2 suites 🍴 Breakfast.*

$$$ B&B/INN **Hamanassett.** Innkeepers Ashley and Glenn Mon fill their hilltop country house with Southern hospitality and British style: breakfast by candlelight, evening cordials served on the Empire sideboard, a solarium with wicker hampers perfect for impromptu picnics. **Pros:** friendly innkeepers; gourmet breakfast; pet-friendly. **Cons:** some bathrooms are small; some inconsistencies with service. *[$] Rooms from: $225 ✉ 115 Indian Springs Dr., Chester Heights ☎ 610/459–3000, ⊕ www hamanassett.com ⇨ 6 rooms, one 2-bedroom house 🍴 Breakfast.*

$$ B&B/INN Fodor's Choice ★ **The Inn at Grace Winery.** This historic property—part of William Penn's land grant to the Hemphill family—carves out a tranquil 50 acres of Brandywine Valley countryside. **Pros:** elegant decor; well-maintained grounds; accommodating staff. **Cons:** some guest rooms are small; some may not like presence of pets; late breakfast not available. *[$] Rooms from: $190 ✉ 50 Sweetwater Rd., Glen Mills ☎ 610/459–4711, 800/793–3892 ⊕ gracewinery.com/accommodations ⇨ 7 rooms, 8 cottages 🍴 Breakfast ☞ Pet-friendly and family-friendly cottages available.*

CENTREVILLE, DELAWARE

5 miles south of Chadds Ford via U.S. Route 1 and PA Route 52 (Kennett Pike).

The village is aptly named: Centreville, Delaware, founded in 1750 and listed in the National Register of Historic Places, was a midway point between the farms of Kennett Square and the markets of Wilmington. The tiny village, with a historic tavern and some art and antiques shops, is in the middle of the Brandywine Valley's attractions. Longwood Gardens, Winterthur, and the Brandywine River Museum are all less than 5 miles away. Kennett Pike (Route 52) runs through the village; the surrounding two-lane roads take you through some of the still-bucolic parts of the valley.

GETTING HERE AND AROUND

Traffic on both Kennett Pike and Route 1 picks up on weekends, especially in the spring and fall.

EXPLORING

FAMILY **Hagley Museum and Library.** A restored mid-19th-century mill community on 235 landscaped acres along the Brandywine River, the Hagley Museum and Library provides an enlightening look at the development of early industrial America. This is the site of the first of the du Pont family's black-powder mills, family estate, and gardens. Live demonstrations depict the dangerous work of the early explosives industry.

"Du Pont Science and Discovery" traces the company's evolution and displays a NASCAR car and a space suit. Admission includes a narrated bus tour through the powder yards with stops at Eleutherian Mills, the 1803 Georgian-style home furnished by five generations of du Ponts; Workers' Hill, where costumed interpreters describe the life of a typical mill worker; demonstrations in a machine shop and power yard; and a French Renaissance–style garden. Allow about two hours for your visit. The coffee shop, Belin House Organic Cafe, is open for lunch year-round. ✉ *298 Buck Rd., Wilmington* ✥ *Rte. 141 between Rte. 100 and U.S. 202* ☎ *302/658–2400* 🌐 *www.hagley.org* 🎟 *$14* 🕒 *Daily 10–4:30.*

FAMILY dor's Choice ★ **Winterthur.** Henry Francis du Pont (1880–1969) housed his 85,000 objects of American decorative art in a sprawling nine-story country estate called Winterthur. The collection, displayed in 175 rooms, is recognized as one of the nation's finest. Its objects, made or used in America between 1640 and 1860, include Chippendale furniture, silver tankards by Paul Revere, and Chinese porcelain made for George Washington. To view the collection, you can choose between an hour-long introductory tour, different one-hour theme tours (such as "American Interiors"), and two-hour tours that delve into ceramics, textiles, or furniture. The museum also has galleries with permanent displays and changing exhibitions of antiques and crafts to study at your own pace. No children under 8 are allowed except on the daily family tours (March–October), which are open to all but geared to kids ages 4 to 12. Surrounding the estate are 982 acres of landscaped lawns and naturalistic gardens, which you can visit on a 30-minute narrated tram ride or on your own. The Enchanted Woods is a fantasy-theme 3-acre children's garden with an 8-foot-wide bird's nest, a faerie cottage with a thatch roof, and a troll bridge. A gift shop and cafeteria, which serves Sunday brunch, are also on the grounds. ✉ *5105 Kennett Pike, Rte. 52, 5 miles south of U.S. 1, Winterhur* ☎ *800/448–3883* 🌐 *www.winterthur.org* 🎟 *$20 for house, garden, and introductory tour; ticket good for 2 consecutive days; $30 for house, garden, and 1-hr specialty tour; $40 for house, garden, and 2-hr specialty tour* 🕒 *Tues.–Sun. 10–5; introductory tours offered 10:30–3:30.*

WHERE TO EAT

$$ AMERICAN 🍴 **Buckley's Tavern.** Though this 1817 roadside tavern serves your typical burgers and beers (local microbrews are on tap), the menu surprises you with Thai noodle soup, shrimp and grits, and crab Cobb salad. The sweet-potato chips and the crab, artichoke, and spinach dip are favorites. There's a sunny porch and a dining room with a fireplace. You can pick from the wine list or buy a bottle from the shop next door. If you wear your pajamas to the Sunday brunch, your entrée will be half off. You won't be alone, either, about a third of brunch diners eat in their PJs. [$] *Average main: $17* ✉ *5812 Kennett Pike, Centreville* ☎ *302/656–9776* 🌐 *www.buckleystavern.com.*

$$$$ FRENCH 🍴 **Krazy Kat's.** Oil paintings of regal felines watch over diners at this plushly furnished restaurant in a former blacksmith shop at the Inn at Montchanin Village. Animal-print chairs add to the atmosphere of elegance with a grin. The unique setting and creative menu draw regulars from Philadelphia and beyond, who come for crab bisque,

7

shrimp squash-blossom poppers, New Zealand grilled venison, and apple-walnut bread pudding. Try breakfast here before you start your day of sightseeing. $ *Average main: $30* ⊠ *Inn at Montchanin Village, 528 Montchanin Rd., Montchanin* ☎ *302/888–4200* ⊕ *www. krazykatsrestaurant.com* ⊗ *No lunch Sat.*

WHERE TO STAY

$$ 🛏 **Inn at Montchanin Village and Spa.** This luxurious lodging includes 11
HOTEL painstakingly restored 19th-century cottages that once housed workers from the nearby Du Pont powder mills. **Pros:** good mix of new amenities and period charm; gorgeous bathrooms; beautiful gardens. **Cons:** sprawling property; inconsistent service; some street noise. $ *Rooms from: $192* ⊠ *528 Montchanin Rd., Montchanin* ✛ *Rte. 100 and Kirk Rd.* ☎ *302/888–2133, 800/269–2473* ⊕ *www.montchanin.com* ☜ *12 rooms, 16 suites* ⦿ *No meals.*

KENNETT SQUARE

8 miles northwest of Centreville via PA Route 52 and U.S. Route 1.

Kennett Square is where mushroom cultivation began in the United States. By the mid-1920s, 90% of the nation's mushrooms were grown in Southeastern Pennsylvania. The town celebrates its heritage with its annual Mushroom Festival in September. Most visitors come to visit Longwood Gardens, a lovely spot about 3 miles northeast of Kennett Square. The town itself, with its Victorian-era homes lining the tree-lined streets, is also worth a visit; there are shops, galleries, and restaurants along East State Street between Broad and Union.

EXPLORING

FAMILY **Longwood Gardens.** Longwood Gardens has established an international
Fodor's Choice reputation for its immaculate, colorful gardens full of flowers and blos-
★ soming shrubs. In 1906 Pierre S. du Pont (1870–1945) bought a simple Quaker farm and turned it into the ultimate early-20th-century estate garden. Attractions include magnolias and azaleas in spring; roses and water lilies in summer; chrysanthemums in fall; and camellias, orchids, and palms in winter. You can stroll in the Italian water garden or explore a meadow full of wildflowers on the garden's 350 acres. Bad weather is no problem, as 4 acres of cacti, ferns, and bonsai plants, and the biggest green wall in North America, are housed in heated conservatories. Outdoors is the Bee-aMazed Children's Garden, with a honeycomb maze, queen bee throne, and small splashing fountains. The Indoor Children's Garden has a bamboo maze, a grottolike cave, and a drooling dragon. There is a regular summer concert series, as well as special fireworks and fountain events. The cafeteria (open year-round) and dining room (closed January–March) serve reasonably priced meals. ⊠ *1001 Longwood Rd., 3 miles northeast of Kennett Sq. along U.S. 1* ☎ *610/388–1000* ⊕ *www. longwoodgardens.org* ⊠ *$20 off-peak, $27 peak season, including the winter holiday season* ⊗ *Apr. and May, daily 9–6; June–Aug., Sun.–Wed. 9–6, Thurs.–Sat. 9–10; Sept.–late Nov., daily 9–6; late Nov.–early Jan., daily 9–10; early Jan.–Mar., daily 9–5* ☞ *Some nighttime events keep the gardens open as late as 11 pm but require separate admission tickets.*

WHERE TO EAT

$$$$ ✕ **Sovana Bistro.** Chef Nicholas Farrell transforms local and organic
ITALIAN ingredients into satisfying meals at this popular rustic restaurant, which
is part French bistro and part Italian trattoria. A turkey "cheesesteak,"
hand-cut pasta in a wild-boar sauce, harissa-marinated skirt steak, and
warm blueberry crisp with lemon gelato are highlights of the seasonal
menu. Though a lunch of a BLT might sound mundane, it's anything
but: the turkey bacon is local, the rye bread made in-house, and the
toppings include avocado and chipotle mayonnaise. $ *Average main:*
$28 ✉ *696 Unionville Rd.* ☎ *610/444–5600* ⊕ *www.sovanabistro.com*
⊘ *Closed Mon. No lunch Sun.*

$ ✕ **Talula's Table.** Talula's has its own artisan cheeses, house-cured meats,
AMERICAN and handmade breads and pastas, along with a coffee bar and prepared
dor's Choice meals for takeout. The menu, which changes daily, includes treats like
★ pulled pork enchiladas, exotic mushroom soup, roasted beet salad with
candied pecans, and ham and Gruyère *gougères*. You can pick up the
makings for a picnic or eat at the farmhouse table. Dinner at Talula's—
with a prix-fixe offered only at night—is a particularly special treat that
is so popular you have to book almost a year in advance, making it
one of the Northeast's top restaurant reservations. But while only the
select few can have dinner here, lunch is a more relaxed and inclusive
experience. $ *Average main: $12* ✉ *102 W. State St.* ☎ *610/444–8255*
⊕ *www.talulastable.com.*

¬ILMINGTON, DELAWARE

15 miles southeast of Kennett Square via PA Route 52.

Delaware's commercial hub and largest city has handsome architecture—with good examples of styles such as Federal, Greek Revival,
Queen Anne, and Art Deco—and abundant cultural attractions. Wilmington began in 1638 as a Swedish settlement and later was populated
by employees of various du Pont family businesses and nearby poultry
ranches. The four-block Market Street Mall marks the city center and
is distinguished by the Grand Opera House. The four-story theater,
built by the Masonic Order in 1871, has a white cast-iron facade in
French Second Empire style to mimic the old Paris Opera. The adjoining Giacco Building houses a smaller theater and art galleries. Outside
Wilmington's compact city center are several outstanding museums,
including some that are legacies of the du Ponts.

GETTING HERE AND AROUND

The city of Wilmington is less than 45 minutes by car via I–95 South
from Philadelphia and is easily accessible by AMTRAK. But since you
won't want to miss visiting Longwood Gardens, Winterthur, or some
of the other stately mansions in the area, you'll want to have a car.
Typically, those driving south from Philadelphia to Wilmington during rush hours will encounter some traffic, but not gridlock, because
the commute mostly runs the opposite way. Downtown Wilmington is
compact and walkable, but it tends to shut down after business hours.

7

ESSENTIALS

Visitor Information Greater Wilmington Convention and Visitors Bureau. ✉ *100 W. 10th St., Wilmington* ☎ *800/489–6664, 800/489–6664* ⊕ *www. visitwilmingtonde.com.*

EXPLORING

Delaware Art Museum. A treat for art lovers, the Delaware Art Museum is housed in a splendid 85,000-square-foot building. The lighted roofline changes colors according to the celestial calendar, and Dale Chihuly's Persian Window installation draws attention to the entrance. The museum's holdings include a good collection of paintings by Howard Pyle (1853–1911), a Wilmington native known as the "father of American illustration," as well as works by his students N. C. Wyeth, Frank Schoonover, and Maxfield Parrish. Other American artists represented are Benjamin West, John Sloan, Winslow Homer, Edward Glackens, and Edward Hopper. The museum also has the largest American collection of 19th-century English pre-Raphaelite paintings and decorative arts and a children's interactive gallery. *The Crying Giant*, by Tom Otterness, is one of the highlights of the 9-acre Sculpture Park. ✉ *2301 Kentmere Pkwy., Wilmington* ☎ *302/571–9590* ⊕ *www.delart. org* ☎ *$12, free all day Sun. and Thurs. 4–8* ◷ *Wed. and Fri.–Sun 10–4, Thurs. 10–8.*

Nemours Mansion and Gardens. For a look at how the very wealthy lived, visit Nemours Mansion and Gardens, a 300-acre country estate built for Alfred I. du Pont in 1910. This modified Louis XVI château, which underwent a $39 million restoration that was completed in 2008, showcases 102 rooms of European and American furnishings, rare rugs, tapestries, and art dating to the 15th century. The gardens, reminiscent of those at Versailles, are landscaped with fountains, pools, and statuary. The estate can be seen only on guided two-hour tours. Visitors must be at least 12 years old. ✉ *850 Alapocas Dr., between Rte. 141 and U.S. 202, Wilmington* ☎ *302/651–6912* ⊕ *www.nemoursmansion.org* ☎ *$15 for mansion and gardens, $10 garden walk only* ◷ *May–Dec., Tues.–Sat. garden tours at 10, noon, 2, and 4; house tours at 9:30, noon, and 3; Sun. garden tours at noon, 2, and 4; house tours at noon and 3; closed Jan.–Apr.*

Rockwood Museum and Park. Rockwood, a quietly elegant English-style country house and a fine example of rural Gothic architecture, stands in contrast to the opulent, French-inspired du Pont homes in the area. Built in 1851 by Joseph Shipley, a Quaker banker, and occupied by his descendants until 1972, the house is now a museum filled with Victorian furnishings and decorative arts. Tours are given on the hour. Beyond the English landscape garden, the 72-acre public grounds feature 2½ miles of paved, lighted trails. In summer Rockwood Park hosts the Delaware Shakespeare Festival, as well as a weekly farmers' market. ✉ *4651 Washington St. Extension, south of Shipley Rd., Wilmington* ☎ *302/761–4340* ⊕ *www.rockwood.org* ☎ *$10; free 1st Sun. of every month* ◷ *Grounds: daily dawn–dusk. Mansion: Wed.–Sat. 10–4, Sun. noon–4.*

WHERE TO EAT

$$$ ✕**Domaine Hudson Wine Bar & Eatery.** Wine enthusiasts Mike and
AMERICAN Beth Ross oversee this sophisticated bistro that makes wine tasting
approachable. They offer 40 to 50 wines by the glass—served in high-
end German crystal—so you can try several varieties in an evening.
Recipes, such as glazed Berkshire pork belly, duck confit, toast and
pressed leg of lamb, were chosen to complement the wines, and many
are available in half-size versions, leaving room for a cheese course.
The handsome dining room, with faux leather walls and dark woods,
has a clubby feel. $ *Average main: $22* ✉ *1314 N. Washington St.,
Wilmington* ☎ *302/655–9463* ⊕ *www.domainehudson.com* ☾ *Closed
Sun. No lunch.*

WHERE TO STAY

$$$$ ⌷**Hotel du Pont.** Built in 1913 by Pierre S. du Pont, this luxury hotel in
HOTEL downtown Wilmington has hosted everyone from Charles Lindbergh
to John F. Kennedy. **Pros:** fine dining; luxe ambience; responsive service.
Cons: small elevators; staff can be too formal; few restaurants or shops
in immediate vicinity. $ *Rooms from: $439* ✉ *42 W. 11th St., Wilming-
ton* ☎ *302/594–3100, 800/441–9019* ⊕ *www.hoteldupont.com* ⇖ *206
rooms, 11 suites* ⦿*No meals.*

ALLEY FORGE

20 miles northeast of downtown Philadelphia via I–76.

A major site of the Revolutionary War is near the suburban village of
Valley Forge. The town was named for an iron forge built in the 1740s.

The monuments, markers, huts, and headquarters in Valley Forge
National Historical Park illuminate a decisive period in U.S. history.
The park, with its quiet beauty that seems to whisper of the past, pre-
serves the area where George Washington's Continental Army endured
the bitter winter of 1777–78.

GETTING HERE AND AROUND

When traffic is flowing on I–76, the major east–west highway between
Philadelphia and Valley Forge, the trip can take just 35 to 40 minutes.
But frequent gridlock, especially during rush hour, can stretch the trip
to 90 minutes, so try to time your visit accordingly. Once you're at the
park, you can access the major sites via a free shuttle bus. Other area
attractions will require a car for access, however.

TOURS

The self-driven Valley Forge National Historical Auto-Tour can be pur-
chased from the Welcome Center ($14.95 CD), or a free cell phone audio
tour is available at ☎ *484/396–1018.* A narrated trolley tour of the park
is available from June through Labor Day for $16.50 per person.

ESSENTIALS

Bus Information SEPTA. ✉ *1234 Market St., 4th fl., Philadelphia* ☎ *215/580–
7800* ⊕ *www.septa.org.*

Visitor Information Valley Forge Convention and Visitors Bureau. ✉ *1000
1st Ave., Suite 101, King of Prussia* ☎ *610/834–1550,* ⊕ *www.valleyforge.org.*

7

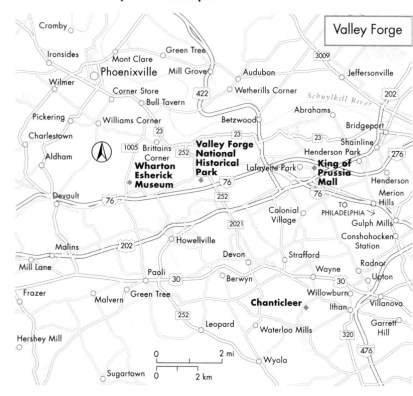

The Welcome Center at Valley Forge. ⊠ 1400 N. Outer Line Dr. ✛ Rte. 23
and N. Gulph Rd. ☎ 610/783–1077 ⊕ www.nps.gov/vafo/learn/historyculture/
welcome-center.htm.

EXPLORING

Chanticleer. Chanticleer, the onetime estate of the owner of a local phar-
maceutical company, is now a 30-acre garden that bursts with colo
in the spring when 10,000 bulbs bloom. The grounds offer a range o
settings, including lush woodlands with rare Asian specimens, a forma
house garden, and a serpentine-shaped "avenue" lined with young juni
pers, wheat and barley, and gingko trees. ⊠ 786 Church Rd., Wayn
☎ 610/687–4163 ⊕ www.chanticleergarden.org ⊠ $10 ⊙ Apr.–Nov.
Wed.–Sun. 10–5; May–Aug., Fri. 10–8; some 8 am openings schedule
in summer ☞ Vistors may be turned away if the parking lot is full.

Valley Forge National Historical Park. Valley Forge National Historica
Park, administered by the National Park Service, is the location of the
1777–78 winter encampment of General George Washington and the
Continental Army. Stop first at the Valley Forge Welcome Center to
see the 18-minute orientation film (shown every 30 minutes) and view
exhibits. In summer you can take a narrated trolley tour for $16.50

per person. Stops include reconstructed log huts of the Muhlenberg Brigade and the National Memorial Arch, which pay tribute to the soldiers who suffered through the brutal winter. Other sites are the bronze equestrian statue of General Anthony Wayne, in the area where his Pennsylvania troops were encamped; Artillery Park, where the soldiers stored their cannons; and the Isaac Potts House, which served as Washington's headquarters.

The park is quiet today, but in 1777 the army had just lost the nearby battles of Brandywine, White Horse, and Germantown. While the British occupied Philadelphia, Washington's soldiers were forced to endure horrid conditions here—blizzards, inadequate food and clothing, damp quarters, and disease. Although no battle was fought at Valley Forge, 2,000 soldiers died here.

The troops did win one victory that winter—a war of will. The forces slowly regained strength and confidence under the leadership of Prussian drillmaster Friedrich von Steuben. In June 1778 Washington led his troops away from Valley Forge in search of the British. Fortified, the Continental Army was able to carry on the fight for five years more.

The park contains 6 miles of jogging and bicycling paths and hiking trails, and you can picnic at any of three designated areas. A leisurely visit to the park takes no more than half a day. ⊠ *1400 N. Outer Line Dr.* ⊕ *Rte. 23 and N. Gulph Rd.* ☎ *610/783–1077* ⊕ *www.nps.gov/ vafo* ⊠ *Free; optional Trolley Tour in warm weather, $16.50* ⊙ *Park daily 7 am–dark (½ hr past sunset); visitor center daily 9–5 (9–6 June 14–Aug.15); Washington's Headquarters, Mar.–Dec., daily 9–5 (9–6 June 14–Aug. 15), Jan. and Feb., weekends and Presidents Day 10–4; Washington Memorial Chapel, Mon.–Sat. 11–5, Sun. noon–5; Varnum's Quarters, June–Aug., weekends noon–4.*

Wharton Esherick Museum. The Wharton Esherick Museum preserves the former home and studio of the "Dean of American Craftsmen." Best known for his sculptural furniture, Esherick (1887–1970) shaped a new aesthetic in decorative arts by bridging art with furniture. The museum, a National Historic Landmark, houses 200 examples of his work—paintings, woodcuts, furniture, and wood sculptures. The studio, in which everything from the light switches to the spiral staircase is hand-carved, is one of his monumental achievements. The museum is 2 miles west of Valley Forge National Historical Park. Reservations are required for the hourly tours. On weekdays a minimum of five people is required for a tour. ⊠ *1520 Horseshoe Trail* ☎ *610/644–5822* ⊕ *www. whartonesherickmuseum.org* ⊠ *$15* ⊙ *Mar.–Dec., Mon.–Sat. 10–4 (for groups of 5 or more), Sun. 1–4* ☞ *Tours by reservation only; children's tour offered Sat. at 11; not handicapped accessible.*

HOPPING

Chapel Cabin Shop. The Chapel Cabin Shop is staffed primarily by volunteers from the Washington Memorial Chapel parish on the grounds of the Valley Forge National Historical Park, who make the cakes, candies, and jams that are sold here. Proceeds help keep the privately owned chapel afloat. You can also find fine pewter, Colonial art, and souvenirs related to the American Revolution. The shop includes a tiny luncheonette—and outdoor picnic tables—where there are daily specials, such as Martha's 16-Bean Soup. There is also a used-book store directly behind the chapel. ⊠ *Alongside Washington Memorial Chapel on Rte. 23* ☎ *610/783–0576* ✉ *cabinshop@wmchapel.org* ⊙ *Daily 10–5.*

King of Prussia Mall. The King of Prussia Mall, one of the nation's largest shopping complexes, is a tourist destination in itself. Comprising two main buildings—the Plaza and the Court—the mall contains more than 40 restaurants, 400 shops and boutiques, and seven major department stores, including Bloomingdale's, Nordstrom, and Neiman Marcus. Dining options include Morton's of Chicago, Legal Sea Foods, the Cheesecake Factory, and three food courts. ⊠ *U.S. 202 at Schuylkill Expressway, 160 N. Gulph Rd., King of Prussia* ☎ *610/265–5727* ⊕ *www.simon.com/mall/king-of-prussia* ⊙ *Mon.–Sat. 10–9, Sun. 11–6* ✆ *Extended holiday shopping hrs.*

BUCKS COUNTY

Bucks County, about an hour northeast of Philadelphia by car, could have remained 625 square miles of sleepy countryside full of old stone farmhouses, lush hills, and covered bridges if it hadn't been "discovered." First, New York artists and intelligentsia bought country homes here in the 1930s. More recently, suburbanites and exurbanites bought or built year-round houses, eager to live in an area of relative peace and quiet within a long commute of New York and Philly.

Over the years Bucks County has been known for art colonies and antiques, summer theater, and country inns. Cookie-cutter housing developments are now planted where grain once grew, however. It's not unusual to find suburban sprawl and hyper-development adjacent to an old clapboard farmhouse or ancient stone barn. Yet many areas of Central and Upper Bucks County remain as bucolic as ever—a feast of lyrical landscapes, with canal and river vistas, rolling hills, and fertile fields. Driving back roads is one of the county's pleasures, and making your way through quiet little towns, stopping at historic sites, checking out antiques shops, and staying overnight in an appealing inn make for a classic weekend getaway.

WASHINGTON CROSSING

35 miles northeast of Philadelphia via I–95 and Route 32.

The small village of Washington Crossing is home to a smattering of basic services and residential areas as well as Washington Crossing Historic Park. Upriver from its central crossroads is a research library dedicated to the American Revolution, while just to the west, where Route 532 crosses the canal, you'll find access to the towpath with parking.

GETTING HERE AND AROUND

Washington Crossing Historic Park stretches along River Road (Route 32). The Lower Park, at the intersection with Route 532, is the site of both the actual crossing and the visitor center. There is a narrow

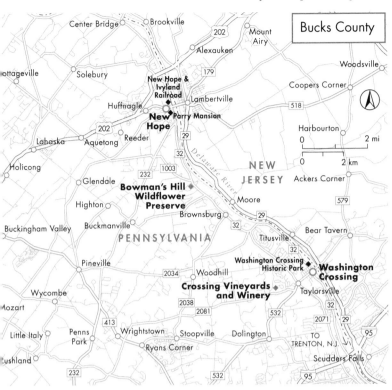

Bucks County

0   2 mi

0   2 km

7

bridge here, which makes crossing to New Jersey somewhat easier today. The Upper Park and wildflower preserve are 5–6 miles north of the visitor center.

EXPLORING

Crossing Vineyards. On a 200-year-old estate near where Washington crossed the Delaware, the family-run vineyard mixes vintage charm with modern wine-making techniques. Despite a nod to the rustic (a beam ceiling in the tasting room and gift shop), the old gambrel-roofed barn feels fresh and upscale. In a 15- to 20-minute tasting ($10), the staff lets you know what to expect from eight different types of wines. Ask to see Lucy and Ethel, the computerized press and crusher-destemmer, respectively. Concerts are offered in summer. ✉ *1853 Wrightstown Rd., off Rte. 532* ☎ *215/493–6500* ⊕ *www.crossingvineyards.com* ☉ *Daily noon–6.*

Washington Crossing Historic Park. Most people recognize Emanuel Leutze's famous 1851 painting of Washington crossing the Delaware (which hangs in New York's Metropolitan Museum of Art), but far fewer know where or why he crossed. It was from the site of what is now this park that on Christmas night in 1776 General Washington and 2,400 of his men crossed the ice-studded river, attacked the Hessian stronghold at Trenton, and secured a much-needed victory for the Continental Army.

Today park attractions, including historic houses and memorials, are divided between the Lower Park and Upper Park.

In the Lower Park, the visitor center screens a 15-minute introductory movie as part of the guided tour. Here you can purchase tickets for guided tours of the Lower Park, which include the McConkey Ferry Inn, where tradition has it that Washington and his staff had Christmas dinner while waiting to cross the river. You can also see replicas of the Durham boats used in that fateful crossing.

In the Upper Park, 125-foot-tall Bowman's Hill Tower offers a commanding view of the Delaware River. An elevator takes you up the 1931 tower, but be prepared to walk the last 23 steps. A half-mile farther north, the Thompson-Neely House, an 18th-century miller's house, offers tours that tell of life in Bucks County during and after the American Revolution. The house was used as a hospital during the 1776–77 encampment of Washington's army. Some Revolutionary soldiers are buried near the home.

The park holds special events throughout the year, including a reenactment of the crossing in December. ✉ *1112 River Rd. (Rte. 32)* ☎ *215/493–4076* 🌐 *www.washingtoncrossingpark.org* 🎟 *Grounds free, 1 tour or tower $6, all 3 $11* 🕒 *Grounds daily dawn–dusk; visitor center daily 10–5; Lower Park and Thompson-Neely tours Apr.–Dec., daily 10–4; Jan.–Mar., weekends only; Bowman's Hill Tower Apr.–Dec., daily 10–4; Jan.–Mar., weekends only* ☞ *Bowman's Hill Tower tours are weather-permitting. Please call 215/862–3166 the day of planned tour for updates.*

WHERE TO EAT

$$$ ITALIAN

🍴 **Francisco's on the River.** Cozy rooms, including an enclosed front porch, beamed ceiling, white tablecloths, and windows all around, give a refined but undeniably country feel to this river-view, BYOB restaurant. Chef Francisco Argueta breathes new life into old favorites like lobster ravioli; a thin-sliced, layered eggplant *parmigiano;* linguine *al frutti di mare fradiavolo;* and lasagna with a hint of smoked bacon. Nightly specials lean heavily to seafood, while pasta portions are large. If you don't have access to a fridge for your leftovers, consider sharing. [$] *Average main: $22* ✉ *1251 River Rd.* ☎ *215/321–8789* 🌐 *www.franciscosontheriver.com* 🕒 *Closed Mon. No lunch.*

$ AMERICAN FAMILY

🍴 **It's Nutts.** If this place had been here in 1776, you can bet that George Washington and company would have stopped in for some lemon-chiffon pancakes, ice-cream treats, or tomato pie (a yummy thin-crust pizza native to the Trenton area) before heading off to stomp the Hessians. Don't let the drive-in facade fool you. There's more here than a good old-fashioned soda fountain, though that certainly draws a steady stream of return visitors. The "little dive," as it calls itself, serves breakfast, lunch, and dinner. It's just a little north of the Washington Crossing bridge on the New Jersey side. [$] *Average main: $12* ✉ *1382 River Rd.* ✥ *Off NJ Rt. 29, ½ mile from Washington Crossing–Pennington Rd.* ☎ *609/737–0505* 🌐 *itsnuttsrestaurant.com* 💳 *No credit cards* ☞ *ATM on premises. Accepts personal checks.*

:W HOPE

8 miles north of Washington Crossing via Rte. 32, 40 miles northeast of Philadelphia via I–95 and Route 32.

For a small town, New Hope is a mix of many things. A hodgepodge of old homes, narrow streets and alleys, courtyards, busy restaurants and bars, and shops, it attracts artists, shoppers, and hordes of day-trippers. Festivals feature everything from classic cars to films to gay pride. In summer, Friday-night fireworks over the river bring still more crowds.

The town, listed on the National Register of Historic Places, is easy to explore on foot; the most interesting sights and stores are clustered along four blocks of Main Street and on the cross streets—Mechanic, Ferry, and Bridge streets—which lead to the river. Some parts of town are older than others. As you might guess from their names, Ferry Street dates back to Colonial times; Bridge Street is Victorian.

GETTING HERE AND AROUND

Getting to New Hope is easy. Both U.S. 202 and Route 32 run through it. Getting around New Hope on a busy weekend is harder. If you see cars backed up along Main Street, drive around the periphery instead, as it can take a fair amount of time to inch your way through town. Grab a parking spot when you find one—either on the street or in a municipal lot (bring change for the meter or metered ticket)—and walk where you want to go.

VISITOR INFORMATION

New Hope Visitors Center. ⊠ *1 W. Mechanic St., at Main St.* ☎ *215/862–5030* ⊕ *www.newhopevisitorscenter.org* ☽ *Mon.–Thurs. 11:30–5, Fri. and Sat. 11:30–7.*

EXPLORING

FAMILY **New Hope & Ivyland Rail Road.** The passenger train, pulled by an authentic steam locomotive or vintage diesel, makes a 9-mile, 45-minute scenic round-trip between New Hope and Lahaska. The route crosses a trestle used in the rescue scenes in silent films like *The Perils of Pauline*. The New Hope depot is an 1891 Victorian gem. Special events, which require reservations, include dinner trips on Saturday evenings and holiday excursions in December. ⊠ *32 W. Bridge St.* ☎ *215/862–2332* ⊕ *www.newhoperailroad.com* ⊟ *Coach $20.95, First Class $30.90; holiday and special excursion fares may vary* ☽ *Jan.–Mar., limited weekends; Apr.–late May and Nov., Fri.–Sun.; late May–Oct. and late Dec., daily; early Dec., Thurs.–Sun.; daily departure times vary.*

QUICK
BITE

✕ **The Last Temptation.** The Last Temptation dishes up delicious Thomas Sweet ice cream, a local favorite. You can blend in M&Ms and other decadent delights. Open year-round, but call ahead in the off-season to verify hours. ⊠ *115 S. Main St.* ☎ *215/862–3219* ☞ *Hrs and days may vary in off-season; call to verify.*

Parry Mansion. Built in 1781, and home of the New Hope Historical Society, this stone house is notable because the furnishings reflect decorative changes from 1775 to 1900—including candles, whitewashed walls, oil lamps, and wallpaper. Wealthy lumber-mill owner Benjamin

Parry built the house, which was occupied by five generations of hi family. ⊠ *45 S. Main St.* ☎ *215/862–5652* ⊕ *www.newhopehs.or* 🎟 *Free* ☉ *Tours May–Nov., weekends 1–5.*

WHERE TO EAT

$$ ╳ **Karla's.** This longtime casual hangout in the heart of New Hope
ECLECTIC offers hearty American food (meat loaf, burgers, and sandwiches with an emphasis on exciting international ingredients. Green gaz pacho, panko-crusted mac-and-cheese, and a pulled-chicken-chipotl quesadilla are a few examples of dishes. The decor is an assemblag of mismatched tables under a corrugated-plastic ceiling, with plant in retro macramé hangers. Part indoors and part out, half restauran and half bar, some shabby and some chic, Karla's feels like an olc comfortable pair of jeans. 🆂 *Average main: $15* ⊠ *5 W. Mechanic St* ☎ *215/862–2612* ⊕ *www.karlasnewhope.com.*

$$ ╳ **Sprig & Vine.** This vegan restaurant is chic, BYO, and attracts plent·
VEGETARIAN of non-vegetarians. Located in Union Square, an old-converted-ware house-meets-new-construction complex that backs on the vintage rail road, Sprig & Vine is like the first green of spring, a fresh and welcom· addition to the sometimes tired New Hope dining scene. The menu i small—only a handful of large-plate dinner options—but offers inter esting dishes with unusual flavors, made with ingredients from loca farms. You may not have come in craving tamarind-glazed tempet with a rum-grilled peach, but you'll leave wishing you could have i again. 🆂 *Average main: $18* ⊠ *450 Union Square Dr.* ☎ *215/693–142* ⊕ *sprigandvine.com* ☉ *Closed Mon. No dinner Sun. No lunch Tues.*

WHERE TO STAY

$$$$ 🛏 **Inn at Bowman's Hill.** South of New Hope on the road leading to Bow
B&B/INN man's Tower, this modern interpretation of country charm was built i the late 1970s as a private home and converted to a high-end B&B in th mid-2000s by its energetic, world-traveled owner, Mike Amery. **Pros** rates include full breakfast; not a frilly B&B; many luxurious touches **Cons:** expensive; some rooms are small. 🆂 *Rooms from: $395* ⊠ *51* *Lurgan Rd.* ☎ *215/862–8090* ⊕ *theinnatbowmanshill.com* ⇄ *4 rooms 4 suites* ⦿ *Breakfast.*

$ 🛏 **Logan Inn.** Established in 1727 as an extension of the Ferry Tavern
B&B/INN this inn once accommodated passengers riding the ferry to Lambertville **Pros:** tidy rooms—and free parking!—in the thick of New Hope. **Cons** no breakfast. 🆂 *Rooms from: $145* ⊠ *10 W. Ferry St.* ☎ *215/862–230(* ⊕ *www.loganinn.com* ⇄ *16 rooms* ⦿ *No meals.*

$ 🛏 **Wedgwood Inn.** Accommodations at this B&B are in a variety o·
B&B/INN buildings—two 1870s-era "painted ladies," a Federal-style manо· house, and a carriage house that works equally well for families anc romance. **Pros:** lovely grounds near, but set apart from, the middle o· town; welcomes children and dogs. **Cons:** rooms are tasteful, but if yоu don't like Victoriana, wall stencils, and Wedgwood blue, this may no· be for you. 🆂 *Rooms from: $95* ⊠ *111 W. Bridge St.* ☎ *215/862–257(* ⊕ *www.wedgwoodinn.com* ⇄ *14 rooms, 5 suites* ⦿ *Breakfast.*

NIGHTLIFE AND PERFORMING ARTS

Bowman's Tavern. The piano that once graced Odette's, the restaurant, bar, and cabaret that was a New Hope institution until it was flooded out one too many times, now resides at Bowman's Tavern, a quintessential tavern halfway between New Hope and Washington's Crossing. Many of those who loved Odette's have followed, too, making the piano lounge's seven-nights-a-week entertainment quite popular and gay-friendly. ⊠ *1600 River Rd.* ☎ *215/862–2972* ⊕ *www.bowmanstavernrestaurant.com.*

Bucks County Playhouse. This longtime summer theater, housed in a historic mill by the Delaware, stages Broadway revivals and is also used for community events and performances. Shows range from *25th Annual Putnam County Spelling Bee* to a *Simply Sondheim* benefit concert. The season generally runs from April to December, but check the website for what's on. ⊠ *70 S. Main St.* ☎ *215/862–2121* ⊕ *www.bcptheater.org* ↝ *The Riverview Cafe Deck Bar is open Mon.–Thurs. 4–8, Fri. 4–10, Sat. noon–10, and Sun.1–6, weather permitting, whether or not a performance is scheduled, during the summer season.*

Havana. Havana has karaoke on Monday and a variety of live music from jazz to the house cover band Friday through Sunday. National acts leaning heavily toward classic rock are sprinkled in for good measure. ⊠ *105 S. Main St.* ☎ *215/862–5501* ⊕ *www.havananewhope.com.*

John & Peter's. Since 1972, John & Peter's has featured live, original music seven nights a week. Jazz musicians, singer-songwriters, and plenty of rockers all take the stage, as do the not-yet-famous on Monday's open-mike night. ⊠ *96 S. Main St.* ☎ *215/862–5981* ⊕ *www.johnandpeters.com.*

Triumph Brewing Company. Shiny vats are the tip-off to what's on tap at Triumph Brewing Company, a brewpub whose exposed-brick walls, beams, and ductwork give it an industrial feel. Entertainment includes live music Friday, Saturday, and some Wednesday nights; Texas Hold 'Em on Monday and Wednesday; open mike on Sunday; Cornhole on Tuesday; trivia and Paint Nite on Thursday; and a ceremonial barrel tapping the first Friday of the month at 6. ⊠ *400 Union Sq.* ☎ *215/862–8300.*

SPORTS AND THE OUTDOORS

Bucks County River Country. Join the more than 100,000 people a year who take to the water in inner tubes every summer. Bucks County River Country also rents rafts, canoes, and kayaks. Even when the Delaware River is a mass of yellow and green tubes, it's still peaceful. ⊠ *2 Walters La., Point Pleasant* ☎ *215/297–5000* ⊕ *www.rivercountry.net* ⊗ *Closed Tues. and Wed. mid-May–June and mid-Sept.–Oct.; otherwise open weekday 9–6 and weekends 9–7, conditions permitting.*

New Hope Cyclery. New Hope Cyclery rents hybrid bikes for $25 for five hours, $35 for the whole day, with helmets and locks included in the rental price. You can also rent family-friendly trailers and tagalongs. The staff can direct you to scenic bike routes. ⊠ *404 York Rd.* ☎ *215/862–6888* ⊕ *newhopecyclery.com.*

SHOPPING

New Hope's streets are lined with shops selling a touristy mix of upscal and lowbrow. Very nice arts and crafts and handmade accessories clothing, antiques, and jewelry are juxtaposed with campy vintage items, doggie treats, tarot readers, and gargoyle-related gifts.

BOOKS

Farley's Bookshop. The crowded shelves at Farley's Bookshop, a New Hope institution, hold plenty of choices, including books about the region. ⊠ *44 S. Main St.* ☎ *215/862–2452* ⊕ *www.farleysbookshop com* ☉ *Sun.–Thurs. 10–9, Fri. and Sat. 10 am–11 pm.*

CRAFTS

A Mano Gallery. A branch of the Lambertville store of the same name A Mano Gallery stocks jewelry, clay, wood, glass, garden doodads, and other decorative items. ⊠ *128 S. Main St.* ☎ *215/862–5122* ⊕ *www amanogalleries.com* ☉ *Sun.–Wed. 10–6, Thurs.–Sat. 10–9.*

Topeo. You can find art glass and jewelry at Topeo. A sister store, Topeo South, located at 15 North Main Street, offers art pottery, garden art and Judaica as well. ⊠ *35 N. Main St.* ☎ *215/862–2750* ⊕ *www.topeo myshopify.com* ☉ *Sun.–Fri. 10–6, Sat. 10–7.*

FOOD

Pierre's Chocolates. For chocolate, including yummy truffles, turtles and chocolate-covered pretzels, head a little outside the main busi ness district to the delectable Pierre's Chocolates. ⊠ *360 W. Bridge St* ☎ *215/862–0602* ⊕ *www.pierreschocolates.com* ☉ *Weekdays 10–6 Sat. 10–5; closed Sun.*

Suzies Hot Shoppe. This shop, quirky in comparison to others in New Hope, sells spicy sauces, snacks, and "hot" chocolate year-round Among its hottest of the hot peppers are ghost peppers and scorpion peppers. ⊠ *19A W. Bridge St.* ☎ *215/862–1334* ⊕ *www.squareup.com market/suzies-hot-shoppe* ☉ *Sun.–Thurs. 11:30–7, Fri. and Sat. 11:30–8*

TRAVEL SMART
PHILADELPHIA

GETTING HERE AND AROUND

▌AIR TRAVEL

Flying time from Boston is 1 hour, 20 minutes; from Chicago, roughly 2 hours; from Miami, 2 hours, 40 minutes; from Los Angeles, 5 hours, 40 minutes.

AIRPORTS

The major gateway to Philadelphia is Philadelphia International Airport (PHL), a seven-terminal airport located roughly 7 miles southwest from downtown. Elaborate renovations over the past decade-plus, adding multiple dining and shopping venues in addition to entire new terminals, have brought PHL into modern times and added some decent retail and dining options.

An alternative is Newark Liberty International Airport (EWR), about 85 miles northeast of Philadelphia in New Jersey. From EWR, a United Airlines hub, you can take an AirTrain shuttle to the Newark Airport station, then take a NJ Transit train to Trenton, and from Trenton ride a Southeastern Pennsylvania Transportation Authority (SEPTA) train into Philly. Expect a cost of roughly $30 per person and a minimum of an additional two hours to your travel time.

Airport Contacts Philadelphia International Airport (PHL). ⊠ 8000 Essington Ave., South Philadelphia ☎ 215/937–6937, 800/ PHL–GATE automated flight information ⊕ www.phl.org. **Newark Liberty International Airport** (EWR). ⊠ 3 Brewster Rd. ☎ 973/961–6000 ⊕ www.panynj.gov/airports/ newark-liberty.html.

Airline Security Issues Transportation Security Administration. ⊕ www.tsa.gov.

GROUND TRANSPORTATION

For $8 (cash only), you can take SEPTA's Airport rail line directly into Center City directly from any of the airport terminals. It leaves the airport every 30 minutes from 5:09 am to 12:13 am. The trip to Center City takes about 20 minutes. Trains serve the Eastwick, University City, 30th Street, Suburban (Center City), Jefferson and Temple University stations.

By car from the airport, the city is accessible via I–95 south or I–76 east. Allow at least a half-hour, more during rush hour for the 8-mile trip. Taxis at PHL are plentiful; follow signs in the airport and wait in line to catch one. Destinations that fall within the zone demarcated by Fairmount Avenue to the north, South Street to the south, the Delaware River to the east and 38th Street to the west are eligible for a $28.50 flat rate, not including tip. If you're heading to a location south of South Street, you can ask the driver to run the meter, as you'll likely end up paying less than the flat rate.

Limousine and shuttles are also available from PHL. Shuttle buses cost $10 and up per person and will make most requested stops downtown as well as the suburbs. You can make shuttle arrangements at the centralized ground transportation counter in the baggage claim areas.

Limousines Allways Transportation. ⊠ Northeast Philadelphia Airport, 11301 Norcom Rd., Suite 1 ☎ 215/669-0522 ⊕ service.londonlimousine.net. **Carey Limousine Philadelphia.** ☎ 610/667–1576 ⊕ www.carey.com.

Shuttles Priority Shuttle. ☎ 215/632-2885 ⊕ www.priorityshuttle.com.

Train Southeastern Pennsylvania Transportation Authority (SEPTA). ☎ 215/580-7800 ⊕ www.septa.org.

FLIGHTS

Most major U.S. airlines offer service to and from Philadelphia (PHL), which is a hub for American Airlines.

tacts **American Airlines.** ☎ 800/433–
0 ⊕ www.aa.com. **Frontier Airlines.**
'01/401–9000 ⊕ booking.flyfrontier.com.
Blue. ☎ 800/538–2583 ⊕ www.jetblue.
. **Southwest Airlines.** ☎ 800/435–9792
/www.southwest.com. **Spirit Airlines.**
'00/955–8771 ⊕ www.spirit.com. **United.**
:00/864–8331 ⊕ www.united.com.

BOAT AND FERRY TRAVEL

e RiverLink Ferry, a seasonal (May–
•tember) passenger ferry, offers service
ween Philadelphia and Camden, site
the Adventure Aquarium, the Susque-
na Bank Center, the battleship *New
sey,* and Campbell's Field. Ferries
•art every hour from Penn's Landing
ly between 10 and 6 Monday through
ursday, and 10 and 7 Friday through
day, and from Camden's waterfront
the half-hour, daily from 9:30 to 5:30
onday through Thursday, and 9:30
6:30 Friday through Sunday, with
ended hours and continuous service for
n's Landing and Susquehanna Bank
iter concerts, and Camden Riversharks
eball games. The cost is $7 round-trip,
ride takes 12 minutes, and the ferry is
eelchair-accessible.

IP➡ **Payment can be made by cash only.**

itacts **RiverLink Ferry.** ✉ Columbus
1. and Walnut St. ☎ 215/625–0221
www.delawareriverwaterfront.com/places/
rlink-ferry.

BUS TRAVEL

GIONAL BUSES

bus is generally the cheapest option
reach Philadelphia, particularly when
1 are coming from New York City.
w Jersey Transit stops at the Grey-
und terminal and offers service between
ladelphia and Atlantic City and other
w Jersey destinations. There is a Bolt
s and Megabus stop adjacent to 30th
eet Station, offering service to and from
town Manhattan in New York City.

Tickets are best purchased online prior to
your trip.

Contacts Bolt Bus. ⊕ boltbus.com. **Megabus.**
⊕ www.megabus.com. **New Jersey Transit.**
☎ 973/275–5555 ⊕ www.njtransit.com.

COMMUTER BUSES

Buses make up the bulk of the SEPTA system, with more than 120 routes extending
throughout the city and into the suburbs.
Although the buses are comfortable and
reliable, they should be used only when
you're not in a hurry, as traffic on the
city's major thoroughfares can add some
time to your trip. The distinctive purple
minibuses you see around Center City
are SEPTA's convenience line for visitors,
the PHLASH. The 22 stops run from the
Philadelphia Museum of Art through
Center City to Penn's Landing, stopping
near high-profile destinations such as The
Barnes Foundation, Eastern State Penitentiary, the Philadelphia Zoo, and Reading
Terminal Market. Since a ride on the
PHLASH costs $2 for a one-way ticket
(seniors, SEPTA pass holders, and children four and under ride free), consider
the all-day, unlimited-ride pass available
for $5 per passenger. These buses typically
run daily from 10 am to 6 pm. There's
service every 15 minutes.

The base cash fare for subways, trolleys, and buses is $2.25, paid with exact
change or a token. Transfers cost $1.
Senior citizens with proof of age are permitted to ride free. Up to two children
four or younger may ride free with each
paying adult.

If you plan to travel extensively within
Center City, consider a SEPTA pass. A
one-day Convenience Pass costs $8 and
is good for a total of eight rides on any
SEPTA bus, trolley, or subway train,
excluding regional rail. A one-day Independence Pass costs $12 and is good for
24 hours of unlimited use on all SEPTA
vehicles within the city, including regional
rail, the PHLASH bus, and the Airport
Express train. Passes, as well as tokens,
can be purchased both online and in the

SEPTA sales offices, in the concourse below 15th and Market streets; in the Jefferson Station (10th and Market streets); and in 30th Street Station.

Contacts Philly PHLASH. ☎ *484/881–3574* ⊕ *www.phlvisitorcenter.com/tour/philly-phlash*. **Southeastern Pennsylvania Transportation Authority** (*SEPTA*). ☎ *215/580–7800* ⊕ *www.septa.org*.

▌ CAR TRAVEL

Getting around Philadelphia by car can sometimes be difficult—and at rush hour, it can be a nightmare. The main east–west freeway through the city, the Schuylkill Expressway (I–76), is notorious for its traffic and delays. The main north–south highway through Philadelphia is the Delaware Expressway (I–95). To reach Center City heading southbound on I–95, take the Vine Street exit.

From the west the Pennsylvania Turnpike begins at the Ohio border and intersects the Schuylkill Expressway (I–76) at Valley Forge. The Schuylkill Expressway has several exits in Center City. The Northeast Extension of the turnpike, renamed I–476 and often called "The Blue Route" by locals, runs from Scranton to Plymouth Meeting, north of Philadelphia. From the east the New Jersey Turnpike and I–295 access U.S. 30, which enters the city via the Benjamin Franklin Bridge, or New Jersey Route 42 and the Walt Whitman Bridge into South Philadelphia.

With the exception of a few thoroughfares (e.g. the Benjamin Franklin Parkway, Broad Street, Vine Street, Spring Garden Street, parts of Market Street), streets in Center City are narrow and one-way. Philadelphia's compact 5-square-mile downtown is laid out in a grid. The traditional heart of the city is Broad and Market streets, where City Hall stands. Market Street divides the city north and south; 130 South 15th Street, for example, is in the second block south of Market Street. The diagonal Benjamin Franklin Parkway breaks the grid

pattern by leading from City Hall out o Center City into Fairmount Park.

GASOLINE

Most downtown gas stations can b found on Broad Street or Delaware Ave nue. A majority are 24-hour operations except in rural areas, where Sunday hour are limited and where you may drive lon stretches without a refueling opportunity

PARKING

In most cases, a spot at a Philadelphi parking meter will cost $2.50 an hou Parking garages are plentiful, especiall around Independence Hall, City Hall, an the Pennsylvania Convention Center, an rates vary. Philadelphia Parking Author ity (PPA) employees are famously vigilan about ticketing illegally parked cars an vehicles with expired meters. Fortunately Center City is compact, and you can eas ily get around downtown on foot or b bus after you parking. If you plan to sta in a hotel in Center City, check ahead o time to see if they have their own parkin facility or if they'll direct you to a nearb parking garage for a reduced rate, as thi can significantly affect your overall park ing budget.

ROAD CONDITIONS

Traffic flows relatively freely through th main thoroughfares of the city. Just pa attention: You will often see Philly native employing both the "rolling stop" at sto signs (found plentifully in South Philly and the "red light jump" when driver sitting at a red light will drive throug it just as (or just before) it turns green Road and house construction is a wa of life for residents, particular in Sout Philly neighborhoods, so be prepare to detour if you plan on driving in an around this area. Use extra caution whe maneuvering the narrow one-way street of Center City. Drivers on the Philadel phia stretch of the Schuylkill Express way (I–76) routinely drive well over th speed limit, and frequent accidents o this highway attest to this. If you're a slower motorist, consider gentler, mor

cenic routes to your destination, such as
Kelly Drive or West River Drive.

RULES OF THE ROAD

Pennsylvania law requires all children
under age four to be strapped into
approved child-safety seats, and children
from ages four to eight to ride in booster
seats. All passengers must wear seat belts.
In Pennsylvania, unless otherwise indicated, you may turn right at a red light
after stopping if there's no oncoming traffic. When in doubt, wait for the green.
Speed limits in Philadelphia are generally
25–40 mph on side streets, 55 mph on the
surrounding highways.

CAR RENTALS

If you plan on spending the majority of
your time within the immediate city centres, especially in Center City, you don't
need to rent a car, but you may want to
rent them if you plan to do a lot of day
trips. For rental cars, rates in Philadelphia
begin at around $50 to $60 a day.

Generally, you must be at least 21 years
old to rent a car in Philadelphia and the
surrounding areas, though there are a
handful of areas that hold to a 25-and-older rule. (Rates may be higher if you're
under 25.) Non-U.S. residents need a reservation voucher (for prepaid reservations
that were made in the traveler's home
country), a passport, a driver's license,
and a travel policy that covers each driver,
when picking up a car.

Contacts **Avis.** ☎ 800/633–3469 ⊕ www.avis.com.
Budget. ☎ 800/218–7992 ⊕ www.budget.
com. **Hertz.** ☎ 800/654–3131 ⊕ www.hertz.
com. **National Car Rental.** ☎ 888/826–6890
⊕ www.nationalcar.com.

SUBWAY TRAVEL

The orange-colored Broad Street Line
(BSL) runs from Fern Rock Station in
the northern part of the city to Pattison
Avenue, aka AT&T Station, in South
Philadelphia, where Citizens Bank Park,
the Wells Fargo Center, Lincoln Financial
Field, and XFINITY Live! are located.

The blue-colored Market-Frankford
(MFL) runs across the city, from
Street Transportation Center in the western suburb of Upper Darby to Frankford
in Northeast Philadelphia.

Sunday through Thursday, most trains
on the BSL and MFL begin suspending
service for the evening between midnight
and 1 am, resuming around 5 am. During these times, "Night Owl" buses operate along the same routes. On Friday and
Saturday nights, both lines run continuously throughout the night. While subway
travel in Philadelphia does have its limitations, it's a safe, accessible, and affordable
way to maneuver around the city without
the cost and hassle of driving and parking.

Contacts **Southeastern Pennsylvania Transportation Authority** (SEPTA).
☎ 215/580–7800 ⊕ www.septa.org.

TAXI TRAVEL

Cabs in Philadelphia begin with a flag-drop fee of $2.70, then charge 23¢ for
each 0.10 mile and 37.6 seconds of wait
time thereafter. They're plentiful downtown and throughout Center City, especially along Broad, Walnut, Chestnut, and
Market streets and near major hotels and
travel hubs. At night, during prime-time
hours, try your luck on a busy street corner or ask a hotel doorman to hail a taxi
for you. Smartphone users can also download 215-Get-A-Cab, a free Android/iOS
app that allows you to schedule pickups
instantly. It saves you the trouble of getting stuck on hold with a dispatcher, a
common occurrence on busy evenings.
All Philadelphia cabs accept credit cards,
though most drivers prefer cash transactions. The standard tip for drivers is 20%
of the total fare. Smartphone-powered
ride-sourcing services, like Uber and Lyft,
have a strong presence in Philadelphia in
addition to the cabs sanctioned by the
PPA, which regulates taxis and limos.

Contacts **215-Get-A-Cab.** ☎ *215/438–8888* ⊕ *www.215getacab.com.* **All City Taxi.** ☎ *215/467–6666* ⊕ *all-city.taxi.philadelphiapa. tel.* **Quaker City Cab.** ☎ *215/726–6000* ⊕ *www. quakercitycab.com.* **Yellow Cab Co.** ☎ *856/963– 4100* ⊕ *www.yellowcabnewjersey.com.*

▌ TRAIN TRAVEL

Philadelphia's beautifully restored 30th Street Station, at 30th and Market streets, is a major stop on Amtrak's Northeast Corridor line. The 90-minute Philadelphia–to–New York trip can cost anywhere from $50 to $200 each way, depending on the type of train, class, and when tickets are purchased. Both Amtrak's Northeast Regional trains and its high-speed Acela line cater to business travelers, and are equipped with conference tables and electrical outlets. You can travel by train between Philadelphia and New York City more cheaply by taking the SEPTA's Trenton rail line to Trenton, New Jersey, then transferring to a NJ Transit commuter line to Manhattan. The trip takes an extra 30 minutes, but the savings is considerable ($16 to $25.50 each way). Amtrak also serves Philadelphia from points west, including Harrisburg, Pittsburgh, and Chicago.

SEPTA's network of commuter trains serves both the city and the suburbs. The famous Main Line, a cluster of affluent suburbs, got its start—and its name—from the Pennsylvania Railroad route that ran westward from Center City. SEPTA commuter trains stop at 30th Street Station and connect to Suburban Station (16th Street and JFK Boulevard, near major hotels), and Jefferson Station (10th and Market streets), which is close to historic Old City. Fares, which vary according to route and time of travel, range from $3.75 to $10 each way. These trains are your best bet for reaching neighborhoods to the northwest, like Germantown and Chestnut Hill, as well as numerous suburbs.

The PATCO (Port Authority Transit Corporation) High Speed Line trains run underground, from 16th and Locust streets to Lindenwold, New Jersey. Trains stop at 12th and Locust, 9th and Locust, 8th and Market, and City Hall, then continue across the Delaware River to Camden. It's one way to get to the Adventure Aquarium or the Susquehanna Bank Center; round-trip fares range from $2.80 to $6.

Contacts **Amtrak.** ☎ *800/872-7245* ⊕ *www.amtrak.com.* **New Jersey Transit.** ☎ *973/275-5555* ⊕ *www.njtransit.com.* **Port Authority Transit Corporation** (*PATCO*). ☎ *215/922-4600* ⊕ *www.ridepatco.org.* **Southeastern Pennsylvania Transportation Authority** (*SEPTA*). ☎ *215/580-7800* ⊕ *www.septa.org.*

▌ TROLLEY TRAVEL

Philadelphia once had an extensive trolley network, and a few good trolley lines are still in service and run by SEPTA. Route 10 begins west and north of Center City and ends on Market Street; routes 11, 13, 34, and 36 each come from the west and south of Center City and also end on Market.

SSENTIALS

HOURS OF OPERATION

st banks in Philadelphia follow stan-
d hours. (TD Bank, which has a
ong presence in the city and its sub-
s, tends to stay open later, until 7 or
m.) ATMs accessible 24 hours a day
located all over the city, and Wawa, a
al convenience chain, offers surcharge-
e teller machines. United States Post
ice locations, can close from anywhere
m noon to 6 pm, depending on loca-
n and day of week. Many museums
d sights of interest are open 10 to 5; a
* stay open late one or two evenings a
ek, and a number are closed on Mon-
. Historic-area sights are open daily,
h longer hours in summer, but it's
e to check ahead. Bars and nightclubs
se at 2 am, but there are several after-
urs clubs for the serious night owls.
wntown shopping hours are gener-
* 9:30 or 10 to 5 or 6. Some stores are
en until 9 pm on Wednesday. Smaller,
ependently owned businesses like
iques stores, vintage shops, and art
leries may be closed some mornings
weekdays; it's wise to call ahead or
ck online.

HOLIDAYS

w Year's Day (Jan. 1); Martin Luther
g Day (3rd Mon. in Jan.); Presidents'
y (3rd Mon. in Feb.); Memorial Day
t Mon. in May); Independence Day
ly 4); Labor Day (1st Mon. in Sept.);
umbus Day (2nd Mon. in Oct.);
anksgiving Day (4th Thurs. in Nov.);
ristmas Eve and Christmas Day (Dec.
and 25); and New Year's Eve (Dec. 31).

PACKING

ladelphia is a fairly casual city,
ough men will need a jacket and tie in
ne of the better restaurants. Jeans and
akers or other casual clothing is fine

for sightseeing. You'll need a heavy coat
and boots for winter, which can be cold
and snowy. Summers are hot and humid,
but woman may wish to bring a shawl
or light jacket for air-conditioned restaurants. Many areas are best explored on
foot, so bring good walking shoes.

▌ PHONES

Philadelphia has two area codes: 215 and
267, which is being assigned to new num-
bers. Because of this, you must dial all 10
digits, even for local calls. For the Main
Line, as well as other suburbs, the prefixes
610 and 484 are often used.

▌ SAFETY

Center City and the major tourist destinations are generally safe and well lit, but it's
always smart to take certain precautions.
You should always be aware of your
surroundings—take care not to count
change on the street or regularly flash
an extremely expensive camera, phone,
or tablet. Keep your purses and bags on
your lap—not on the floor or dangling
on the back of your chair—in restaurants
and theaters. (Many thoughtful eateries
install hooks on bars and tables for this
purpose.) Ask hotel personnel or guides
about the specific feel of places you're
interested in visiting. As you would in
any city, keep your car locked and mind
your possessions carefully. Remember to
remove valuable items from your car.

During the day, subway cars are crowded
and safe, but some platforms and cars can
be relatively empty during late-night hours.
Although crime is relatively low in areas
like Rittenhouse Square, other hot spots
can be a bit trickier. South Street and Old
City attract a young crowd that can get
rowdy, though the areas are well patrolled
by police, both on foot and by bicycle.

▮ TAXES

The main sales tax in Philadelphia and the surrounding areas is 8%. This tax also applies to restaurant meals. Various other taxes—including a 10% liquor tax—may apply. There's no sales tax on clothing. Hotel taxes are 8.5% in Philadelphia, 3% in Bucks County, and 5% in Lancaster County.

▮ TIPPING

TIPPING GUIDELINES FOR PHILADELPHIA	
Bartender	$1 to $5 per round of drinks, depending on the number of drinks
Bellhop	$1 to $5 per bag, depending on the level of the hotel
Hotel Concierge	$5 or more, if he or she performs a service for you
Hotel Doorman	$1 to $2 if he helps you get a cab
Hotel Maid	$1 to $3 a day (either daily or at the end of your stay, in cash)
Hotel Room-Service Waiter	$1 to $2 per delivery, even if a service charge has been added
Porter at Airport or Train Station	$1 per bag
Skycap at Airport	$1 to $3 per bag checked
Taxi Driver	15%–20%, but round up the fare to the next dollar amount
Tour Guide	10% of the cost of the tour
Valet Parking Attendant	$1 to $2, but only when you get your car
Waiter	15%–20%, with 20% being the norm at high-end restaurants; nothing additional if a service charge is added to the bill
Restroom and Coat-Check Attendant	Restroom attendants in more expensive restaurants expect some small change or $1. Tip coat-check personnel at least $1 to $2 per item checked unless there is a fee.

▮ TOURS

BICYCLE TOURS

Bike tours are a great way to see a wide expanse of Philadelphia in a short period of time. Philadelphia Bike Tours offers both guided, customized tours and bike and moped rentals. You can also organize an independent tour of sorts by renting an Indego bicycle from one of the many kiosks situated throughout the city.

Contacts **Philadelphia Bike Tours.** ☎ 215/514-3124 ⊕ www.philadelphiabiketour.com.

BOAT TOURS

The *Spirit of Philadelphia* runs lunch and dinner cruises along the Delaware River. This three-deck ship leaves Penn's Landing for lunch, dinner, and a variety of specialty cruises. Dinner cruises include entertainment and music. Between April and October, Patriot Harbor Lines offers cruises that on both the Delaware and Schuylkill rivers, including wine-centric events and a ride to Bartram's Garden, a National Historic Landmark in Philly's southwest.

Contacts **Patriot Harbor Lines.** ☎ 800/979–3370 ⊕ www.phillybyboat.com. *Spirit of Philadelphia.* ☎ 866/455–3866 ⊕ www.spiritcruises.com/philadelphia.

BUS AND TROLLEY TOURS

Philadelphia Trolley Works offers narrated tours in buses designed to resemble Victorian-style open-air trolleys. Trolleys depart frequently from the corner of 5th and Market; The $27 fare is an all-day pass, allowing unlimited stops. There are nearly 30 sites on a route covering the Historic Area, the Benjamin Franklin Parkway, the Avenue of the Arts, Fairmount Park, the Philadelphia Zoo, Eastern State Penitentiary, and Penn's Landing. For a different kind of Philly experience, you can also try the Philadelphia Mural Art Tour, a trolley ride that visits some of the more than 2,000 public murals the city has to offer; or the Philly By Night Tour, which gives patrons a chance to see the city under the stars in the comfort of a double-decker open-top bus.

tacts **Mural Arts Tour.** ☎ *215/925–3633*
www.muralarts.org/tour. **Philadelphia**
lley Works. ☎ *215/389–8687*
www.phillytour.com. **Philly By Night Tour.**
215/389–8687 ⊕ www.phillytour.com.

RRIAGE RIDES

merous horse-drawn carriages wind
ir way through the narrow streets of
Historic Area. Tours last anywhere
m 20 minutes to an hour and cost from
D to $100 for up to four people. Car-
ges line up on 5th and Chestnut streets
ar Independence Hall between 10:30 am
d 3:30 pm and 6:30 pm and 10:30 pm
nday through Friday, and 10:30 am to
30 pm Saturday and Sunday. Carriages
erate year-round, weather permitting.

tacts **'76 Carriage Company.**
215/923–8516 ⊕ www.phillytour.com.

GWAY TOURS

eel Fun Rentals operates tours on
torized Segway scooters that travel
oughout the city, allowing patrons to
around the museum corridor, through
toric Old City, and more. The tours,
ich run from two to three hours
ending on destination, include hands-
Segway training, and run anywhere
m $70 to $100.

tacts **Wheel Fun Rentals.** ☎ *215/523-5827*
hiladelphia.segwaytoursbywheelfun.com.

ALKING TOURS

ntipede Tours offers tours of Inde-
dence Park led by guides in Colonial
ss; other tours, focusing on faith, gar-
is, and ethnic heritage, among other
ics, are available, as well. For food
ffs, the Taste of Philadelphia tour of
ading Terminal Market offers a fas-
ating look behind some of Philly's
st well-loved edibles, including soft
tzels and cheesesteaks. That tour
offered at 10 am every Wednesday
d Saturday morning ($16.95 adults,
.95 children). The more gourmet-
ded might appreciate the City Food
irs Decadent Gourmet, which leads
through Center City to meet with

chefs and owners of multiple establishments, tasting cheeses, Middle Eastern
fare, desserts like chocolate and gelato,
and more ($35 adults). Founding Father
fanatics should take right to a Constitutional Walking Tour or a tour of noted
Philly landmarks, with the multifaceted
Lights of Liberty experience juggling
history and entertainment. Finally, mild
scares can be found during the Spirits of
'76 Ghost Tour ($19 adult, $12.50 children), which begins at 4th and Chestnut
streets and guides its patrons through
some of the ancient architecture of Old
City, including famous film locations
from spooky Philly-based films like
The Sixth Sense.

Contacts **Centipede Tours.** ☎ *215/735–*
3123 ⊕ *www.centipedetourspa.com.*
City Food Tours Decadent Gourmet.
☎ *215/546–1234* ⊕ *www.cityfoodtours.*
com. **Constitutional Walking Tour.**
☎ *215/525–1776* ⊕ *www.theconstitutional.*
com. **Landmark Tours.** ☎ *215/925–2251*
⊕ *www.philalandmarks.org.* **Lights of Liberty.**
☎ *215/629–4026* ⊕ *historicphiladelphia.*
org/night/lights-of-liberty. **Spirits of '76**
Ghost Tour. ☎ *215/525–1776* ⊕ *www.*
spiritsof76.com. **Taste of Philadelphia:**
Walking Tour. ☎ *215/545–8007* ⊕ *www.*
readingterminalmarket.org.

▌VISITOR INFORMATION

Contacts **Independence Visitor Center.**
✉ *1 N. Independence Mall W, 6th and Market*
Sts., Old City ☎ *800/537–7676* ⊕ *www.*
phlvisitorcenter.com. **Pennsylvania Office**
of Travel and Tourism. ☎ *800/847–4872*
⊕ *www.visitpa.com.* **Philadelphia Conven-**
tion & Visitors Bureau. ✉ *1601 Market St.,*
Suite 200, Center City West ☎ *215/636–*
3300, ⊕ *www.discoverphl.com.* **Visit Philly.**
☎ *215/599-0776* ⊕ *www.visitphilly.com.*

ONLINE TRAVEL TOOLS

The online home of the *Philadelphia Inquirer* and the *Philadelphia Daily News* (⊕ *Philly.com*), features numerous articles on the region, as does the website for *Philadelphia* magazine (⊕ *phillymag. com*). Visit Philly's blog, UWISHUNU (⊕ *uwishunu.com*), previews happenings throughout the city. The alternative newsweekly, the *Philadelphia Weekly* (⊕ *phillyweekly.com*), focus heavily on local events, as well.

NDEX

PHOTO CREDITS

NOTES

NOTES

NOTES

NOTES

NOTES

Fodor's PHILADELPHIA

Publisher: Amanda D'Acierno, *Senior Vice President*

Editorial: Arabella Bowen, *Editor in Chief*; Linda Cabasin, *Editorial Director*

Design: Tina Malaney, *Associate Art Director*; Erica Cuoco, *Production Designer*

Photography: Jennifer Arnow, *Senior Photo Editor*; Mary Robnett, *Photo Researcher*

Production: Linda Schmidt, *Managing Editor*; Evangelos Vasilakis, *Associate Managing Editor*; Angela L. McLean, *Senior Production Manager*

Maps: Rebecca Baer, *Senior Map Editor*; Mark Stroud (Moon Street Cartography), *Cartographers*

Sales: Jacqueline Lebow, *Sales Director*

Marketing & Publicity: Heather Dalton, *Marketing Director*; Katherine Punia, *Publicity Director*

Business & Operations: Susan Livingston, *Vice President, Strategic Business Planning*; Sue Daulton, *Vice President, Operations*

Fodors.com: Megan Bell, *Executive Director, Revenue & Business Development*; Yasmin Marinaro, *Senior Director, Marketing & Partnerships*

Copyright © 2016 by Fodor's Travel, a division of Penguin Random House LLC

Writers: Adam Erace, Drew Lazor

Editors: Perrie Hartz, Douglas Stallings

Production Editor: Elyse Rozelle

Fodor's is a registered trademark of Penguin Random House LLC. All rights reserved. Published in the United States by Fodor's Travel, a division of Penguin Random House LLC, New York, and in Canada by Random House of Canada, a division of Penguin Random House Limited, Toronto. No maps, illustrations, or other portions of this book may be reproduced in any form without written permission from the publisher.

1st Edition

ISBN 978-0-14-754622-7

ISSN 2381-5302

All details in this book are based on information supplied to us at press time. Always confirm information when it matters, especially if you're making a detour to visit a specific place. Fodor's expressly disclaims any liability, loss, or risk, personal or otherwise, that is incurred as a consequence of the use of any of the contents of this book.

SPECIAL SALES

This book is available at special discounts for bulk purchases for sales promotions or premiums. For more information, e-mail specialmarkets@penguinrandomhouse.com.

PRINTED IN THE UNITED STATES OF AMERICA

10 9 8 7 6 5 4 3 2 1

ABOUT OUR WRITERS

Adam Erace has been writing about food and travel for more than a decade. In addition to Fodor's, he has contributed to such publications as *Details, Fortune, Southern Living,* and over 50 more. He lives in South Philadelphia with his wife, Charlotte, and two maniacal Chihuahua-mixes.

Drew Lazor covers food, drink, travel, and the arts locally in Philadelphia as well as nationally. In addition to Fodor's, he's contributed to *Bon Appétit, Condé Nast Traveler, Lucky Peach,* the *Philadelphia Daily News,* and the *Philadelphia Inquirer.* His work has also appeared on the Food Network, Food Republic, Serious Eats, and PUNCH. He's the co-author, with chefs Jeremy and Jessica Nolen, of *New German Cooking,* which was released in 2015 by Chronicle Books.